You Can Renovate
Your Own Home

FLOYD GREEN
AND SUSAN E. MEYER

You Can Renovate Your Own Home

A STEP-BY-STEP GUIDE TO
MAJOR INTERIOR IMPROVEMENTS

WITH PHOTOGRAPHS BY SUSAN E. MEYER

DOLPHIN BOOKS
Doubleday & Company, Inc.
Garden City, New York
1980

Library of Congress Cataloging in Publication Data

Green, Floyd
    You Can Renovate Your Own Home
    Includes index
    1. Dwellings—Remodeling.   I. Meyer, Susan E.,
    joint author.   II. Title
ISBN: 0-385-17006-8

For Bobbie,
the hands and heart behind this book

Acknowledgments

This book was started as a collaborative effort between two authors, but by the time the project was completed, many others had participated—either directly or indirectly—in its creation. To them we are most grateful.

With Barbara Emmerth our duet became a trio from beginning to end. Although her assistance was required most frequently during a particularly intense period at graduate school, she never faltered. Many times Bobbie was forced to push aside her studies on the weekends because her hands were summoned to help with a project or to serve as a model for photos, yet she withstood this added pressure with good cheer.

To those friends in Warwick, New York—where the renovation was completed for the book—we are also grateful: for the special assistance of George Van Strander at the lumber and building materials dealer Conklin and Strong, Inc., and to those who helped us at Warwick Hardware and Warwick Photo.

Our timing was always dictated by the requirements of the book, and so we put special demands on the electrician, Clayton Eurich, to fit his schedule in with ours, and on the plumber, Edmund Andryshak, to work around us. Both came through every time.

Our families gave still further assistance; we are grateful to Joan and Sandy Green, for patiently withstanding Floyd's absences on the cherished weekends; to Bruce McKeever and John Nolan, for working alongside, when added muscle power was needed; to Dorothy Meyer, whose contribution, both monetary and psychological, enabled us to do more than we had originally planned; to Rosemary and Wayne Blake, who reg-ularly restored us and our grounds with loving care.

Our friends—even those who thought we were slightly crazed—helped in many ways. Kathryn Baker and Ruth LeDrew got us started in the first place; Rebecca Bounds always volunteered to pitch in with great vigor and enthusiasm; and we owe thanks to the others who contributed so much in so many ways: Helga Borisch, Susan Bonhomme, Lee and Diane Hines, Ted and Carol Sattler, Faith Stern, Becky Johnston, Clermonde Dominicé.

Several manufacturers generously supported this project also, and we owe them thanks as well:

Andersen Corporation
Arrow Fastener Company, Inc.
Dosch Manufacturing Company
Johnson Products Co.
Milwaukee Electric Tool Corp.
Red Devil, Inc.
Skil Corporation
The Irwin Auger Bit Company

Once we entered into the real throes of creating the book itself, we relied on still others who worked patiently with us: Wayne Atkinson made the fine pen and ink drawings; Ben Ness Cameras & Photo Studio and Nathan Schorr performed the darkroom work on the vast majority of photographs; Marcy Shain typed the manuscript. And, last but not least, thanks to Jim Craig, a good friend who rescued the book at the very last minute, and to our editor at Doubleday, Karen Van Westering, who naturally assumed it would all work out well in the end.

Contents

Introduction

BY SUSAN E. MEYER

I didn't have a book to consult when I first began to think about home renovating. My total education in carpentry had only amounted to a few shop classes in elementary school, from which I learned to make a not-very-appealing shoeshine box. But knowing how to grip a hammer and how to assemble an odd assortment of boards was a far cry from the ambitious undertaking I was contemplating.

HOW THIS BOOK CAME ABOUT

The idea I had in mind seemed crazy at first. On my property in Warwick, New York, a vacant barn stood only thirty-five feet from my house. Not a large, picturesque cow barn, mind you, but a two-story, altogether sad-looking structure that seemed to serve no function whatsoever except as an eyesore. Its presence in my back yard became intolerable, not so much because it was an unattractive and useless building, but because it was a challenge, daring me to reshape it, to render it into something worthy of the handsome landscape surrounding it.

Inside, the barn seemed harmless enough: the top floor was an open space 20′×30′; the lower floor was divided into two sections—a concrete floor at the end, and a wood-floored storeroom in the back, the two areas separated by an old wall. The windows in the barn had been boarded up for years because the panes were broken and the frames rotten. There was no water or heat, and only one electric cable, with two antiquated outlets, served to illuminate the entire structure. As an added feature, the empty barn seemed to have been a long-standing residence hotel for every bird and rodent in the neighborhood.

Hiring someone to renovate this unsightly mess was out of the question. The cost of labor is prohibitive, as we all know, and I hardly needed two houses on a single piece of property. But I couldn't abandon my idea. The barn continued to taunt me.

Floyd Green provided the solution. Before meeting him, I had already known him by reputation as a contractor: he could erect an entire house single-handedly; he had remodeled old homes on his own; he was a mason, a cabinetmaker, and a designer. When an architect designed a round house near Warwick, I had heard Floyd Green was the only man in the area who would undertake the job of building it.

When Floyd and I became friends, I discussed the barn with him, confessing—with some embarrassment—that I had nurtured this private fantasy of transforming the barn into a kind of Cinderella house, of doing it myself. I anticipated that Floyd would guffaw loudly and dismiss the whole notion as silly, "not woman's work," or some equally reasonable response. On the contrary, he urged me to begin, not the least put off by my lack of skill, brawn, or funds. In fact, he offered to teach me. (I guess if building a round house appealed to him, the prospect of training *me* must have been a real challenge!) We agreed to start immediately.

Although I admit that I lacked some know-how about carpentry in the beginning, I can also boast that my dear friend Barbara Emmerth made me look like an expert in comparison. Bobbie wanted to learn, too. Would Floyd teach her at the same time? "Sure, why not?" he responded. And so, like the Keystone Kops, we began.

IF WE COULD DO IT, SO CAN ANYONE!

The book was a natural outgrowth of this three-way collaboration. Bobbie and I learned together, and as we progressed, I photographed what we were learning, using her hands as evidence of our joint education. Everything you see in this book

—in photographs and in spirit—is the result of that education received on weekends. Floyd's confident attitude was contagious, and we felt that "if we could do it, so can anyone!" And this is the approach we maintained throughout the book.

In the end, what we discovered is that renovating a home is just not very difficult. The margin for error in much of the work is far greater than in other skills we already had—cooking or sewing, for example—and the physical demands are only as great as those expected of any sport or dance activity. As our skills grew, so did our stamina, and we learned to accomplish more in two hours than we had in an entire day.

We deliberately chose to do as many different kinds of things in the barn as we could, to expand our knowledge of all aspects of home renovation —from ceramic and vinyl tile to hardwood floors, from barnboard paneling to Sheetrock on the walls. But we also avoided anything that would be too unconventional. We wanted to learn the kind of basics we could later apply to more original work, to undertake a foundation course for more complex jobs ahead. And this is how we conceived the book.

WHAT THIS BOOK INCLUDES

This book contains just about everything we needed to know in order to transform a vacant, shabby barn into a comfortable home. But we don't want to give you the impression that you, too, must be so ambitious to benefit from this book. We also concentrated on the aspects of home renovation that seem common in most homes, even the smaller jobs that can improve an interior, like hanging a door, or placing vinyl asbestos tile on a kitchen floor. We have assumed that your home is like ours: nothing is quite plumb or level, and the structure may not conform to contemporary building standards. In short, your home is imperfect, and you want to improve it.

We never were so advanced ourselves that we forgot the fundamental problems every amateur encounters. Too many books we had seen assume that an amateur knows more than he or she actually does. We assume that you are now where Bobbie and I began.

We also discovered that other books were inadequately illustrated. No matter how thorough Floyd and I may be at explaining everything in words, the pictures still convey more than what we say. So we photographed everything! We decided against drawings because we found that they tend to oversimplify and can be discourag-

ing when you discover that the procedure is not quite so simple. Photographs also tell more because they are less selective. You may find in the photographs some specific information you need for your particular job that we may have neglected to point out in a caption.

Moreover, we did not retouch or doctor the photographs in any way. We wanted you to feel you are on location with us, sharing in the chips and sawdust, so that you don't get the impression that home renovation is like working in a medical laboratory where utensils are sterilized and everything is in order. We photographed tools that have been used for the jobs they were designed to do.

WHAT THIS BOOK DOES NOT INCLUDE, AND WHY

Obviously, no single book can show you how to do everything. Any book that pretends to do so is misleading, because it will only tell you a little bit about a lot of things, information that is insufficient to follow any but the simplest of procedures. We've done the reverse: we eliminated what we couldn't show in the greatest detail, advising you instead to purchase books that specialize in these subjects alone. And there are some very fine books on such subjects as masonry, cabinetmaking, painting and wallpapering, and home repair. By omitting these more specialized areas we could focus on procedures less well presented in other books, discussing only what you need to know when you undertake the major jobs of interior home improvement.

We have also limited our scope to only those procedures we feel you can do yourself. This point of view explains the absence of information on wiring and plumbing. From experience, we've learned that it's wisest to contract this work with a plumber or electrician well versed in the local codes and regulations. To capsulize this technical information in a short space would only be incomplete and could be potentially dangerous. So we urge you to go elsewhere for this kind of assistance.

IS IT WORTH THE TROUBLE?

After clearing out the debris, ripping out walls, windows, and doors, and rebuilding it all, would we do it again? Tomorrow. If you catch any of our enthusiasm, the sheer joy of doing this job creatively, you'll have gained something extra from this book. You see, Floyd was right all along!

Warwick, New York

PART ONE

The Basics

CHAPTER 1

Basic Tools and How to Use Them

In undertaking any kind of interior home renovation you will be tackling some very big jobs. Considering the nature of the work ahead, it's surprising how small the initial investment is. If you're planning to do this work simply because it *must be done,* the cost of the tools is far less than what you would spend to hire someone to do these jobs for you. If you're planning to do this work because you also regard carpentry as a hobby, you'll find that the initial expense is not nearly so great as for some of the other hobbies you might have chosen!

But let us be perfectly clear, right at the outset: we're not recommending that you economize in your purchase of tools. Throughout this book we will assume that you are working with only the very best. The saying "A craftsman is only as good as his tools" is very appropriate here. The best tools will give you the best performance; poor tools will fail when you need them most.

While we're quoting epithets, let's not forget another pearl of wisdom on the same subject: "A poor craftsman blames his tools." This, too, has particular meaning here. Unless you know how to use your tools properly, you'll never get the results you seek, regardless of how fancy the utensil! Here we do not intend to recite the words given in the instruction manuals. Experience has taught us some techniques that are not so obvious, and we're eager to pass these tips on to you so that you can get better performance from your tools. Even if you have had experience with these tools, we think you'll find some handy bits of information in this chapter.

Here we will discuss only the basic tools you'll require for the work ahead. For more specialized jobs—tiling, trimming, spackling, for example—we'll describe the specific tools and procedures needed in those particular chapters. For now we will restrict our discussion to the tools you'll find indispensable for nearly all the work ahead.

In each project your work will consist of four stages: you'll remove old work, measure and plan for the new installation, cut down or cut away the materials, and install the new materials. For these four stages you'll need wrecking tools, measuring and marking tools, cutting and boring tools, and fastening tools. Most of these are hand tools; some are power-driven. Within each category there are variations in size, capabilities, and, of course, price. We'll limit this selection to the barest minimum. (Naturally, you can augment this initial selection later with other tools if you so choose.)

WRECKING TOOLS

Just what kinds of wrecking tools you need will depend on what you are removing. In our work, we dismantled the interior of an entire barn, extracting spike nails that ran as long as 6″, pulling out old broken windows, and breaking apart everything from walls and shelving to a large area in the rafters that must have served as headquarters for every squirrel in the neighborhood! We pried and pulled, pounded and scraped, and managed to collect an assortment of tools that assisted us in this arduous task. Your work may not be quite so extensive, so select only enough wrecking tools for the job you anticipate.

Cat's-paw: A nail imbedded so deeply that its head is either flush with or recessed below the surface of the wood is difficult to extract. A cat's-paw is a tool with sharpened claws. You hammer this sharpened claw into the surface of the wood, alongside the nailhead, catch the nail beneath the surface with the tool, and pry it loose. This tends to damage the surface of the wood but is an ideal method of ripping out undesirable nails.

Ripping Bar: This handy tool is also called a *crowbar, wrecking bar,* or *goose-necked ripping bar.* It operates on the principle of leverage: the longer the handle, the greater its force as you pry out the object in question. We used two sizes of crowbars, one heavier than the other, because we had so much heavy removal. One will probably be sufficient for normal wrecking. Incidentally, a ripping bar is also an effective wrecking instrument if you swing it—like a baseball bat or sledge hammer—against whatever you'd like to knock down.

Flat Bar: Also called a *pry bar* or a *Wonder Bar,* this tool is like an extended hammer claw. It is ideal for pulling out nails and for prying apart a small piece of wood fastened to another object. It is also an excellent tool for prying together tongue-and-groove lumber, as we show in our chapter on hardwood flooring.

MEASURING AND MARKING TOOLS

In nearly all the building described in this book, you have a tolerance of ¼″. This is meant to reassure you that there is more latitude than you might have imagined, certainly more tolerance than permitted in sewing or in fine cabinetmaking. But don't assume from this that your measurements can be inaccurate. Used properly, your measuring tools will save you from the frustrations of doing work over because of a minor miscalculation.

Folding Wood Ruler: This will be your most indispensable measuring device. It is used for general measuring, especially where its rigidity is needed, across an opening, for example. It is made from several 6″- or 8″-long wooden sections hinged together in a zigzig that opens to 6′, 8′, or 12′. (We found 8′ most practical and compact.) At one end a metal extension slides out an additional 6″ for precise inside measurements.

Retractable Steel Tape Ruler: Compact and easy to use, flexible steel tapes come in both short and long sizes, ranging from 2′ to 100′ lengths. Although a 12′ tape is the one most commonly used by carpenters, we found that renovation work frequently involved still greater lengths, so we purchased a 50′ ruler. The tape recoils automatically into the case, so be sure that your tape has the handy feature of locking into an extended position. The first 6″ of the tape are usually graduated in eighths of an inch; later inches are in sixteenths. At the end of the tape is a hook or loop, its 1″ dimension calculated as part of the ruler to permit outside and inside measurements to be precise. The tape's flexibility enables you to measure round as well as straight objects, and its compactness saves space.

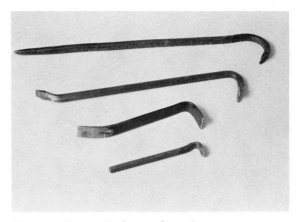

Two crowbars, a flat bar, and a cat's-paw.

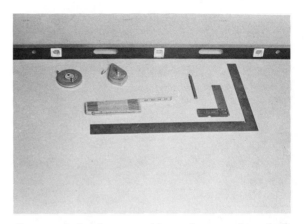

Carpenter's level, retractable steel tape ruler, chalk line, folding wood ruler, pocket square (or right angle), steel square, and chisel-point pencil.

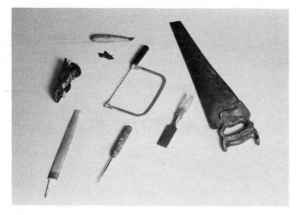

Utility knife and blades, block plane, coping saw, small handsaw, wood rasp, awl, and 1" chisel.

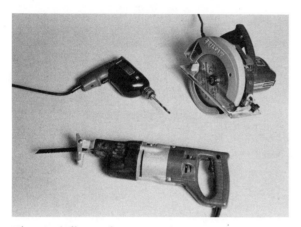

Electric drill, circular saw, and reciprocating saw.

Squares: There are a whole variety of *carpenter's squares* designed to facilitate the measuring and marking of right angles, but only two squares are vital. A *try square, pocket square,* or *right angle* (called by any of these three names) is used to test adjoining surfaces for squareness and to mark for right-angle cuts. We recommend one that is only 6" long, making it ideal for marking construction lumber for square cuts, and easily carried in the apron or pocket. A 2' *steel square* is also considered one of the most adaptable layout tools, permitting you to lay out angles on the wall or floor where a perpendicular line is needed.

Level: As its name implies, a level enables you to check the true level of horizontal surfaces and the plumb level of vertical surfaces. Standard levels are made of wood, aluminum, or lightweight alloys. We used two levels for our work—a 2' and a 4' level—the latter being the more useful of the two because it could extend across the broad span needed for window and door openings. At the tool's center, a glass tube holds an air bubble in oil. When the lines marked on the tube's surface exactly frame the bubble, the surface is level. A similar tube near each end of the tool indicates plumb. A mason's level is the best of these tools because it is constructed to withstand abuse without losing accuracy. Other levels tend to be more fragile and should be handled with care.

Chalk Line: To make a very long straight line mark—for flooring tile, for example—you can pop a taut chalk line between two points. A chalk line is available on a reel that applies chalk automatically to the cord. Purchase chalk in a color that contrasts with the surface you intend to mark: use white for dark surfaces, blue for light surfaces. Avoid using the red chalk on finished surfaces because its oxide content is impossible to remove entirely.

Pencil: Don't underestimate the importance of a reliable pencil; you'll be using it a great deal. We recommend a chisel-point carpenter's pencil. It is easily sharpened with a knife and its tough lead is sturdier than that of an ordinary writing pencil, so it won't break easily under pressure. For finishing work, where detail is so important, use a regular pencil with a fine point.

HAND CUTTING AND BORING TOOLS

Because your materials are always longer or wider than required, you'll be cutting down nearly everything delivered to your home for installation. Other abuses to which your materials will be subjected include puncturing and drilling. So it's vital that you have on hand the proper tool for the proper activity.

Handsaw: There are a variety of handsaws designed for carpentry, each variation affecting the shape of the saw, blade, size, and position and number of teeth along the blade. You should use an 8-point for regular cutting and a 10-point for trim or paneling. The *crosscut saw* will serve all your needs for home renovation. Made to cut across wood grain, it also does all-purpose cutting of plywood, hardboards, and other wood-base materials. Saw lengths vary from 12″ to 36″, the longer being easier to use but the shorter lengths more serviceable when cutting in tight areas.

Coping Saw: This saw has a thin, wiry blade held in a spring steel rectangular frame. A tension adjustment holds the blade taut. It makes very thin, accurate cuts and saws along very tight curves with ease. Cutting is limited to surfaces that the frame will fit around. Cutting blades for both wood and metal fit in the frame, and the blades mount to face in any direction.

Plane: Planes are used to trim wood to size, to smooth it, to straighten irregular edges, to bevel, and—in special forms—to groove and shape wood into moldings. Types of planes vary according to use. For home renovation, we recommend only a *block plane,* the smallest regular shop plane (about 6″ long). The blade, or plane iron, is mounted bevel up at a low angle for planing along the grain or across ends. The best type for small smoothing and fitting jobs, the block plane can be operated with one hand.

Chisel: Chisels are used to make small grooves, notches, and cuts. They come in sets, which you might obtain if you anticipate a number of cuts of different sizes. We used only one chisel—a 1″—with a metal-capped plastic handle that could be driven with a hammer.

Utility Knife: There are a number of instances where you will require the services of a razor-sharp knife. A utility knife consists of a handle into which a blade is inserted. The blade is disposable and should be replaced as soon as it dulls. Purchase a good supply of blades. (They come in boxes of five to one hundred.)

Awls: An awl is an all-around tool designed to puncture holes into relatively soft surfaces. The awl comes to a sharp point and can be driven through a surface with a hammer.

File: There are a wide variety of files available, but most are designed for finer work than you are likely to encounter. You'll need only one file, a *wood rasp.* It has coarse teeth and is designed for the rapid removal of wood or other soft materials.

POWER TOOLS

Here's where the expense comes in. Power-driven tools will be more costly than any of the other items, but there's no avoiding them. They are well worth whatever you pay. They perform their jobs efficiently and with a minimum of exertion, and what they cost you initially will pay off over and over again in savings of time, effort, and improved results. Only two or three power tools are vital to home renovation. If you are serious about doing a big job well, you won't hesitate to purchase these few.

Circular Saw: If we were to vote on the most indispensable power tool of all, the circular saw would win hands down. It is capable of making relatively straight cuts in unwieldy pieces of lumber or paneling. Using this saw, you can cut painlessly ten times the amount of wood that you could cut in the same time with a handsaw. And the portable circular saw can be taken to the project and operated without assistance. Choose a saw that is large enough to handle the materials you'll be working with. Any portable circular saw you buy should be capable of cutting a 2×4 at a 45-degree angle. In general, saws that have a blade diameter of 7″ or 7½″ are good choices. The saw should have a depth adjustment, which enables you to make shallow cuts when required; an angle adjustment for cutting miters and bevels; and a ripping fence, which guides the saw when you want to rip a board to a specific width. It should also have an automatic spring-actuated blade guard that retracts as the blade enters the work, then covers the exposed part of the blade as soon as the cut has been completed. There are also a wide variety of blades to choose from: we recommend the combination blade for all-around use. A carbide-tipped blade, though far more expensive, will last much longer.

Reciprocating Saw: The reciprocating saw is one of the most undervalued of tools. We would say, without hesitation, that this saw is indispensable for any kind of heavy renovation work. The blades are interchangeable among different manufacturers, available in lengths from 2½″ to 12″. The blades range in purpose from cutting metal to cutting wood up to 6″ thick. You can use the

Nail set, 20-ounce hammer, screwdrivers, stapling hammer, compression staple gun, and pliers.

saw to cut right through a wall, after making sure wiring and plumbing won't be endangered. Blades for this can cut through any nails that you encounter. We preferred the Milwaukee "Sawzall" to all the other models of reciprocating saws because its unique design makes it possible to get into the tightest spots from just about any angle. We used the tool innumerable times in unexpected situations, cutting through areas that would have been otherwise unreachable.

Electric Drill: This tool is optional. We would advise your purchasing it because you'll find all sorts of places to use it, even if not in heavy home renovation. Because of its versatility you'll find uses for this drill above and beyond what we describe in this book. It can drill metal, wood, plastic, and concrete and perform many other operations as well. The size of the drill is determined by the largest drill shank its chuck will accept, which may be ¼", ⅜", ½", or ¾". The ¼" is the handiest for the average job, but you'll probably find greater over-all use for the ½". It can take drills (or bits) that will perform a wider variety of jobs, including those you'll be encountering in home renovation. Speed usually decreases with size, the slower speeds of the larger drills providing the greater turning power necessary for driving large-diameter bits and hole saws.

FASTENING TOOLS

When you install the materials you have measured and cut down, you'll either nail them, screw them, or staple them. Each of these operations requires the tools designed for the job. Most of these tools should be familiar to you.

Hammer: You may already have a hammer around the house, but it's probably not designed for heavy-duty renovation. Professional builders tend to use one hammer for everything. So the hammer should be versatile and sturdy. First of all, it should be fairly heavy—20 ounces is a good size—because you will be driving in some pretty hefty nails. Second, it should be constructed of a tough material. A wooden handle will only splinter and loosen from the abuse to which you'll be subjecting it. Select a steel-handled hammer instead. These 20-ounce hammers are called ripping hammers because they are designed for rough work and dismantling. They have straight claws that fit more readily between boards for prying. The head should be drop-forged steel rather than brittle cast iron. "Rim-tempering" of the striking face also greatly reduces the chance of breakage or chipping. It may come as a surprise to you as well that a hammer with a fairly large head is preferable for *all* work, including finishing, to a hammer with a small head. A large head mars the surface far less than a small one. Strike two hammers into soft wood and make the comparison yourself!

Screwdriver: For heavy renovation work you'll need only two screwdrivers: one with a standard blade and tip, and a Phillips screwdriver. Remember, screwdrivers are designed to do only one job: to drive and draw screws. They are not pries, putty knives, paint paddles, or chisels. If your work calls for a good many screws, you might consider the purchase of a ratchet screwdriver. With this you simply push down on the handle and the spiral ratchet spins the blade. It can be set in reverse to remove screws or locked for use as an ordinary screwdriver.

Pliers: There are several kinds of pliers available, each designed for a different purpose. It's unlikely that you'll need anything more than the standard *slip-joint pliers,* so named for the two-position pivot that provides both normal and wide jaw openings.

Staple Gun: You'll be using at least one kind of staple gun. We made the greatest use of a *stapling hammer*—in which the staples are released when the stapler is whacked against the surface. A *compression stapler*—the staples being released by squeezing the handle of the tool—is also handy for tacking light materials to wood in hard-to-reach places.

Nail Set: For finishing work, particularly trimming around windows and doors, nails should be concealed. A nail set placed on the head of a nail and driven with a hammer will sink the nail below the surface of the wood. Lacking a nail set, you can usually use another nail for the same purpose.

OTHER ITEMS YOU'LL NEED

This list is far from comprehensive. We've tried to eliminate as much as possible so that we would not alarm you with the amount of tools you need to begin. As you work, you may find a use for tools not mentioned here—a *sanding machine* or a *saber saw,* perhaps—but these items will follow later. To begin, you need only what we have described above.

Meanwhile, give some thought to your working area. Two *sawhorses* will always come in handy, particularly when you want to place your mate-

rials for sawing. And a *carpenter's apron,* tied around your waist, is ideal for carrying nails and small tools. A *hammer loop* that fits on a belt and hangs at your side is a good place to carry your hammer so that it is nearby at all times.

One further item: you'll find plenty of use for *cedar shingles,* strange as this may sound. Shingles are wedge-shaped, paper-thin along one edge and graduating to about ¾" along the other. They are ideal for shimming, or building up a surface so that it is level or plumb. As you slide them through the space, they will adapt to exactly the thickness you need to fill the space. So add a small bundle of shingles to your list of materials.

BETTER MEASURING

Accurate measuring begins with using the right measuring tools for the right job. Try to use the longest ruler for the longest dimensions. For long measurements, use a 12' ruler, rather than an 8' ruler, for example. Each time you begin again with the ruler, you run the risk of adding or losing a fraction of an inch. Across a long span this can add up to quite an error.

In using the tool—even if it is the correct one for the purpose—be sure you are operating it at maximum efficiency by taking advantage of all its features. For example, a fold-out ruler is designed for taking both inside and outside measurements. The metal extension enables you to slide the ruler out to the point where it touches the other side of the item or space you are measuring. Use the extension for very small measurements, too. Rest the top of the ruler against the side of the item and slide the extension along the surface of what you are measuring until it touches the other side. The end of the ruler will stay in place as you slide out the extension.

Also notice if your ruler is printed in more than one color. In most fold-out rulers the numbers are mainly black, but printed in red every 16". You will be laying out a good deal of your work in intervals of 16", so this feature is designed to assist you. Use it.

Figure out two ways to measure and see if you get the same answer twice. Whenever possible, fit things together without measuring. Just cut the material to workable lengths. This is particularly true in trimming, where accuracy to a fraction of an inch is critical. It's more effective to hold the trim against the door or window and mark it against the actual object than to measure both the object and the wood.

If you want to mark a board or panel to a certain length, draw the steel tape down along the

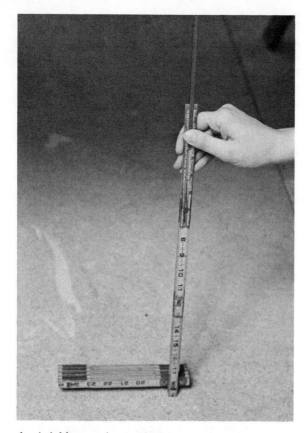

1. *A fold-out ruler is ideal for inside measurements between two objects. Slide out the metal extension.*

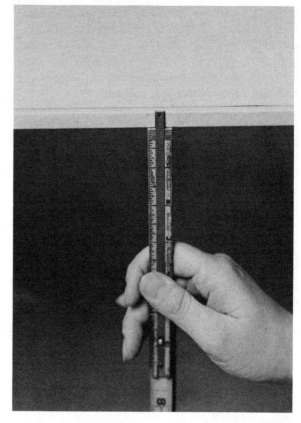

2. *The metal extension can also be used for smaller measurements to a fraction of an inch.*

3. *When measuring, avoid placing the ruler at an angle like this.*

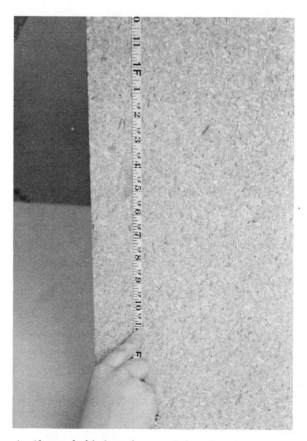

4. *Always hold the ruler parallel to the edge you are measuring.*

edge and hold it parallel to the edge. If the tape is slightly out of parallel, an error will result.

If you have a number of figures to keep straight, don't try to memorize them. You'll only jumble the calculations. Draw a rough diagram and label the dimensions you're working with. This way you have a written and a visual record of your calculations.

In the next chapter we will discuss the dimensions used in the building trade. Here it is sufficient to say that you should distinguish between the *nominal* dimension of an item (such as 2×4) and its *actual* measurement ($1\frac{1}{2}'' \times 3\frac{1}{2}''$). If you are in doubt, always order a material by the actual measurement you calculated rather than naming the wood you think you need.

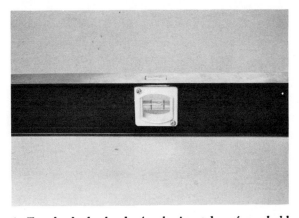

1. *To check the level of a horizontal surface, hold the instrument flat and look at the bubble in the middle of the level. When it is perfectly centered between the two marks, the surface is level.*

USING A LEVEL

The level will tell you if the surface is horizontally level or vertically plumb. Always use the longest possible level for the job at hand. Taking a reading of a 5' span with a 12'' level will tell you only if the particular *section* of the surface is level; this may have no bearing on the entire surface.

Before you lay down the level, wipe the surface clean. Even the smallest particle on the surface can throw off the reading level. As you look at the level, always check the same bubble. First place the level on one end, then turn it and check the same bubble again. It should read correctly in both directions with the bubble perfectly centered between the two marks in the vial. If the bubble is off center, the surface is not level or plumb and adjustments must be made.

POPPING A LINE

The chalk line is an excellent tool for extending a mark across a long span. In several of the projects ahead you will lay out an entire wall or floor based on only two points that are particularly important. And two points are all you need to make a line. Mark these two points on the floor or wall. If one of these marks is at the extreme end of the line, tack a nail into that point. Shake up the chalk marker to distribute the chalk powder in the container, and unwind the line. The cord is now charged with chalk powder, so handle it carefully to avoid depositing chalk in unwanted areas.

Place the loop at the end of the chalk line on the nail, and draw the line along the surface so that it passes over the two points and extends to

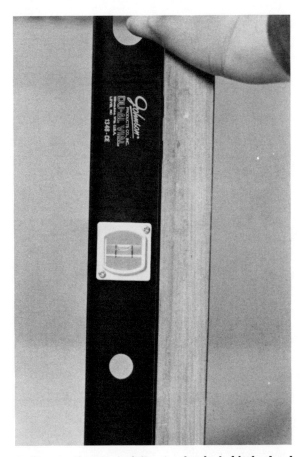

2. *To see if a vertical line is plumb, hold the level against the surface and check the bubble at the end.*

1. *Two points are needed to make a straight line. A nail is tacked at one extreme end to indicate the first point, and a second is marked with a pencil.*

2. *Place the loop of the chalk line on the nail and bring the line over the second mark.*

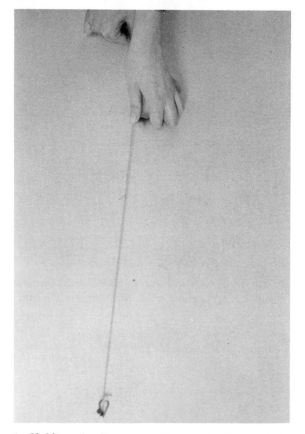

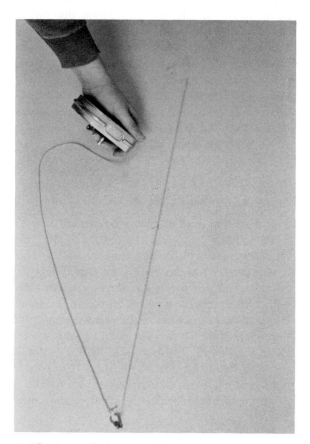

3. *Holding the line taut with one hand, grasp the cord with the other and snap it.*

4. *The line will deposit a chalk mark along the surface.*

the other side of the wall or floor. Always keep the line above the surface so that it doesn't touch and mark up the area. With one hand pull the line taut about ½" above the surface, and with the other hand lift the line and snap it back. This is called "popping a line." The chalk marks the line.

If you have two marks near the center of the wall or floor, you won't know precisely where the extreme point will fall along the line. You'll need an assistant here to hold the other end. Position the cord over the two marks, extend the cord to the other extreme, and pop the line.

GETTING BETTER CUTS WITH A HANDSAW

Unless you get a good start, your cut will not be accurate and you'll have several grooves disfiguring the wood. To begin, use the butt portion of the blade near the handle and use the knuckle of the thumb of your free hand as a guide for the first few strokes. Use several pulling strokes to make the starting groove. Don't cut directly on the marked line but on the waste, or throwaway, side to reduce chances of cutting short.

As you saw, consciously make an effort to cut with as much of the blade as possible, sawing back and forth in long, slow, even motions. Using the entire blade in one slow motion is ultimately faster and cleaner than several short, quick strokes. Because the crosscut saw cuts on both the forward and the back strokes under its own weight, you need apply only light pressure in using it. The stroke of the sawing should be in a rocking motion, following a normal arc as the arm swings from the shoulder. This helps the saw carry the weight for you.

As you cut, steady the lumber with your free hand so that the motion of the arm working the saw won't move the board out of position. Allow at least 3" clearance from the support on which you are working in order to avoid sawing into it. If the saw wanders off the line, bring it back to the spot where it veered and start again. This is easier than twisting the saw back to the line.

At the finish of the crosscut, always support the waste piece while you are making the final cutoff strokes. Never break the piece off by twisting the saw blade.

BETTER RESULTS WITH A CIRCULAR SAW

Every feature on the circular saw is designed for a good purpose. Taking advantage of these fea-

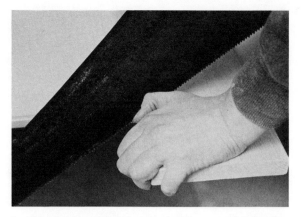

1. Use the knuckle of your thumb to guide the first few strokes of the saw.

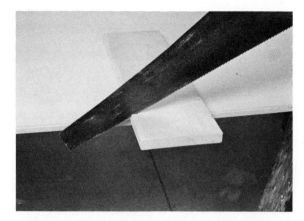

2. Pull the saw toward you as you begin to cut.

3. With the entire blade of the saw, use long, slow motions as you cut.

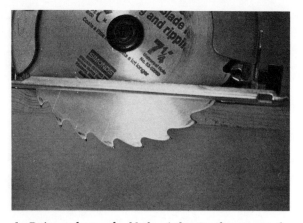

1. *Raise or lower the blade of the circular saw to the appropriate depth of the wood you are cutting. The blade here is too low for the wood.*

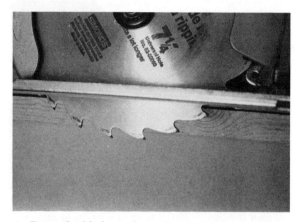

2. *Raise the blade so that only one full tooth extends beyond the width of the wood, as shown here.*

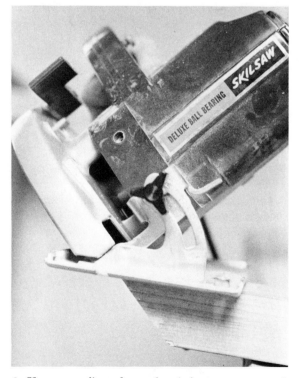

3. *You can adjust the angle of the saw to a maximum of 45 degrees.*

tures makes the difference between a good cut and a poor one.

First, you can raise or lower the blade. Although many amateurs tend to leave the blade at the full-depth adjustment, you can improve the performance of the machine by using the depth adjustment feature. Always adjust the saw so that one full tooth of blade extends beyond the wood. Deeper than this, and you have less control over the saw. For example, if you are cutting a sheet of plywood along a line 48″ long, you'll find that the saw will veer off the line uncontrollably if the blade is at its full depth. By raising the blade, you can easily direct the saw to stay on the line.

If you want to make a groove in the surface of the wood or a *pocket cut* into the wood—scooping out a section so that it is recessed below the surface—you can do so with the circular saw. Here you raise the blade to just enough depth for the cut, yet not so deep that the blade will penetrate through to the other side of the wood. Retract the guard of the saw and tilt the saw so that it rests on the front of the base, then lower the rear until the blade starts to cut into the wood.

You can also adjust the angle of the saw to a maximum of 45 degrees. It's not easy to judge the angle by looking at the scale of the saw. Check the angle first by cutting a scrap piece and seeing if it's where you want it. If you have changed the tilt angle of the saw at a previous stage of the job, be sure that it is correctly readjusted the next time you use it. You can check for right-angle cuts by cutting a scrap piece and using a try square on the cut section.

When you try out a new saw, familiarize yourself with all the adjustments by cutting up several pieces of scrap wood. In this way you'll learn how accurate the settings on the saw really are. The calibration on the saw, showing the angles and distance, should be used only as a guide, never for actual measurements. Remember, too, that the width of the saw blade itself and the types of blades used in construction work will affect the precision of the final cut.

HOW TO RIP WOOD

You will probably have to saw off long continuous sections from your lumber. For example, you may have to take 1″ off a long piece of 1×6 lumber. Removing this piece is call *ripping*.

Draw a pencil line down the length of the board as a guide for your cut. Tack the board lengthwise onto the sawhorse with the pencil line extending over the edge. Place large nails, one at each end of the board, where they will not interfere with the sawing operation. Don't hammer the nails in all the way; leave just enough head so that you'll be able to extract them easily after you've finished ripping.

Adjust the blade of the circular saw so that it is one tooth below the thickness of the wood. Cut on the pencil line, holding the saw steadily, and guiding it across the piece of wood. The saw has an attachment for ripping, a *ripping fence,* which adjusts to the desired width of the cut and acts as a guide. We never used it because it took too much time to assemble it; simply following the pencil line seemed easier, especially when we ripped a section that was of an irregular dimension. If you think you will feel more comfortable with the fence, try it out.

SAFETY PRECAUTIONS WITH THE CIRCULAR SAW

The circular saw is a dangerous tool and must be carefully handled. When using the saw, always be sure that the work to be cut is firmly supported or held so that it will not shift during the cut. Start the saw before the blade enters and guide it straight along the cutting line. Veering can cause jamming, stalling, and even possible motor damage. When cutting a long piece of lumber, have a helper support the wood. It must not be moved during the cut in such a way that it closes the cut and binds the blade.

Keep a firm grip on the saw with one hand and keep your other hand well away from it. Make certain, too, that the cord is well out of the way so that it will not be cut by the blade.

Maintain a strong grip on the saw to keep it from tipping or dropping at the end of the cut. Keep your hands clear of the blade during the time required for it to come to a complete stop. Never adjust the saw without first disconnecting the power cord.

When replacing a blade, make sure that it will be turning in the correct direction. This is generally indicated by an arrow on the blade. Also, always be sure to use a sharp blade. A dull blade requires more power to cut through the work, tends to scorch the wood, and is a hazard to use because you tend to push the saw into the wood, instead of letting the saw do the work.

If you've been working for long hours and feel fatigued, don't use the circular saw. A slight miscalculation can be one of the most dangerous errors of all. Quit for the day, and return when you are fresh.

CUTTING WITH THE RECIPROCATING SAW

The reciprocating saw is ideal for rough-cutting lumber to size, for general trimming, and—best of all—for cutting openings into the side of a building. To begin the cut, rest the blade against the surface at a point along the line you plan to cut. Turn on the saw and hold it firmly in place as it rubs against the surface. As soon as it enters the line, lift the saw and insert it more deeply into the cut. The saw will cut through the wallboard first; then, after you've checked for wiring or plumbing installations that have been hidden by the wall, you can saw directly into the siding of the house.

The reciprocating saw must be grounded before you use it, particularly in view of the kinds of tasks you'll be using it for. Always connect a three-pronged plug to a properly grounded outlet or use an adapter with a ground wire (available at any hardware store), which you attach to the receptacle cover mounting screw at the outlet.

When you return the saw to its box, don't twist and bend the electric cord into a compact unit, which will shorten its life. Lay it loosely in the box with the saw.

USING THE CHISEL PROPERLY

Work only with sharp chisels, and use them only for the removal of material that other tools can't handle. Never use them to cut anything other than wood, and don't pry with them.

The chisel is a knife, its tapered edge slicing and separating wood fibers just like a wedge. Splits will break free if the blade travels into downhill grain. Let one hand firm and guide the blade while the other hand applies pressure on the handle. It's more efficient to take several small bites with the chisel than to try to get all the wood off in one piece. Control the cutting action by holding the angle of the chisel constant. Always limit the length of your cut by making a cut across the grain before driving the chisel parallel to the grain; otherwise, the wood may split beyond your cutting.

The cleanest cut comes from a sidewise slip as the chisel advances—like the slide of a sharp razor—and the chisel is ideal for this purpose if you are rounding off sharp edges at a corner. A chisel is also used to make a mortise (a recess in the wood), a process we have described in detail in our chapter on hanging doors.

USING THE BLOCK PLANE

First be sure that the cutting edge of the plane is set properly. Its edge should align with the plane mouth at the underside of the plane. To adjust the blade, run your thumb lightly along—or sight

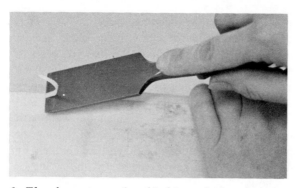

1. *The cleanest cut of a chisel is made by advancing the tool along the grain of the wood at the edge of the board. It works like a sharp knife.*

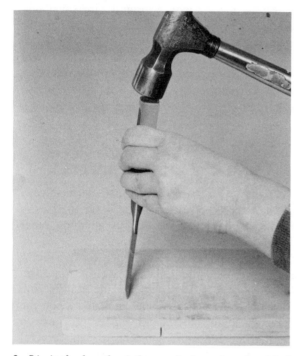

2. *Limit the length of the cut by inserting the chisel into the wood across the grain.*

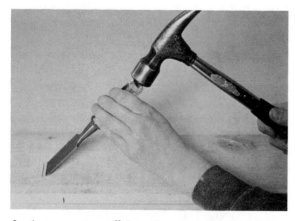

3. *As you cut parallel to the grain, the first groove made by the chisel will prevent the chisel from slipping and cutting more than you want. Always take several small bites with the chisel rather than trying to dig out the wood in one piece.*

down—the bottom of the plane. For a smooth cut, the blade should extend a hair's width. (Extended farther, the plane will cut too deeply into the wood and make a rough cut in doing so.) For even shaving, keep the blade parallel with the plane mouth. This keeps the wood from getting high on one edge, low on the other.

For straight planing, start with the plane level and flat on the surface. Apply even pressure during the stroke to produce a continuous shaving. Always plane in the direction of the grain to minimize chipping. Planing against the grain leaves a rough surface. Hold the plane at a slight angle to the cut you're making. It should shave wood off, not tear or chip it. Try for ribbon-like shavings by practicing on scrap pieces of wood until the plane is set for the job.

To plane across the end grain of a board, set the plane for a shallow cut, making sure the blade is sharp. Before starting the cut, be sure to bevel (round off) the ends of the wood slightly. If you don't, the plane will split the wood as it nears the end of the cut.

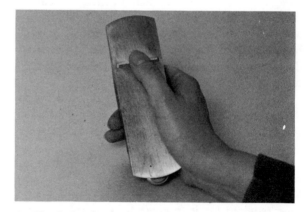

1. *Check the depth and angle of the blade at the underside of the plane. Keep the blade a hair's width beyond the mouth and parallel to it.*

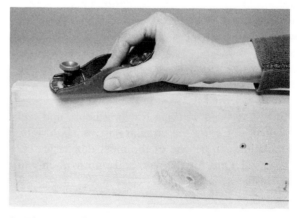

2. *Plane in the direction of the grain, at a slight angle to it, applying even pressure to achieve ribbon-like shavings.*

GETTING MORE FROM YOUR HAMMER

Follow these suggestions for handling a hammer to get better results with less effort and less chance of accident.

In nailing, grasp the hammer near the end of the handle, not near its head. This will give you greater leverage and force behind the swing. Hold the hammer firmly, but not too tightly. A lighter grasp will help the hammer land more squarely on the head of the nail.

Develop good habits right from the start. Don't hold the nail with more than two fingers. If you should—and someday you will—miss the nail-head, at least you'll affect only two fingers, rather than the whole hand. Hold the nail fairly high in the shank so that you'll knock your fingers, rather than smash them.

Tap the nail so that it stands up in the wood, then release your hold, and drive the nail home. As you raise your arm, keep your eye on the head of the nail, and use your entire arm from

3. Never hold the nail with several fingers, like this.

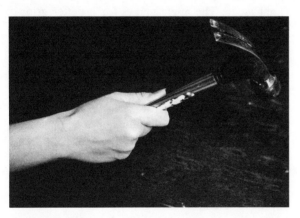

1. Don't "choke" the hammer by holding it near the head, this way.

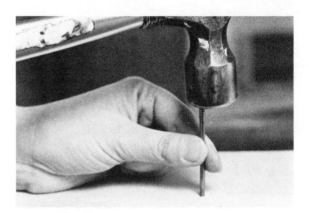

4. Always grasp the nail between two fingers only, fairly high on the shank.

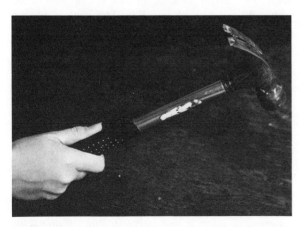

2. Grip the hammer near the end of the handle for better leverage.

5. A wood block under the hammer head prevents marring the surface when you want to extract a nail and gives better leverage with longer nails.

33

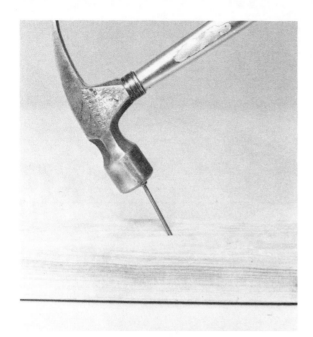

6. Nail at a slight angle for a better join.

7. To attach a board through the side, the nail is placed at a 45-degree angle. This is called toenailing.

8. Toenail through the opposite side of the wood as well, the two angled nails holding the wood in place. A third toenail is required for framing by most building codes. In some communities, four nails may be required.

the shoulder in the swing. The less wrist action you use, the more accurate and efficient your swing. (You might wear a wrist bandage for extra support, and as a deterrent to flexing.)

Use the claw of the hammer to extract nails or to pry loose two pieces of lumber. You will get greater leverage for pulling out long nails if you place a wood block under the hammer head. (A block will also prevent the hammer from marring the surface of the wood below.)

For finishing work, always check the head of your hammer before using it to be sure it is clean. Dirt can be transferred almost indelibly to the surface on which you're hammering.

SOME TIPS ON NAILING INTO WOOD

You'll be reading a good deal more about nails in the next chapter, but here's some general advice on doing a better job with them.

You will get a better join if you nail in at a slight angle. The angle makes for a better grip; it is less likely that the two pieces of lumber will part, even under stress. For rough framing, where appearance doesn't count, drive the nail deep into the wood, below the surface of the lumber, so that the head won't interfere with the material— flooring or wallboard, for example—you will be placing on the face of the lumber. When the final appearance of the surface is important, stop hammering when the nail is just above the surface, and sink it into the wood with a nail set.

As your nailing improves, you'll learn when you have to stop to straighten a bending nail and when it's not necessary. If a nail bends slightly as you are hammering, you can correct the bend by meeting the angle with a square blow of the hammer. This slight change in the swing will come naturally to you with practice. The trick is *always to keep your eye on the head of the nail*.

Not all nails are driven through the wood head on. Sometimes you must nail at an angle through the side of one board into the surface of the other. This is called *toenailing* and requires some practice. The object is to angle the nail so that it penetrates both pieces of wood being joined without shifting the position of the wood as it is struck with the blows of the hammer. Hold the nail at a 45-degree angle and tap it into the wood, just to the point where the nail is about to enter the second wood surface. Position the wood where you want it and drive the nail home with one or two solid blows. Drive the nail downward so that you don't shift the wood any more than necessary. If the wood slips, toenail the opposite side of the lumber and force it back to the original position. The board is anchored only when it is toenailed from two opposite sides, both nails angled to prevent the board from shifting. For framing, you'll need to toenail on three sides of the board to meet building code requirements in some communities, four sides in other communities.

When nails must be driven close to the end of a piece, you can avoid splits in any of several ways. You can drill holes slightly smaller than the nails if it isn't important that you lose some holding power. Or you can blunt the nail point by tapping on it with the hammer while the head is on a solid surface. The blunt point shears the wood fibers instead of wedging them apart, reducing the chance of splitting.

You'll find yourself nailing small blocks of wood into place with fairly heavy nails from time to time. Small blocks—particularly in pine—tend to split when penetrated with nails. One way of reducing the chances of splitting is by inserting a nail—*before* you've cut down the wood—into the side of the block so that it penetrates across the grain. Then saw the wood down to size. The nail at the side seems to hold together the grain and the wood, and the block is less likely to break apart when you nail it at the face. (You can leave the nail in.)

You can also minimize split ends by cutting wood longer than necessary for the joint, nailing it, and sawing off the excess. Avoid nailing several nails into the same grain line in the wood— this will split the lumber. Using finishing nails instead of common nails will reduce the chances of splitting wood.

When you are spiking together two pieces of lumber, always position the nails in an angled pattern. Don't line up the nails in a straight row. You will get greater strength when you nail across more surface of the boards you are tying together. Our illustration suggests two patterns for you to follow.

Avoid nailing into hardwood with anything but tempered nails (see Chapter 2). If common nails must be used, drill holes first, slightly smaller than the nail shank, before driving in the nails.

Use nails that are 2½ to 3 times longer than the thickness of the wood they must hold, and always nail light work to heavy. If the nails exit at the other end of the wood, bend them over from the other side (this is called *clinching*), and flatten them into the wood for a tight grip.

A FINAL WORD ABOUT SAFETY

Although this makes tedious reading, there is no way to avoid mentioning safety measures. They

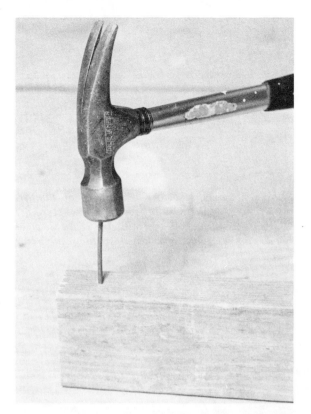

9. *If you must nail a small block of wood with heavy nails, here's a way to avoid splitting the wood. Before cutting the block, first drive a nail through the side of the wood. Then cut the block to size.*

10. *Drive a second nail through the face of the small block. The nail through the side helps bind the wood fibers together.*

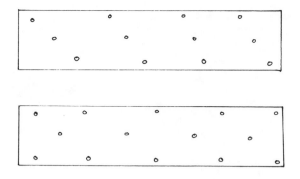

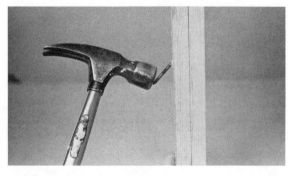

11. When spiking together two pieces of lumber, avoid lining up the nails in a straight row. Here are two patterns for nailing that will give you a stronger bond with less chance of wood splitting along the grain.

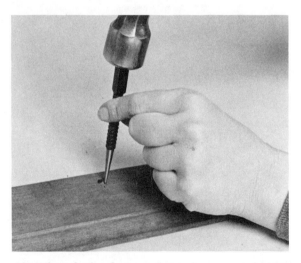

12. If the nail exits through the opposite side of the wood, bend it over and flatten it into the wood for a tight grip. This is called clinching.

13. When the head of a nail is to be concealed, drive it below the surface of the wood with a nail set.

are just too important. Too many accidents can happen because you didn't take the proper precautions.

•Always read the manufacturers' instructions. Read what they say about your power tools; read the warnings on adhesives, insulation, joint compound. And, most important, follow their advice!

•You may be ripping out a good deal of old wood, and it may contain some very nasty-looking rusty nails. Always bend the nails over before you lay the wood down on the floor. You can easily impale yourself on a rusty nail in an old board.

•Wear gloves whenever you rip out old work. They will help protect you from punctures, splinters, broken glass, and animal bites. Why take chances?

•If you are wearing an apron, pay attention to what you put into the pockets. Don't deposit the utility knife there.

•Always leave your cutting tools in a place where you're not likely to bump into them or step on them.

•Be certain that your ladder, step stool, or whatever means you use to reach heights is absolutely sound. Falling off is bad enough. If you also happen to have a saw or hammer in your hand, you can cause even further damage. Don't take chances by standing on something rickety.

•Always work in a well-lighted area, with plenty of room for maneuvering. You only invite disaster when you work blind and bump into every item scattered through the room. Keep your working areas free from debris as much as possible, and try your best to return your tools to the same place each time.

•Don't wear loose clothing, ragged sleeves, or a scarf. They can easily get caught.

•Always cut away from your body, so that if your hand should slip, you will not run the tool into your body.

•Use safety glasses whenever you strike or cut metal that might fly, when sawing materials that are coarse and create pellets of dust—such as particle board—and any other time there is danger of splinters, metal, chips, or glass falling into your eyes.

CHAPTER 2

Basic Building Materials

There's no point in overwhelming you with the vast assortment of materials available at your neighborhood lumberyard. In fact, you'll be using relatively little of that vast assortment. What's more important is that you understand some of the general characteristics of building materials, and the lingo used to describe them, so that you can adapt this information to the variations in your own specific projects.

You will notice that we don't mention screws in this chapter. This may come as a surprise to you, but it's not an oversight on our part. In the projects ahead you'll encounter screws when you remove old work, perhaps, but rarely when installing new work. The screws you will use here will most likely be packaged with the hardware you're installing—hinges and doorknobs, for example. If you nail properly—and you can find our tips for better nailing in the previous chapter—you will not need to depend on the greater holding power of screws. So we have eliminated them from this chapter altogether.

LUMBER

Wood is the basic building material. With the exception of concrete-and-steel-foundation buildings, wood is what is behind every wall and under every floor, regardless of how it is covered. So it's the first material you should learn about.

All woods are composed of approximately 60 per cent cellulose and 28 per cent lignin. These substances make up the woody and fibrous cell walls of plants and trees and the cementing material between them. The remaining 12 per cent consists of the elements that give each species individual qualities, like the rich color of mahogany used in cabinets, the aroma of cedar in blanket chests, and the rot resistance that makes redwood so ideal for lawn furniture. The other characteristics that match lumber to specific uses are the result of the way it is sawed from the log and seasoned. After that, it's up to you and your tools to handle it in whatever way you have in mind.

Lumber is generally classified into two principal kinds: softwoods and hardwoods. These terms, often misleading, refer to the kind of tree the wood comes from, not the characteristics of the wood. The term *softwood*, as used in the lumber industry, does not always refer to a tree whose wood is soft any more than the term *hardwood* necessarily refers to a tree whose wood is hard. For example, the softwoods yew and Douglas fir are actually harder than so-called hardwoods like poplar, aspen, and Philippine mahogany. And the softest wood of all—balsa—is technically a hardwood. So there is no definite or precise means of determining the difference between many trees in respect to hardness or softness.

Hardwoods

Hardwoods come from the broadleaf, or deciduous, trees, such as oak, walnut, maple, or mahogany. Woods in this group tend to cost more than softwoods, but—as a very general rule—hardwoods tend to be stronger and more durable. The lumber industry classifies the following trees in the hardwood group:

Ash	Gum
Aspen	Maple
Balsa	Mahogany
Basswood	Oak
Beech	Philippine mahogany
Birch	Poplar
Butternut	Rosewood
Cherry	Teak
Chestnut	Walnut
Elm	

Softwoods

Softwood is lumber from evergreen, or coniferous, trees, such as pine, cedar, and spruce. It is usually sold sawed and, since the timber from the saw is rough, planed to finished dimensions. Later we will discuss some of the drying and shrinking qualities of these softwoods because these characteristics affect the way in which you call and order these woods from the lumberyard. Softwoods vary in their resistance to weather. Some, like pine, must be protected with preservatives or paints. Others, like redwood, have natural weather-resistance. Many softwoods also have hard, brown pockets, called *knots,* that give off a sticky liquid, and softwoods are also susceptible to rough or split ends.

The lumber industry classifies the following trees as softwoods:

Cedars	Pines
Cypress	Redwood
Douglas fir	Spruce
Firs	Tamarack
Hemlock	Yew
Larch	

Of all these woods, pine is what you will be using more than anything else for the projects in this book.

Shrinking and Warping of Wood

At the time lumber is cut from the trees, it is said to be "green," because it contains a considerable amount of moisture. Until much of that moisture has been eliminated, the lumber is unsuitable for carpentry. As the moisture content diminishes, the lumber changes in size. Actual shrinkage takes place, which reduces the over-all size of the lumber. For example, when a piece of green wood measuring 2″×4″ dries, the shrinkage reduces both the 2″ and the 4″ dimensions. The precise amount of shrinkage depends on the kind of wood and the geographical location. Shrinkage hardly affects the length of lumber during the drying process: only about ⅛″ shrinks every 12″.

Lumber must be dry for a number of reasons. Nails don't have full holding power when driven into green wood. They may partially work their way out as the wood dries and cause loose joints, squeaking, and even unsafe conditions. Furthermore, the structural items reduce in size (unequally) as the wood dries, resulting in warping, which can cause cracking, force windows and doors out of plumb and floors out of level, and so on.

Lumber is dried in one of two ways; either naturally or artificially. In natural drying, the lumber is air-dried, placed in piles where horizontal pieces are laid between each layer. The air circulates freely throughout the pile, so that drying takes place gradually. The artificial method of drying is with kilns, the method that is becoming increasingly more common for construction lumber. The kilns are large ovens in which controlled heat over a given period of time can be used to drive out the moisture.

Once the lumber has dried, it should be kept dry. Whenever it is stored out in the open, it should be protected from rain and snow. In hot climates the sun can cause splitting or checking unless the lumber is stored properly.

You can recognize dry lumber without having to test it scientifically. Dry lumber generally weighs less than green lumber. Dry lumber sounds hollow when rapped with the knuckles. Dry lumber has greater spring and is likely to have small and brittle slivers on it. Green lumber has a sharp odor and feels damp to the touch.

As the lumber dries out, it tends to warp because the shrinkage takes place unequally. Warping can be corrected somewhat by stacking the lumber with one layer in one direction and the next layer at right angles. (This is also a good way to store lumber if you buy it in quantity.) Warping of two boards can be corrected by placing them together, convex sides outside, and clamping the centers together. Wetting the wood thoroughly before clamping will hasten the straightening process. But, in general, you will simply have to work around warped wood. In construction you can pretty well force the wood to the correct position, nailing it firmly so that it is secured and straight.

Crowns on Lumber

Construction lumber contains what is called a *crown.* This is the configuration in the grain that causes the lumber to arch up slightly along its narrow edge. In some boards this is more obvious than in others because of the natural variations in the configurations of softwood. The best method of spotting the crown is to stand holding the

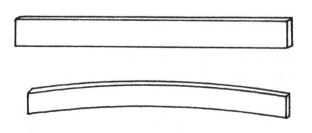

The configuration of the grain in construction lumber causes the wood to arch up along the edge. The crown here has been exaggerated to show how this arch compares to a straight board.

board by one end, the other end resting on the floor. Turn the board so that the narrow edge is resting on the floor and bring the other end up to eye level. As you look down along the narrow edge, you should see a slight arching midway down the board. If you don't see it, flip the board and look along the other narrow edge. You may see it here. This is the crown side.

The crown is important when you frame out anything that will eventually support a weight. In floors and over windows, for example, the lumber will support weight. The crown always faces the stress, so that when weight is pressed against it, the lumber has greater strength to resist it.

Wood Grades

Presumably the grading of lumber is a method of protecting the consumer, so that you know exactly what you're buying, and why one thing is more costly than the other (much like the grading of beef, for example). But we don't know any consumer who really understands the system. We can only assume that it is recognized by the dealer, and that the standards are passed on to us.

In general, the grade names and broad division into grades conform to the requirements set forth in "American Lumber Standards" by the National Bureau of Standards. Then various lumber associations establish grade requirements and grade marking procedures for species of lumber produced in their regions. The lumber industry itself is responsible for marking the lumber with the appropriate grade, but in some areas private agencies provide grade marking services. So the marks tend to differ from one company to the next, from one region to the next. Confused? So are we!

To simplify it as much as possible, here's how we understand it. Lumber is divided into two basic classifications: *select* and *common*. Select lumber is of excellent quality, for use when appearance and finishing are important; common lumber has defects and is used for construction and general-purpose projects. Now, this *is* important: *don't buy select when you need only common lumber*. Most of the work shown in this book has been performed with common lumber. Don't go to the extra expense of good-looking wood when it will only be concealed later.

The complications arise when we try to describe the grades of lumber within each of the two categories mentioned above. Each has its own lingo. For example, in select lumber you can have B and Better Grade or 1 and 2 clear as the highest quality, devoid of any but minor blemishes; then there are C select grade and D select grade, in diminishing order. Among hardwoods, you also have firsts, seconds, and a third grade, which is still further broken down into No. 1 common, No. 2 common, etc.

If grading referred only to appearances, we could judge everything by our personal taste. But grading also refers to such things as moisture content, seasoning, and strength as well. And what may be true of wood in our region may not apply to it in yours.

So we can only recommend that you make friends with your lumber dealer as soon as possible, relying on his judgment and advice for the kind of wood—at the most reasonable price—you need for the job at hand. Study the situation, and all the choices open to you, and make the selection based on your findings. Above all, don't walk into the lumberyard and simply say, "Give me 300 pieces of 2×4." Know exactly what you're buying first!

Wood Sizes: Nominal vs. Actual

There were times when we were convinced that the entire building industry conspired against amateurs by developing a secret language to describe its materials. Fortunately for us, the terms used for dimensions are not nearly so confusing as those used for grades, but they are still very tricky. Unless you understand them, you can make considerable errors in calculating your needs.

At the mill, lumber is usually sawed in dimensions of even inches in thickness and width and in 2′ increments of length, generally from 8′ to 20′ or 24′. But, as we explained, green wood shrinks, and is planed and surfaced, and the size of the wood can be reduced by as much as ½″ to ¾″ in width. Although we *call* the lumber by its original size, in fact we purchase the smaller size.

Lumber is ordered by thickness, width, and length: 2″×4″×8′, for example. The 2×4 measurements refer to the *nominal* dimensions of the lumber (as it comes from the saw). Though you order and pay for the 2×4 size, the *actual* size is 1½″×3½″.

Although this may sound complicated, it's in fact a lot simpler now than a few years ago when the actual size of a 2×4 was 1⅝″×3⅝″. Recently the sizes of softwood lumber—which is what you'll be working with more than anything else—were revised and approved by the United States Department of Commerce. The new sizes are now uniform, smaller than the original ones, but easier to calculate.

One more piece of lumber lingo: lumber that is less than 2″ thick (nominal size) is called *board lumber;* lumber that is 2″ thick or more is called *dimension lumber*. (Lumber that is thicker than

5″ is called *timber,* but you're unlikely to use anything this hefty.)

We've made up a chart listing the nominal sizes of the board and dimension lumber you're likely to use, comparing these dimensions with the currently uniform actual sizes you'll receive:

Nominal Size for Board Lumber	*Actual Size*
1×2	¾″×1½″
1×3	¾″×2½″
1×4	¾″×3½″
1×5	¾″×4½″
*1×6	¾″×5½″
1×8	¾″×7¼″
1×10	¾″×9¼″
1×12	¾″×11¼″

Nominal Size for Dimension Lumber	*Actual Size*
2×2	1½″×1½″
2×3	1½″×2½″
*2×4	1½″×3½″
*2×6	1½″×5½″
*2×8	1½″×7¼″
2×10	1½″×9¼″
2×12	1½″×11¼″
3×4	2½″×3½″
4×4	3½″×3½″

If you're working on an older home, the lumber used for the framing may correspond to the dimensions previously accepted by the building industry. So figure this difference in your calculations. You can usually compensate for it quite easily in your new installation, but don't overlook it.

One final word of caution, while we're on the subject: never assume that you know what the actual size is unless you really do know it. There seems to be no rhyme or reason to what constitutes the actual vs. the nominal size. For example, you'll hear wood referred to as five-quarter (5/4). Do you know what this means? It's the accepted term for wood that is actually 1″. If you're in doubt about the actual size, therefore, always check with the dealer before you order it, so that you won't be surprised later.

Other Lingo You May Encounter

By now you have acquired a rudimentary vocabulary of the trade. You should know, for example, that you refer to a piece of wood 2″ by 4″ simply as a 2×4 (a two-by-four), wood that is 2″ by 6″ as a 2×6 (a two-by-six), and so forth. Wood that is 2″ thick will be the kind of lumber most frequently ordered, and particularly 2×4's. They are thick and strong, what you might expect to find behind your walls, creating the framework.

For hidden framework, where strength is not a requirement (as in paneling), another type of cut is commonly used, a 1×2 or 1×3. These 1″ pieces of wood (actually ¾″ thick) are called *furring strips.*

Another variety of rough wood strips is called *lath,* and it comes approximately ⅜″ thick by 1¾″. You probably won't have much use for this, but you might as well learn the term.

We'll talk more about *molding* later in the book, but this is another kind of wood you'll encounter. It is shaped and molded to a particular design and used for trimming around windows, doors, and corners and at the base of the wall.

How to Order Lumber

When you order lumber, you specify the type of wood you need (select or common), the length, thickness, and width of the wood (8′×2×4) and the type of wood you had in mind (pine). The price of the lumber is calculated according to the *board foot.* This is the unit that equals the amount of wood in a piece of lumber that measures 1′ long, 1″ thick, and 12″ wide. The number of board feet in lumber of any dimension can be found by applying a simple mathematical formula: T (thickness)×W (width)×L (length), all divided by 12, equal the board feet. To find the number of board feet in a piece of lumber 6′ long, 2″ thick, and 6″ wide, for example, multiply 6×2×6, or 72. Divided by 12, you get 6 board feet.

This is the basis on which the price of wood is established. We find it simpler to ask for the price of one 8′ length of 2×4 and multiply that number by the quantity of 2×4's being ordered.

In the building trade, incidentally, the width of a dimension always comes before the height. When you order a 3×5 window, for example, you are asking for a window that is 3′ wide and 5′ high. If you give these dimensions in the wrong sequence, you can easily be misunderstood.

Also be careful in how you specify the quantity of lumber you need. If you ask for 32′ of 2×4's, you may get two 12-footers and one 8-footer, when you really wanted four 8-footers. Rather than take any chances of being misunderstood, specify the precise quantity and lengths of lumber you want. Always be generous in your order, too. If you cut it too close, you may be caught short at a bad time. When in doubt, order more than you need.

It would be impossible to publish a list of prices—even approximate—for the lumber in your area. The price of lumber varies from one region to the next and is as unpredictable as the

* Lumber used most frequently in this book.

stock market; it rises and falls with supply and demand. When a building boom is on, prices skyrocket; when building is down, the prices plummet too.

PLYWOOD

Plywood is a panel product made from thin sheets of wood called veneers. Select logs are peeled in giant lathes to form veneers of uniform thickness. After drying, veneers are bonded together under heat and high pressure with an adhesive, producing a bond between layers (plies) as strong as or stronger than wood itself.

Plywood panels are made from an odd number of veneers adhered face to face, with grains running in alternate directions. Lumber-core plywood has a solid center ply with thin crisscrossed veneers glued to both its surfaces. Use of an odd number of veneers stabilizes the wood for a very good reason: if two veneers are bonded together, tensions created by the glue lines, and inherent in the opposite grain directions, will cause warping. But bonding the two veneers to the opposite sides of a middle panel will equalize the tension. New veneers are added in pairs, one on each side, building up to as many as required. Whatever the thickness, the total is always an odd number.

Types of Plywood

The type of glue and the grade of inside plies determine whether plywood is suitable for exterior use. Exterior plywood, with higher-grade panels, has a glue bond that is so resistant to moisture that it will not delaminate even when boiled in water. You can get interior panels with this same glue but with different face grades.

All plywood is divided into two main types: softwood and hardwood. Hardwood is most often used for fine paneling and furniture; softwood is used for general carpentry and is the type most commonly encountered in home renovation.

Grades of Plywood

Most plywood made today is graded by the American Plywood Association. Look for a rubber stamp at the back or along the edges with the letters *DFPA*, which stand for Department for Product Approval. There are about ten grades of interior plywood and about as many grades for exterior.

The appearance of a panel's face and back determines its grade. Letters *N, A, B, C,* and *D* indicate the different grades. *N* is defect-free, all heartwood or sapwood veneers. Use it where you want a perfect, "natural" finish. *A* has neatly made repairs on a surface that can be painted or finished naturally. *B* surfaces may have circular repair plugs and tight knots. *C* plies can have knotholes slightly larger than 1″. Limited splits are permitted. A grade known as *C-plugged* has a repaired veneer that allows splits up to ⅛″ in width and knotholes up to ¼″×½″. *D* grade may have knotholes as large as 3″ in width and limited splits. A panel may have one grade for the face, another for the back, marked *A–C,* for example.

The stamping on the plywood will also indicate the species group of tree used and the relative strength, ranging from Group 1, the strongest, down to Group 5. For example, Group 1 includes plywood made from birch, various types of pine, and so forth.

The stamp will also indicate interior or exterior use and will provide additional numbers to indicate the amount of spacing suggested when the panels are installed.

Ordering Plywood

Plywood is generally sold in 4′×8′ sheets and in thicknesses ranging from ¼″ to 1″. For the projects shown in this book, there is no reason to go into nonstandard sizes or thicknesses. Bear in mind that plywood, like lumber, is priced according to its appearance as well as other factors. Don't order a plywood for looks if you are planning to cover it later. For home renovation, as shown here, you will probably be covering plywood with siding or flooring, so specify a plywood that is of construction grade (sufficiently strong but not finished in appearance), and save yourself a good deal of money.

OTHER BUILDING MATERIALS

Depending on the project you are undertaking, you will probably need only framing lumber—2×4's, 2×6's, and possibly 2×8's—and perhaps plywood. Other materials—such as gypsum wallboard, hardboard, and moldings—are described in the chapters pertaining to the specific jobs at hand. As you become more familiar with lumber, and as your lumberyard becomes more familiar to you, no doubt you will adopt your own preferences for certain kinds of wood. We hope this background will give you enough information so that you can get started without feeling foolish at the store.

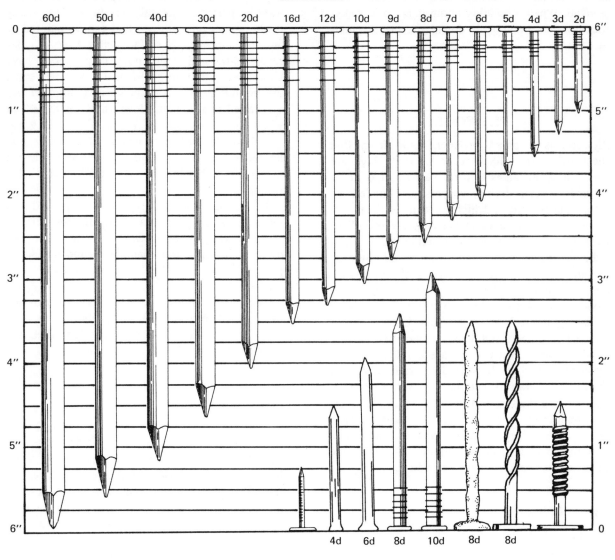

Nails you need

Common nails range in length from 1″ (or 2-penny) to 6″ (or 60-penny). Depending on the extent of the renovation you are doing, you will probably need only eight kinds of nails: ¾″ galvanized nails, 4- and 6-penny finishing nails, 8- and 10-penny common nails, 8-penny coated box nails, 8-penny tempered-steel flooring nails, and 1½″ annular drywall nails.

NAILS

The variety of nails is very extensive. They vary according to their length, their diameter, their design and construction, and the size and shape of their heads. Each type serves its own function. We've counted about twenty categories of nails, nearly each category having its own assortment of sizes as well. We won't subject you to all the fine points that distinguish nails in each of these categories. For all the demonstrations shown in this book, you will need only about five different kinds.

Types of Nails

By way of background, here are the characteristics that describe nails:

Length of Nail: Nail length can be designated in inches, but more commonly in pennies. This is an old English term which, in its original meaning, probably described the number of nails that could be purchased for a penny, or the price of nails per hundred. (It's all legend, anyway.) The term is now used as a measure of length. Since long nails were higher-priced than short ones, they had a higher penny rating, as they still do.

The designation *pennies* is abbreviated as *d,*

42

deriving from the *denarius,* an early Roman coin. A 60d nail is a 60-penny nail, which is 6″ long; at the other extreme, a 2d nail is a 2-penny nail and is only 1″ long.

Diameter of Nail: Since the diameter of most widely used nail types increases with the length, the length designation—whether in inches or in pennies—also implies over-all size and weight. A 6d nail, therefore, is nearly four times the diameter of a 2d nail.

The diameter of the shank also varies according to the type of nail. Three basic types of nails are as follows: box nails, common nails, and spikes. The smallest diameter is among the box nails; the largest, among the spikes. (You will be using common nails primarily.) Each category of nail has a number of sizes as well. Special-purpose nails, however, may come in only one size, or in several lengths but only a single diameter, depending on their purpose.

Design and Construction of Nails: Nails are constructed according to their purpose. Most nails are smooth along their shanks; others are ringed, barbed, or ridged. Nails may also be coated with cement or rosin to increase their holding power.

Nailhead: The shape and size of the nailhead also determines its use. Large heads hold best because they spread the load over a wider area, resisting pull-through. The heads of other nails are designed for appearance, small enough so that they can be concealed easily. There are double-headed nails, and even one kind of nail that has no head at all!

What Nails Will You Use?

We have reduced our selection of nails to the barest minimum.

Common Nails: These will be your mainstay. They are especially useful for rough framing and are required by building codes where the strength of a joint is the first consideration. You need only two kinds of common nails: 8d (2½″ long) and 10d (3″ long).

Coated Box Nails: These nails are exactly the same shape as common nails, but their diameter is slightly less, which helps avoid splitting the wood. The term *coated* means that they have been coated with a cementing agent (rosin) to increase their holding power. As the nails are driven, the coating becomes very hot, melts, and forms an adhesive after driving is completed. They are an ideal nail for flooring—as long as

you are not working in hardwood. They are used for underlayment flooring primarily. You need only one size: 8d. (Incidentally, the coating also makes them pretty tricky to drive, but more on that later.)

Finishing Nails: These nails are mainly used for interior finish work and in cases where you fear splitting the wood. You'll use them for trimming, in particular. Only two sizes are needed: 6d and 4d.

Drywall Nails: If you are planning to install wallboard, you'll need special nails designed specifically for this purpose. They have tapered threads and a broad flat head for better holding. For ½″ wallboard, use nails that are 1½″ long.

Flooring Nails: If you intend to install a hardwood floor or oak steps, you'll need nails that can penetrate this tough wood. Flooring nails are made of tempered steel. You can either work with a cut flooring nail—which has a rectangular cross section and a blunt tip—or a steel threaded nail, which has great holding power and makes a squeak-proof joint. In either case, you'll need the 8d size.

Galvanized Nails: If any of your work brings you outside—installing windows, for example—you'll need nails that will not rust from rain and snow. A ¾″ galvanized coated nail will probably serve most of your needs.

Ordering Nails

Nails are purchased by the pound. Obviously, the larger the nail, the fewer you will receive with each pound. Try to estimate your needs based on the extent of the work you intend to be doing. We ordered our common nails in the 50-pound box and had them delivered with the lumber.

Where nails will be regularly spaced, as in laying floors, you can avoid errors in buying if you know the number of nails per pound in the size you need. Your dealer can probably give you a chart with this information. For the nails you'll be ordering in the greatest quantities, here's a run-down:

8d common nails: 101 per pound
10d common nails: 66 per pound
6d finishing nails: 288 per pound
4d finishing nails: 630 per pound
8d threaded flooring nails: 142 per pound

To avoid running short, allow about 10 per cent more than you expect to need for the job and add any surplus to your workshop assortment.

CHAPTER 3

The Structure of Your House

If all you have at your disposal is the information given in this book, we would not recommed you build a house, or even an addition to a house. We are concerned here with the *interior* work you can do, and the exterior is included only as it affects the installation of windows and doors. But don't get us wrong: in these projects you should have at least a rudimentary knowledge of how your house is built, from the foundation to the roof. You will be working within the framework of the building, removing and replacing portions of it, adding to it, and decorating it. Every aspect of your house—its wiring, plumbing, heating, and construction—will determine the work ahead, so that even a casual acquaintance with the principles of house building is essential to your success. If nothing else, it will introduce you to the building terms used throughout the remainder of this book.

The structure of your home should conform to the regulations set forth by the building codes in your community. If it does not, at least your renovation work must incorporate the current building codes. Consequently, any discussion of home building must also include some reference to the official codes regulating your work.

BASIC HOUSE TYPES

There are numerous variations in design among residential homes, some more common in one region than in another, but in general your house should correspond to one of these basic types:

One-story House: The single-story house, with or without basement, is the most common home of all. It has greater variation in size, shape, and design than any other type. Because it is simply constructed, it is more economical to build. Variations can occur in the pitch of the roof and in the way the ceiling is designed.

One-and-a-half-story House: In this type of house, the first story consists of a full living area, but the second story, although designed as a living area, is only partial. The traditional Cape Cod house is the most familiar of this type of design. Dormer windows are frequently seen in a one-and-a-half-story house; these are windows made into the roof line to admit more natural light.

Two-story House: Here the second story is virtually duplicated over the first, creating a box-like structure that is spacious because it provides the maximum living area, and is most economical per square foot. The second level can also be constructed to overhang the first story, a means of increasing the floor area and breaking up the box-like appearance of the building.

Split-level House: The split level has come into popularity in recent years because it combines the merits of one-, one-and-a-half-, and two-story homes into a more interesting layout in a more compact area. Split levels contain three or more living levels. Rather than the living levels being placed one above the other, they are connected by stairs, which, when totaled, normally amount to no more than one full flight.

Bi-level House: This type of house is built as a two-story house without a basement or a raised one-story house with a finished lower level. Some bi-levels use only the upper level for the living area, creating the lower level for other purposes, such as a garage. Other bi-levels utilize both levels for living areas.

THE FOUNDATION

The foundation is the section of the building below the first level of beams. It supports the

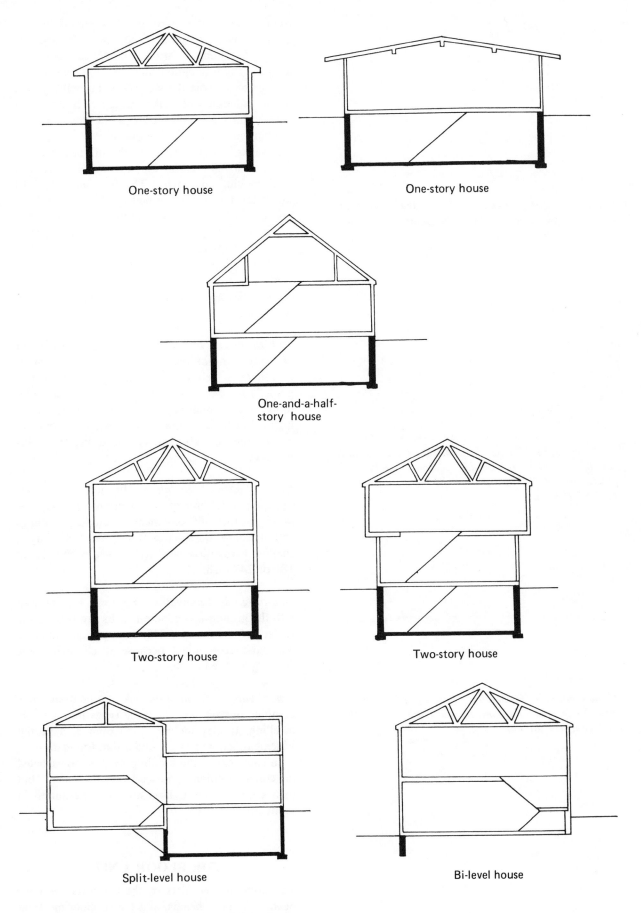

One-story house

One-story house

One-and-a-half-
story house

Two-story house

Two-story house

Split-level house

Bi-level house

Your house should correspond to one of these types. Dark lines indicate masonry walls below ground level.

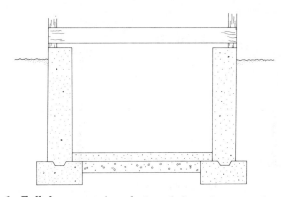

1. *Full basement foundation: below the ground in a one- or two-story house, with footings and masonry walls about 7' high.*

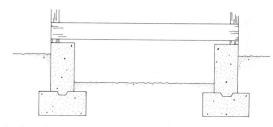

2. *Crawl space foundation: constructed like a full basement—with footings and masonry walls, but placed in a shallow excavation, its walls only about 18" or 24" high.*

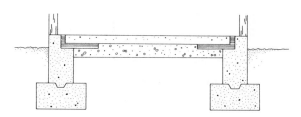

3. *Slab-on-grade foundation: footings are inserted into the ground and concrete slabs are laid on the surface of the ground.*

framing above that rests on it. Foundations are usually made of poured concrete or concrete blocks, fieldstone or bricks sometimes being used as well. The foundation must be built on soil firm enough to support the weight of the building and the installation within the structure. If the foundation shifts or settles because of unstable soil, the building will be forced out of alignment, causing cracks to appear in the walls and masonry.

An excavation is dug into the building site with earth-moving equipment. The type and depth of the excavation is determined by the design of the house foundation and the nature of the soil. Into this excavation the foundation is laid. First, footings—the concrete supports—are laid and then the foundation wall is constructed over the footings.

There are four types of foundations most commonly seen:

Full Basement Foundation: This provides extra area for living or recreation at minimum cost. It is generally below the ground (called "below grade") in one- or two-story houses and includes footings and masonry walls that are about 7' high. (Finishing a basement such as this may be one of the projects you will be doing from this book.)

Crawl Space Foundation: In terms of construction, this kind of basement is precisely the same as the full basement—including footings and masonry walls—but it is placed in only a shallow excavation, and its walls are only about 18" or 24" high.

Slab-on-grade Foundation: Footings are inserted into the ground and concrete slabs are laid on the surface of the ground. This kind of foundation is the most economical because it eliminates the framing for the first floor.

Combination Foundation: A foundation may combine one or more of these types into a single dwelling. It may include, for example, a partial basement, a crawl space, and a slab foundation.

In some cases, the building may be constructed on concrete columns instead of a basement, but this is not common. It is not even permitted in many areas.

THE FLOOR UNIT

The floor unit consists of the supports for floor beams, the floor beams, and the subflooring. First let's consider the construction on the concrete foundation made to support the first-floor beams, including the supports needed for the framing.

No brief description can take into account all the possible methods of constructing these underpinnings. The requirements for a simple cabin will be totally different from those required for a large home built on a hillside, for example. Codes vary, too. And an older home may have been constructed according to methods no longer employed. But, very simply, this construction includes a sill, girders, and Lally columns.

Sill: The sill rests on the foundation wall, carrying all the load of the outside framing of the building. It can be constructed in many ways. It is commonly made up of 2×6's nailed together to form 4×6's and generally is secured to the top of the foundation wall with anchor bolts that protrude up from the foundation. The sill goes around the entire perimeter of the house. (Sills are not needed when the exterior walls are of brick or concrete.)

Girders: The girder is the main supporting beam of the house. In standard houses, there is only one girder. Usually girders are installed across the foundation, midway between opposite parallel foundation walls and usually across the shortest dimension of the building for added rigidity. Usually the foundation wall is notched so that the ends of the girders fit into these pockets and their top is flush with the top of the sill. Depending on the age of the house and the specific building codes, a girder may be made up of timbers or a steel I beam (shaped, in cross section, like the letter *I*), or made from three pieces of 2″-thick boards spiked together to form a support that is 6×8 or 6×12.

Lally Column: One or two posts made of wood or steel also support the girder. Chances are that the girder is resting on a Lally column, a cement-filled steel pipe with steel plates welded on both ends. If the girder is 6×8, the Lallys will be about 7′ apart. In older homes, posts of a hard, extremely durable wood impervious to decay and termites were used instead of Lally columns; they were called *locust posts.*

Box Beams: Around the perimeter of the wall, so-called *box beams* (or *rim joists*) are installed. They are constructed of the same material as the floor beams, and into these the floor beams will be butted and nailed. When the sill is installed, it is squared up on top of the foundation, even if the foundation itself is not perfectly square. It's not always possible to get the sill boards exactly square, so further correction is made when the box beams and floor beams are installed. The box is made as square as possible. If the box isn't square, the whole house will be out of square.

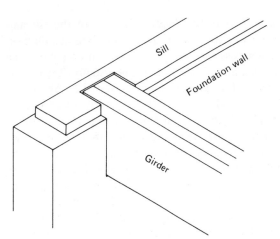

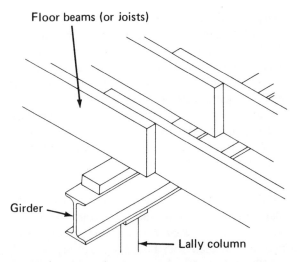

1. The foundation wall is usually notched so that the ends of the girders can fit into these pockets, flush with the top of the sill. These girders are made of three pieces of 2″ boards spiked together.

2. Girders may also be constructed of steel I beams. From below, the girders are supported with posts, usually Lally columns, cement-filled steel pipes with steel plates welded on both ends. The floor beams (or joists) rest on the girders.

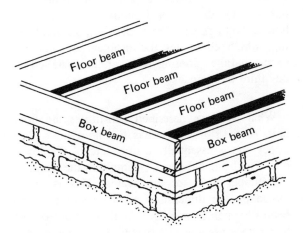

3. While the mid-portion of the floor beams is supported by the girders, the ends of the beams are anchored to the box beams. The box beams have been installed on the sill over the foundation wall.

Floor Beams (or Joists): On top of the sill and girder rest the floor beams. These are installed on edge across the foundation and butted against the box beams. Floor beams are usually 2×8's, although for longer spans—over 12' or 14'—2×10's and 2×12's are frequently used. (These are all subject to local building code regulations.)

The beams are installed with their crown sides facing upwards, toward the stress, so that they will straighten out as the house settles. Beams are laid to accommodate or allow space for plumbing, and extra beams are installed where extraordinary weight is anticipated. Floor beams are nailed at intervals of 16", or what is called *16" on center,* meaning that there is a distance of 16" from the center of one beam to the center of the next one. Older homes may contain beams that have been installed every 20" or every 24".

Bridging: Short pieces of wood or metal are nailed between the floor beams to help distribute the loads on the floor and to stiffen the boards to prevent them from falling over under extreme loads. Most building codes require either wood or steel bridging. Bridging is inserted between the beams with a material the same size as the floor beams (*solid bridging*) or with pairs of 5/4×3 or 2×4 lumber angled so that they cross each other (*herringbone* or *cross bridging*).

Subflooring: Also called a *deck,* subflooring is the platform placed over the sills and beams on which all subsequent framing rests. Subflooring may be installed with boards—generally 6", 8", or 12" wide—often butted edge to edge, or, less commonly, joined with grooved or lapped joints. In some cases subflooring is laid diagonally, and the finished floor is installed at right angles to the beams below. In this way, the subfloor will not loosen or cause squeaking as it can when installed parallel to the finished flooring. In modern homes, builders tend to use plywood for subflooring, which eliminates the problem of diagonal versus parallel flooring and can be installed in one third the time.

What we have described constitutes the floor unit. A two-story house has two floor units. The upper one is essentially a duplicate of the lower one. The basic difference is simply in the width of the lumber used for the beams. This is determined by the dimensions of the room that the beams happen to span, but the floor beams on the lower floor are always larger than the ones on the higher floor because they support two floors. If there are 2×12's on the ground floor, there are 2×10's on the higher floor.

WALL CONSTRUCTION

The wall unit includes all the framing required to construct the exterior walls and the interior partitions of a residence. In the building trade, the term *wall* applies to the framing erected to form the exterior wall of a house. The term *partition* is used to designate what separates one room from another. From the carpenter's viewpoint the work involved in either is virtually identical.

Basically, a wall is constructed of vertical lumber called *studs* and horizontal lumber called *shoes* and *plates.* Openings in a wall or partition require additional framing lumber called *headers, liners,* and *legs.*

We go into far greater detail about wall construction later in this book. Interior partitions are discussed in the next chapter; openings for windows and doors are discussed in the chapters dealing with those subjects specifically. But for now, here are some of the general features that characterize the construction of walls as they affect the over-all framing of the house.

The exterior, or outside, walls of a house rest directly on the sills and subflooring attached to the foundation walls. These walls are bearing units for the upper floors, if any, and the roof of the structure.

Inside walls form the partitions for the rooms inside the dwelling. One type of partition is a *load-bearing wall* that supports the framing above it. (It's like the spinal cord of the house.) Another type is the *nonbearing partition* that carries only the weight of its own materials.

To construct a wall, either interior or exterior, 2×4's called *shoes* (or *sole plates*) are first nailed along the subfloor, anchored into the floor and into the floor beams. To these shoes, *studs*—normally 2×4's also—are attached, and over these studs a *plate* is nailed. This is the rough framing for a wall. Where doors or windows occur, a *header* of adequate size is needed to carry the vertical load across the opening. The ends of these headers are supported with *liner* or *trimming studs.* Studs in walls are placed with the wide faces perpendicular to the direction of the wall. Studs are normally spaced every 16", but in older homes may appear every 24".

There are two basic kinds of home construction. They affect the way the walls are framed.

Balloon Frame Construction: In this type of construction both the studs and the floor beams rest on the sill. The studs run from the bottom of the house to the top in one continuous line no matter how tall the house is. After these tall studs are installed, the floors are added. The second-floor beams rest on a strip of lumber anchored in one continuous strip around the inside edges of the outside wall studs.

Balloon framing is common for two-story buildings where the exterior covering is of brick, stone, or stucco because there is less likelihood of movement between the wood framing and the masonry. Balloon framing was popular years ago, so you'll find it in older homes, but it is seldom used today.

Box or Platform Frame Construction: In platform construction, the subflooring extends to the outside edges of the building and provides a platform upon which exterior walls and interior partitions can be erected. With platform framing, each floor is built like a shallow box with walls added one story at a time. Platform construction is the type of framing most generally used today.

Platform construction is easy to erect because it provides a flat surface at each floor level on which to work. It is also easily adapted to various methods of prefabrication and presents fewer problems for home renovation. With this kind of framing, it is common practice to assemble the wall framing on the floor and then tilt the entire unit into place.

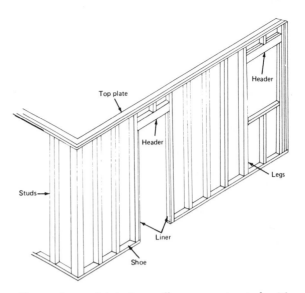

All exterior and interior walls are constructed with the same components: studs are nailed to a shoe and to a top plate. For window and doors, a header of adequate size is installed to carry the vertical load across the openings.

ROOF CONSTRUCTION

The roof of the house is the uppermost structural assembly supported by the exterior walls. The roof provides protection to the dwelling and its occupants, and its shape helps portray the architectural style of the entire building. The roof must be structurally sound and solid and covered with the appropriate roofing material. It is the most complicated of all the framing jobs connected with house construction.

The *rafters* provide the main support of the roof. They may rest right on the plate of the top floor or on a special shoe at the ceiling beam placed there for this purpose alone. In traditional construction, the rafters are notched so that their ends tie into this beam on one end, the notch being called a *bird's mouth.* At the other end rafters are cut to fit so that their ends lie flat against a *ridge rafter.* To about every fourth set of rafters, a *collar beam* may be nailed—parallel to the ceiling beams—near the ridge to counteract the outward thrust of the roof load.

At the gable end of the building—traditionally the narrow side of the house—special studs are cut to fit between the end pair of rafters and the plate below. A carefully framed house will have gable studs directly over the wall studs from the story below—instead of in random locations—to give extra support and to make the nailing of the sheathing (see below) easier. The gable studs are installed so that half of their thickness extends in-

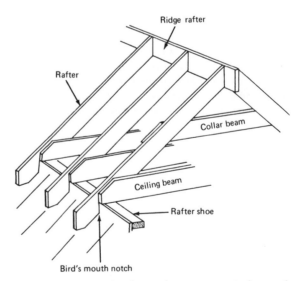

The rafters provide the main support of the roof. Traditionally, the rafters are notched (into a so-called bird's mouth) so that one end ties into a rafter shoe. The other end lies flat against a ridge rafter. A collar beam is installed near the ridge at intervals—usually attached to every fourth set of rafters—to counteract the outward thrust of the roof load.

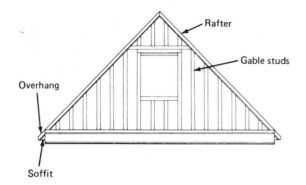

At the gable end of the building, special studs—called gable studs—are cut to fit between the two rafters and the plate below. The framing also allows for the opening needed for a louvered unit that is normally placed near the peak of the roof for ventilation. Notice also the overhang at the end of the rafter that provides the frame for what is known as the soffit.

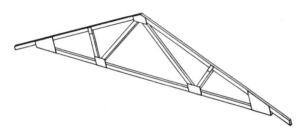

A roof may also be framed with trusses. A truss is a triangular-shaped construction that provides a rigid framework for the roof, and that can be assembled independently and attached to the framing as a complete unit. This is one kind of truss design.

side the rafters, providing a nailing surface for the interior wallboard.

A roof may be framed with *trusses*. This is a triangular-shaped construction that many builders favor today. A truss forms a rigid framework for the roof, can be assembled on the ground before installation, and is simply lifted into place over the framing, set into position, and nailed—as a complete unit—to the framing. (The trusses support the roof, not the interior walls.) As the house is being constructed, trusses look like a row of individual triangles standing in a row across the framing.

The *pitch* is the angle at which the rafters are installed, the mathematical relationship between the total rise and the span of the roof. The *overhang* is the part of the rafter that extends beyond the lower edge of the roof.

ROOF SHAPES

Variation in shape and design is one of the factors that make the roof so complicated to frame. Shapes of roof surfaces vary from the single-surface flat roof—with only a slight pitch to shed water—to a combination of flat, pitched, and even curved surfaces requiring the utmost skill in framing. A roof may be one or more of the following shapes:

Flat Roof: In conventional construction, the flat roof is the easiest to frame. There is no slope or pitch, so that construction is often used in contemporary designs of houses having carports, patios, and courts. The flat roof does not provide an attic space, so adequate insulation must be installed in correct locations.

Shed Roof: Also known as the lean-to roof, this is another single-plane roof, which is given a distinct angle of pitch. The style derives from a relatively small structure built for storage or shelter.

Gable Roof: This most popular and widely used roof is formed by two roof planes meeting at the ridge. A gable roof is characterized by a ridge line running the full length of the house, the two planes on the roof sloping down at equal angles. The gable ends of the structure form triangles. (We used the gable design as our example in the previous drawings to show the construction of a traditional roof.)

Hip Roof: A hip roof forms four roof planes, while a gable roof forms only two. In a hip roof the ridge does not run the full length of the house. Instead, hip rafters extend up diagonally

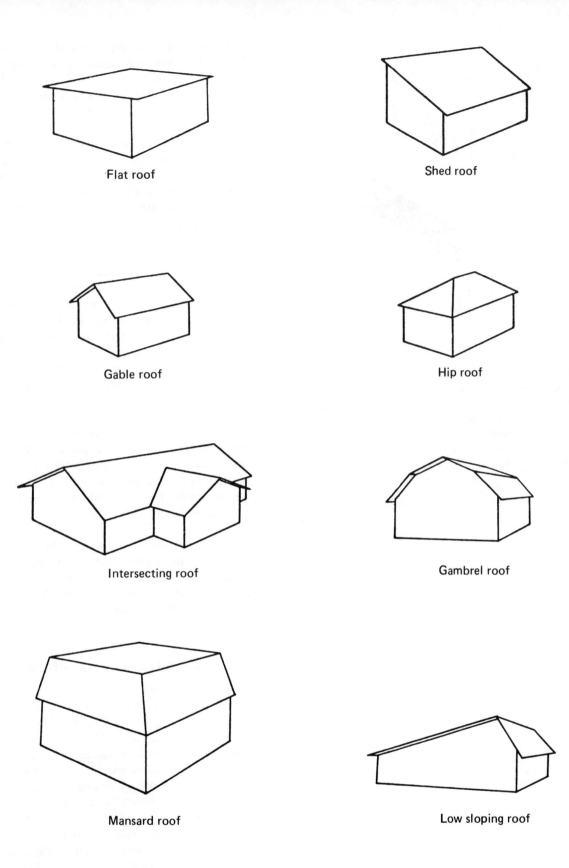

Flat roof

Shed roof

Gable roof

Hip roof

Intersecting roof

Gambrel roof

Mansard roof

Low sloping roof

Roofs can be constructed in any one of a variety of shapes and designs. Here are the basic roof shapes: flat, shed, gable, hip, intersecting, gambrel, mansard, and low sloping.

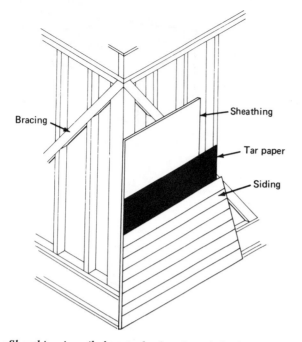

Labels on figure:
- Bracing
- Sheathing
- Tar paper
- Siding

Sheathing is nailed onto the framing of the house for added rigidity and insulation. (If the sheathing has been installed horizontally or if composition board was used, bracing will have been installed diagonally onto the framing.) Over the sheathing is tacked tar paper, which acts as a protection against moisture. Over this, siding is nailed.

from each corner to meet the end of the ridge. A low-pitched hip roof affords a wide variety of room arrangements and so is often used to form a pleasingly low roof on a ranch house or on a rambling contemporary home.

Intersecting Roof: Necessary when the building contains offsets and wings, the intersecting roof may be a combination of shed, gable, and hip roofs, requiring a special rafter for the "valley" where the two different parts of the intersecting roof meet or are joined.

Gambrel Roof: This is the four-planed roof most commonly associated with large homes in a barn-like design. It offers more usable space than a gable or hip roof of equal height with no greater span of rafters. The gambrel roof, like a gable roof, has a single ridge running the full length of the building, but each roof deck is angled outward into two additional planes, with the lower plane much steeper than the higher.

Mansard Roof: A French-style roof designed by François Mansard, it is constructed somewhat like a gambrel roof of four planes. The mansard roof, however, has nine planes formed by rafters meeting at a ridge or at the topmost point of the upper slopes. The mansard roof does not have gable ends like the simple gable or gambrel roof.

Low Sloping Roof: This roof is almost as popular as the simple gable. The larger slope or plane is generally continuous over two or more floor levels so that it is ideal for a split-level or for a one-and-a-half-story house.

SHEATHING AND SIDING

We've now worked our way out—from the internal skeletal structure of the house to its covering. Over the framing is installed *sheathing,* and over the sheathing is installed *siding.*

On most houses constructed today a structural material is utilized on exterior walls to strengthen them against racking—pulling out of shape or out of plumb—which is caused by wind and other natural forces. Sheathing adds rigidity to the building frame and, as an additional layer, helps insulate the house against cold and heat. Sheathing also provides a nailing surface for the siding. (Some houses are constructed with a single material, combining sheathing with siding. This is more frequently seen in economical construction, and in single-story homes primarily.)

Sheathing in older homes was generally installed with 1×6 or 1×8 boards, which were either butted, lapped, or tongue-and-grooved. More contemporary sheathing tends to be accomplished with plywood in thicknesses of ½″ or ⅜″, depending on local codes. Sheathing can also be made of gypsum or some other composition board. If sheathing has been constructed horizontally or if composition boards were used, you'll find bracing installed diagonally, notched into the studs, before the sheathing was attached to the framing.

Sheathing for the roof is generally wood—plywood or boards—because other material won't hold down the roofing material.

Over the sheathing are stapled or tacked sheets of 15-pound *felt paper,* commonly called *tar paper* or *building paper.* This is designed to make the house moisture-proof.

Then comes the siding. Siding is installed in sheets, boards, or shingles, depending on the product. It may be one of a number of materials, chosen on the basis of personal taste, budget, the design of the structure, and the material common to the particular region. Typical siding materials are clapboard, wood shakes and shingles, textured plywood siding, stucco, and aluminum. The siding is nailed to the framing with galvanized nails, and all joint openings around the doors and windows are calked to prevent leakage.

Over the sheathing on the roof, shingles—asphalt or wood—are normally installed, but roofing can also be installed in rolls, or as slate or tile; and even plastic materials are now in use.

When a roof surface intersects with another adjoining wall or a projection, such as a chimney or ventilator, joints are made watertight with *flashing,* strips of sheet metal installed before the roofing goes on. Currently, intersecting roofs are woven into the shingles so flashing is not needed.

STUDY YOUR WALLS

Now that we've given you some of the basic principles of building construction, try to apply this information to your own home. Before you dismantle any part of its structure, you'd better have a pretty good idea of how it's put together.

First study the walls. Can you tell which are bearing and which are nonbearing? Although you may assume from our previous discussion that all exterior walls are bearing, this may not be true. In a gabled house, for example, the exterior walls at the gabled ends (which are normally the narrow ends) do not support the roof and are therefore nonbearing. Even so, it's best to install a header over any wide openings you may make in the exterior wall, the size of the lumber determined by codes in your area.

But what about the interior walls (the partitions)? Any time you decide to rip out or move a partition, you must determine first—before you make any move—which type of wall you're dealing with. Obviously, if you take out a bearing wall, part of the house may collapse. To prevent this from happening, you must replace it with some other kind of support, usually a girder beam. But on the surface all walls look alike. What should you look for?

The best thing to do is to climb into the attic and study the construction of the roof. If the roof has been built with trusses (see our drawing), you'll see individual frames shaped like triangles across the top. And if the roof *has* been installed with trusses, you have no worries: none of the partitions in your home is bearing. The weight of the roof is supported entirely by the exterior walls, and inside bearing walls are unnecessary.

If the roof is not trussed, you'll have to look for other signs. Study the direction of the ceiling beams while you're in the attic. Are they parallel or perpendicular to the partition downstairs? If they are parallel, the beams are supported at their ends by the exterior walls, with no support in the middle, and the wall is not acting as a support. If the beams are at an angle to the partition, look more closely. Are the beams supported midway by a girder? This girder may just be part of the wall. Measure the distance of the girder from the outside walls, then run downstairs and measure the distance of the partition from the outside walls. If the distance is the same, it is a bearing wall. If you remove the wall, you must substitute some other means to support the ceiling beams.

YOU AND YOUR BUILDING INSPECTOR

If you are doing heavy renovation, you'll probably need a building permit. If you are making alterations in the structure or exterior appearance of your home, you will most certainly need a building permit. A permit is meant to be posted, giving full notice that your work is being inspected regularly and that it conforms to the codes set forth in the community.

Building codes and building inspectors are far from uniform. In two towns five miles apart you may find two vastly different requirements. (We know of one community where the installation of a picket fence is regulated by building codes!) So it would be impossible to advise you on what is standard procedure for your area. Some building codes are frightfully outdated; others are very reasonable; still others insist on the most stringent details.

To apply for a permit, you must first submit plans describing the nature of the work you intend to undertake. The building inspector may want to view the premises before issuing this permit. This is the time you will establish the specifications required for the job: what size lumber is required to cover a span of 16′, for example? If you are installing walls, the inspector will want to return again before you actually cover them up, so that he is certain the structure of the framing conforms to code. Then he will allow you to cover up the walls. When you've completed the work, he'll probably want to return for final inspection. In a dwelling being made livable, the inspector will issue a certificate of occupancy (a "C.O.") once he has approved your final work.

And then expect your taxes to go up!

WHAT COMES FIRST?

Even if your work is not being inspected, each project should follow a sequence that makes sense. Assuming that you are doing major renovation—which also affects electricity, heating, and plumbing—here is the ideal sequence to follow. Obviously, not all work can fall into such a neat pattern, but this is what you should strive for. Check off any segment of this list that applies to the work you intend to do. (Incidentally, you'll find that the chapters in this book roughly correspond to this sequence.)

1. Submit plans and apply for building permit.
2. Rip out old installation.
3. Reinforce framing where necessary according to building codes.
4. Partition off room or rooms.
5. Install exterior doors and windows.*
6. Installation of rough wiring, plumbing, and heat ducts (no fixtures).
7. All "rough-in" inspections for framing, plumbing, and wiring.
8. Install insulation in walls and ceilings.
9. Hang wallboard or paneling.
10. Install underlayment on floors.
11. Paint or paper walls.
12. Tile bathroom; tile kitchen floor.
13. Completion of finished wiring, heating, and plumbing (and inspections, if needed).
14. Install finished flooring—carpeting or hardwood.
15. Hang interior doors.
16. Trim doors, windows, and baseboards.
17. Final inspection for C.O.

* If you are planning to have the house re-sided, you can do so any time after the windows and exterior doors have been installed.

PART TWO

Walls, Floors, and Stairs

CHAPTER 4

Partitioning a Room

In the previous chapter we described the way in which the walls of a house are constructed. Called a *partition,* an interior wall is a solidly constructed frame that divides one room from another and can (though does not necessarily) help support the ceiling beams. Partitions are the skeletal structure of a room, the framework on which you will hang your walls and doors.

There are a number of occasions on which you may want to install a partition where none now exists. If you have a large, open attic—as we show in our demonstration—you may want to finish it off so that you can use it for an added living area. You may want to divide a large finished room in the house into two or more smaller rooms. You may want to finish a basement, first separating the space into smaller room units, then hanging walls or paneling on the partitions. Erecting partitions is very enjoyable: here you'll lay out your plans for all the work ahead. Partitioning goes quickly, with immediate and rewarding results.

First we describe the methods of laying out and constructing the partitions for a standard room, then we develop some of the more specific situations you may encounter if you're working in an attic area (where the shape of the ceiling may be angled) or in a basement (where you may encounter masonry surfaces). We show an open attic area primarily because it makes our work more visible by demonstrating how partitions are attached to the framework of a house. You can apply this information to whatever situation you may have in your own home.

CONSTRUCTION OF A PARTITION

Earlier in this book we reproduced a drawing that illustrated the structure of an exterior wall, showing how the doors and windows are framed within a wall. An interior partition contains the same components, and so we show this illus-

tration again. The partitions shown in this chapter are called *stud walls,* the most common method of dividing off rooms, easy and inexpensive to install, strong enough to withstand heavy loads, and providing space through which pipes and electric cables can be run.

Standard partitions are erected with common construction lumber, generally 2×4's. The basic construction of a partition is very simple: the stud walls rest on a base called a *shoe* (also called a *sole plate* in some regions). The standard shoe is a 2×4 nailed to the floor. Vertical pieces of lumber called *studs* stand on the shoe at regular intervals and are toenailed to it. The studs are held in place at the top by a horizontal piece of 2×4 called a *top plate* (or *ceiling plate* or *wall plate,* depending on the region in which you live).

MATERIALS AND TOOLS

Very few materials and tools are needed for partitioning. For standard rooms, only 2×4's are required. Unless you have an unusually high ceiling, precut 8' lengths should be sufficient. For a room 10'×8' we used approximately twenty precuts. Buy construction-grade lumber.

Ten- and 8-penny common nails will serve for the entire project, and a hammer—preferably 20-ounce—for nailing.

A chalk line will also be used. Be certain to select a chalking powder for the chalk line that will contrast visibly with the color of the floor; if the floor is old (as ours is), use white chalking; if you're working on new wood, use blue.

Some builders prefer to use a plumb line for partitioning, but we preferred the level. A 4' level is best. And, naturally, you'll be needing your old stand-bys: circular saw, fold-out ruler, right angle, and pencil.

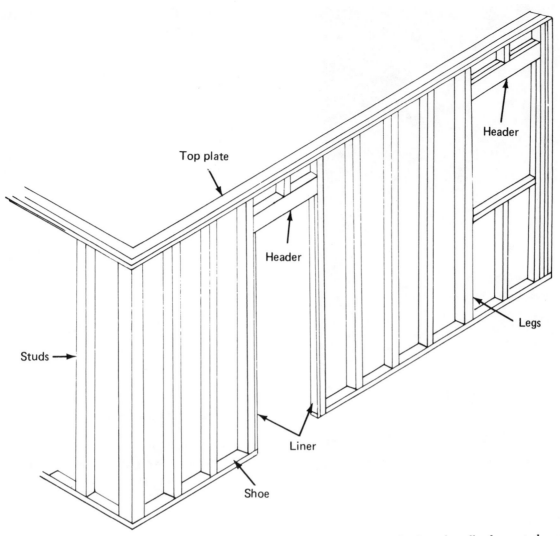

Top plate

Header

Header

Studs

Legs

Liner

Shoe

This is a standard stud wall: shoe, studs, and top plate.

YOUR ROOM

As you can see from our photographs, we are working in a bare attic space. This is very common, and more will be said about attics later in this chapter. But this may not apply to your own situation. A partition can be installed in a finished room just as simply as it can in an incomplete room like ours. The important thing is that the partition be firmly attached at the base and at the top. You can nail directly into a finished floor (provided it is not carpeting) and into a finished ceiling. First determine the direction in which your ceiling beams are running. Tap the ceiling with your hammer. When the sound is hollow, there is no beam above. When the sound in solid, there is a beam above. By tap-

1. This is the corner of an open area that we allocated for a small den. The outer dimensions of the room will measure 8′×10′.

2. *After you've determined the dimensions of the room, measure off its perimeter. Place cross marks on the floor at what will be the corners of the room. At the first outside wall, hammer a 10-penny common nail at the corner where the first wall will be erected.*

3. *Loop the chalk line onto the nail and pull the line across the floor to the point at which the next corner of the room will be located.*

ping systematically, you will discover the intervals between the beams. If they are perpendicular to the partitioned wall, you'll have no problem. Simply anchor the top plate into each of the ceiling beams by nailing the 2×4 onto the ceiling. If your partition runs parallel to the beams, you'd be wise to arrange the dimensions of the room so that the partition runs along the bottom edge of one ceiling beam, so that you can anchor it to the beam along that edge. Otherwise, you'll have to remove the finished ceiling and make other preparations, which will become clear later.

We are showing how to partition off a room with only two walls, by building off two exterior walls. You can also partition a room off with one or with more walls. The procedure is the same, regardless of the number of walls you install.

PLANNING AHEAD

How large do you want the room or rooms to be? Where do you want the door? Do you want a closet? Here are some considerations to bear in mind before laying out the room, factors that may influence your final decisions:

Size of Room: Consider the function of the room as you determine the size. Allow space for the furniture appropriate to the function: one bed or two, double or single? A dresser and a television, perhaps, or a table with four chairs. At this stage it's easy to adjust measurements, but later it will be extremely difficult to do so. Take this time to consider carefully the purpose for which the room is designed.

Door: In planning your room, it's advisable to allow for standard-sized doors, avoiding the extra cost of custom sizes, unless you have no choice. Standard doors are 24″, 28″, 30″, or 36″ wide the most common being 30″. Standard door height is 6′8″. (Much more will be said about doors in Chapter 15, "How to Install Doors.")

Consider also the direction in which the door will swing. Ideally, the door should swing against a wall, rather than against a piece of furniture, so bear this in mind when you select the location for the door. Generally, the corner of the room is a more efficient location for the door than at the center of a wall.

If the ceiling drops at one end of the room (as is common in many attics), be certain to place your door where the ceiling is at least 7′ high. Obviously it's preferable to enter a door that is 6′8″ to one that is 5′10″. So if you have a choice, place the door where the ceiling will permit a standard-height door.

Closets: If you want to build in a closet, now is the time to allow for it in your plan. A standard closet is 24″ deep and as wide as you desire. Remember to allow for a door to the closet and account for the way in which it will swing.

MARKING OFF THE FLOOR

You've established the size of the room by now. Make a drawing of your plan on a sheet of paper, noting the dimensions that are most critical to the room. It may be, for example, that the interior dimensions of the room are most important, or the exterior dimensions of the room may be the determining measure. The outer dimensions of the room will be 3½″ larger along the partitions than those for the inner dimensions. Note the dimensions on your drawing, and follow this guide as you mark the room off on the floor.

Let's assume your room is like ours: 10′×8′, the outer dimensions being most critical. First mark off, with crosses, where you anticipate the corner of your new room to fall. Measure off 10′ from the outside wall and mark a cross at both ends of the proposed wall. Then measure off 8′ from the other wall and indicate with a cross the two extreme points.

Starting at one end, tap a 10-penny common nail into the floor at the first cross you've marked on the floor. Loop the chalk line onto the nail and pull the line across the floor to the next corner of the room that you've indicated with a cross. With the string taut, pop the line. The mark made by the chalk indicates the placement of the first wall of the future room. Do the same with the other wall until you have chalk lines on the floor that indicate the entire perimeter of the room. In our example, these lines indicated the outer perimeter of the walls.

Now mark the line where the door will be placed, allowing for the following: (1) the width of the door itself; (2) the door jamb, which measures ¾″ on each side of the opening; (3) enough space for adjusting the door to a plumb line, ½″ on each side being sufficient for this purpose. In other words, if the door is 30″, your opening will be:

$$
\begin{array}{ll}
30″ & \\
+\ 1″ & \text{(for plumb on each side)} \\
+\ 1½″ & \text{(door jamb on each side)} \\
\hline
\text{Total:}\quad 32½″ &
\end{array}
$$

Although these measurements may have little meaning to you at this stage, you'll find how necessary they are when you install the door (see Chapter 15). (Here we are only concerned with the width of the doorway as it affects the place-

4. When the chalk line has been extended along the full length of the proposed interior wall, pull the cord taut. Place the line precisely at the intersection of the cross indicating the corner of the room. Pull the line taut and, with the free hand, snap the line.

5. The chalk line should produce a visible mark on the floor, as shown here. If you're working on an old floor, use white chalking powder, as we have done. If you're working on a new floor, use blue. Continue to make chalk lines indicating all of the walls, using the same method.

6. *Now mark off the door opening. We are intending to install a door 30" wide. Allowing 30" for the door, therefore, plus 1½" for the door jamb, and 1" for "plumbing," we have marked off 32½" for the door opening.*

7. *At each side of the door opening we have clearly drawn "crow's feet" on the floor.*

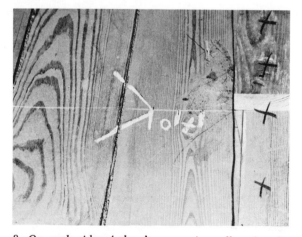

8. *On each side of the door opening, allow for the two studs that will frame the doorway. Allowing 1½" for the first stud (the liner), mark an O, and allow an additional 1½" for the stud directly alongside it, marking an X. Although these marks and terms may have little meaning to you now, they are a good precaution against forgetting to allow for these important studs later, so indicate them clearly even if you don't quite understand their function yet.*

ment of the shoe. In Chapter 15 we will show you how to frame out the height of the doorway as well.)

Returning to the chalk line, mark off 32½" for the door opening. Make your mark clearly visible: "crow's feet" (< or >) work well for all marking.

The door opening will be framed on both sides with two vertical studs, just as they are shown in the drawing. As you mark off the door opening, also indicate on the floor the placement of these two studs, each a 2×4. The stud framing the doorway is called the *liner* (or *trimmer stud*) and is marked with an O. Measure off 1½" for the liner and then mark off another 1½" for the stud that will butt up against the liner. (Remember, although the stud is constructed with a 2×4, this is a nominal dimension only. In fact, 2×4's are 1½"×3½".) Mark this second stud with an X, as shown in the photograph. Mark an O and an X on either side of the door opening on the chalk line.

If you're installing more than one room on the floor, make your chalk lines for all the rooms and allow for all the door openings in the same manner. Before you begin the next stage you should have a clearly marked plan before you: chalk lines on the floor indicating exactly where your partitions will be erected.

LAYING THE SHOE

Now you will lay 2×4's along the chalk lines, the base of your partitions, called the *shoe,* to which vertical studs will be attached later.

Measure off the length of the room from the corner up to the door opening. Cut a 2×4 to this measurement. If your measurement calls for more than 8', simply use more than one length of 2×4. For example, if the measurement is 9½', take an 8' length and cut another piece 1½' long.

Lay the cut 2×4 along the chalk line (remember to lay it on the correct side of the line) and attach it to the floor, using 10-penny common nails. Hammer two nails in each end of the 2×4 and drive in a nail every 12" or 14" in an alternating zigzag direction—rather than in an even line—down the length of the 2×4.

Hammer these shoes along the chalk lines until you have completed the perimeter of the room. If you're constructing more than one room, lay the shoes along the chalk lines for each room, allowing for each door opening, before you proceed with the next step. Always be certain to nail the shoe consistently to the inside or to the outside of the chalk line.

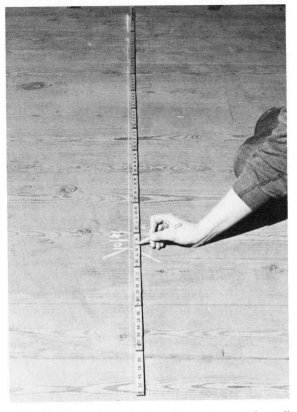

9. Now measure the distance from the outside wall to the nearest door opening. Cut a piece of 2×4 to exactly this measurement.

10. With 10-penny common nails, anchor the 2×4 to the floor, placing it alongside the chalk line. (Decide whether the chalk line will run along the outer edge of the shoe or along its inner edge, and stay consistent throughout.) Place two nails at the end of the 2×4 and drive in nails every 12" or 14" in a zigzag pattern along the length of the piece.

12. The shoes for the room are now complete. The proper amount of space has been allocated for the door opening and the floor has been marked off to indicate where the studs framing the doorway will be placed.

11. Here is another shoe attached to the floor. This one measures 10' long: two pieces of 2×4—one 8' in length, the other 2' in length—butt against each other and are nailed to the floor.

13. Now is the time to allow for all the other rooms and closets you intend to install. Here we have nailed down shoes for two closets, for example: the doorway of one opens into one room, the doorway of the other opens into the room alongside it. The closets are 24" deep.

PREPARING THE TOP PLATE

Each stud will be toenailed into the shoe at the base and anchored to the top plate above. In other words, the pattern laid out on the floor by the shoes must be duplicated exactly overhead. This is basic because the partitions must be plumb. If the top plate is not directly over the shoe, the studs will not be plumb when they are attached above and below. If the studs are not plumb, the wall will hang at an angle. To prevent this from occurring, therefore, it's vital to place the shoe and top plate in their proper relationship.

First you'll cut the 2×4's to the precise measurements of the shoes. This is easy: simply lay the 2×4 directly on top of the shoe and mark it off for proper cutting. Don't cut away for door openings, however. The top plate will run the entire perimeter of the room, with no interruptions for door openings. If you must butt two lengths of 2×4, don't make the joint at the same place on the plate as you did on the shoe. One joint shouldn't occur directly over another one.

After you've cut the top plate to the same measurement as the shoe, simply lay it directly on top of the shoe. If you're planning for more than one room, place all the cut 2×4's directly over all the shoes, creating a running pattern of continuous 2×4's. With 10-penny common nails, tack these pieces of 2×4's onto the shoes so that their position is fixed. This is your pattern, and each should be cut to the precise dimensions indicated on your floor plan. Any errors should be clearly visible here—correct them before you proceed further.

While the top plates are tacked to the shoes, you can conveniently prepare them for the placement of the studs. By marking both shoe and top plates simultaneously at this early stage, you'll guarantee having a precise duplication of each measurement: the marks you make now will provide you with an efficient and precise road map to follow when you're ready to attach the studs to the shoe and top plates at a later stage.

First mark off the door openings, just as you've already done on the floor. (As you know, the shorter dimension of a 2×4 is actually 1½".) Using the right angle, first mark off the liner (or trimmer stud) by drawing an *O* at the edge of the shoe and on the top plate. Exactly 1½" from the edge of this door opening, mark off the placement of the supporting stud with an *X*.

Each time you draw a line to indicate the placement of a stud, inscribe a cross on the side of the line that you intend to place the 2×4. Remember this for all markings: it's a good habit and universally understood.

14. *The shoes describe the perimeter of all the rooms and the top plates must duplicate this pattern precisely. This is most easily accomplished by laying 2×4's directly on top of the shoes, each piece cut precisely the same length as the shoe beneath it.*

15. *Run the top plates continuously from one room to the next, if you're installing more than one room. Don't interrupt the 2×4's with door openings, as you did with the shoes. Simply continue the 2×4's over the door openings, as shown here. Tack these 2×4's temporarily to the shoes with 10-penny common nails, just securely enough so that they remain fastened throughout the next stage.*

16. *Transfer the marks made on the floor directly onto the shoes and top plates. Using the right angle, duplicate your marks clearly, allowing 1½″ for the liner (O) and 1½″ for the stud (X).*

17. *Mark off O and X on each side of each door opening. Later these marks will be meaningful to you, but for the time being perform this operation mechanically.*

18. *Now mark off the shoes and top plates for the studs that will be placed along each wall. Starting from the outside wall, draw off lines every 16″, as shown here.*

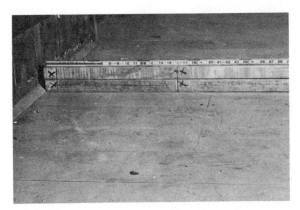

19. *When you attach the studs at a later stage, the edge of the 2×4 will align with the vertical lines you're now drawing on the shoe and top plates. The cross indicates which side of the line the 2×4 will be nailed. Draw these lines every 16″, as shown here.*

20. *Allow for studs at each corner of the room, both the inside and outside corners. You'll need a stud at each corner so that you have a firm support against which to nail the edges of the wallboards at a later stage. You may find that the space between studs at the corners and door openings happens to be less than 16", but it is always safer to have more studs than fewer. In fact, if you find that two studs are actually only 1½" apart, anchor a third between them for added strength.*

After you've marked off each doorway as described above, you're ready to plan for the walls: where will you place the studs? In construction parlance, studs are placed *16" on center*. This is a short method of saying that the space from the center of one stud to the center of the next nearest stud is 16". This 16" spacing is used because all wall panels—such as Sheetrock (gypsum board) and plywood—are manufactured in 16" widths or multiples thereof. (Older buildings may have spacing of 24", but the 4" multiple is still easily adapted to current panel dimensions.) The gypsum board we will be nailing to the partitions measures $4' \times 8'$, and you will see how convenient it is to have the 2×4's predictably placed every 16" as we position the sheets against the vertical studs.

Starting from the outside wall, begin to measure off these 16" intervals on the shoe and top plates. Using the right angle, draw the line alongside which the 2×4 will touch and mark a cross on the side of the line that the stud will be anchored. When the top plate is detached from the shoe and nailed to the ceiling, these marks will clearly indicate where the studs will be attached at the base and overhead.

Mark off the position for studs on all the shoes and top plates. In addition to the studs placed every 16", be sure that there are also studs marked off for every corner in the room, needed for support, to provide a solid surface against which to anchor the edges of the wallboards later. If you're in doubt, don't hesitate to add another stud. It's wiser to have more studs than you need rather than too few.

HANGING THE TOP PLATE

After you've indicated on all the shoes and top plates where the studs will be placed, you're ready to mark off the ceiling. These marks will indicate where to attach the top plates so that they will be directly over the shoes.

Rest the end of a 2×4 directly on the plate so that the edges align precisely. Bring the 2×4 into contact with the ceiling or ceiling beam overhead and lay the level alongside the vertical 2×4. Shift the 2×4 to the left and to the right until the level reads that the 2×4 is standing exactly plumb. This indicates that the point on the ceiling beam touched by the vertical 2×4 is exactly plumb with the shoe below; the point is directly overhead. Mark this point on the ceiling beam (or on the ceiling) and then continue to mark off other points on the ceiling until you have enough marks overhead to indicate where you should nail the top plates so that every point will be plumb with the shoe below.

Remove the top plates that you had tacked to

the shoes. Starting from the outside wall, take the first length and position it overhead along the marks you've just made on the ceiling or the ceiling beams. Attach the end of the top plate to the ceiling beam by driving in one 10-penny common nail. Continue along the length of the top plate, hammering a nail into each successive beam, carefully checking each time to be sure that the top plate is in the position you've indicated with your pencil marks earlier. Continue to attach the remaining top plates to the ceiling in this manner. Whenever two pieces of 2×4 butt against each other, attach them to each other by toenailing 8-penny common nails on each side so that the top plates are firmly and securely joined to each other. By the time you've completed this operation you should have a continuous pattern of top plates overhead, repeating the pattern of shoes below.

In our photographs you'll notice that we're attaching the top plates directly onto the ceiling beams. This is fairly common for open attics. Partitioning off a room within a finished room means that you'll probably be attaching your top plates to another kind of surface overhead. What you see here applies to any situation in which you are installing partitions into a wood-framed house. Once you've determined the location of the ceiling beams through the finished ceiling, attach them in the way described here. Because the ceiling beams are concealed by the finished ceiling, you'll have to locate them first by tapping along the surface until you hear a solid sound. Mark on the ceiling where the beams occur.

If the beams are running parallel to the wall, locate the beam that is closest to where you would want the wall, trace it along the surface of the ceiling, and proceed in reverse: the location of the beam determines the placement of the wall. Plumb the line from the ceiling down to the floor and place your shoe in relation to this mark. Although the procedure is reversed from the one shown above, its principle and method are the same.

CATS

Let's leave a finished ceiling for the moment, returning to our example where the beams are fully exposed. Here, too, we run into a slight problem when the beams run parallel to the partitioned wall, but it's not necessary to shift the position of the top plate because there is no reason why the top plate must be anchored only to the ceiling beams. When the beams are exposed, we can easily insert blocks of wood between the beams, perpendicular to them, to which the top plate can be anchored. These are called *cats*.

1. After all the shoes and top plates have been marked for studs, it's time to position the top plates overhead. Rest one end of a 2×4 directly on top of the plate and bring the other end of the 2×4 into contact with the ceiling overhead.

2. Place your level against the 2×4. Keeping the base of the 2×4 in position, directly on top of the plate, swing the 2×4 gently to the left and to the right until you locate the point where the level indicates that the 2×4 is in a plumb position.

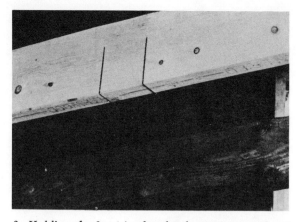

3. Holding the 2×4 in the plumb position, mark off the ceiling at precisely the point touched by the 2×4, so that it is clearly visible from below. These marks on the ceiling indicate the point overhead that is plumb with the plate below.

4. Remove the top plate from the shoe and, with 10-penny common nails, attach it overhead along the marks you've just indicated. If positioned properly, the top plates run exactly parallel to the shoe below: each cross marked on the top plate should be directly above the corresponding cross marked on the shoe below.

Measure the space between one beam and its nearest neighbor and cut a piece of 2×4 to that measurement. Hammer this piece to the beams so that its bottom edge is flush with the bottom edge of the beams. (Two nails at either end, driven through the side of the beams into the 2×4, will hold the piece firmly in place. If necessary, you can also attach the 2×4 to the beam by toenailing two nails at either end.) These cats provide a sturdy surface, at right angles to the rafters, into which the top plates can be attached. Place them intermittently, and mark them off for the top plates in the same manner as described above, using the level to determine the plumb position overhead.

NAILERS

Installing cats between ceiling beams is only one occasion on which you'll be planning ahead by inserting blocks of wood where you need a nailing surface for something else. These blocks are referred to as *nailers;* cats are one kind of nailer.

Unless you know what's coming next, it's not always easy to know where to put nailers. As you go along, you'll find other places where you'll want a firm support to nail against and into, and you'll learn to anticipate these in advance. For example, let's say you intend to attach wallboard to the framing you are now installing. The sheets of wallboard will be nailed to the ceiling beams. To what will you attach the edge of the wallboard at the corner where the wall meets the ceiling? If the top plate is running perpendicular to the beams, you can nail to the beams overhead along the edge of the wallboard. But if the beams are running *parallel* to the top plate, you'll need to provide some other surface to nail into, because there is only open space on each side of the top plate. Blocks of wood—placed at intervals—that extend out along each edge of the top plate are a sufficient nailing surface for wallboard. Try to bear this in mind when you place the top plates in position. If you think far enough ahead, you can nail blocks of wood to the top surface of the plates *before* you nail the top plate into the ceiling beams. This is a lot easier than attaching nailers *after* the top plate is in position (which, by the way, we found ourselves doing very often in the beginning, until we got the hang of it and were able to anticipate further in advance!).

AND NOW THE STUDS

The shoes and top plates have been marked for the placement of the studs. The crosses you've marked on the top plates above should correspond precisely with the crosses marked below on the shoes. Unfolding your ruler, measure the distance from the top plate to the shoe and cut a 2×4 to this measurement. (Measure ever so slightly to the snug side so that with the hammer you can tap the 2×4 into place and have it stand in its proper position without any nails securing it. This makes toenailing much easier.)

Tap the stud at the base until its edge touches your pencil line. Be sure that the stud stands over the cross you've marked alongside the line. Now tap the top of the stud into position overhead. If the top plate has been properly placed, and if the stud had been positioned on the lines correctly, your vertical 2×4 should be plumb. (Check this with the level, just to be sure.)

The stud in position, kneel on the floor and toenail 8-penny common nails into each side and along one or both edges of the stud and anchor it to the shoe. (For further advice on toenailing, see Chapter 1.) Most building codes require three nails for toenailing; some require four nails. Toenail into the top plate as well. If you have an open area above the top plate, spike two 10-penny common nails directly through the top plate into the end of the stud, an easier operation than toenailing.

Here, too, try to anticipate the work ahead. You will probably need nailers along the corners of the room. Do you have an edge to which you can attach the wallboard?

Continue to place the studs until you've anchored them to all the places marked with a cross. For the time being, don't place any studs where you have marked an *O* for the liners at the doorways. You'll frame out the door once you know the precise height of the door. When you are ready to frame out the door, refer to Chapter

2. *Cats aren't the only kind of nailers you'll need. Try to anticipate where you may need a surface onto which you will nail wallboard later. Remember, each edge of the wallboard must be attached to a firm support. Blocks of wood nailed over the plates will catch the edge of the wallboard nailed to the ceiling.*

1. *As long as the top plates run at right angles to the beams, you have several points at which you can anchor them overhead. If the top plates run parallel to the beams, however, you must insert "cats" between the beams, spaced intermittently and marked in exactly the same way as shown above.*

3. *Along the walls, nailers will also be needed to catch the edge of the wallboard at the corners. We anchored 2×4's to the corners so that we had an edge onto which we could nail the wallboard. After you've tried to nail wallboard onto a few partitions, you'll understand the importance of these preparations better. Experience will tell you when and how to place the nailers in advance.*

1. Measure the distance between the shoe and top plate and cut a 2×4 to that measurement. Cut slightly to the snug side: you can tap the 2×4 into position with your hammer so that the stud is wedged into correct position. Tap the 2×4 so that its bottom edge touches the line indicated on the shoe, and is placed over the cross. Tap the edge above so that it touches the line indicated on the top plate.

2. Toenail an 8-penny common nail into each side of the base so that the stud is securely fastened to the shoe. Toenail a third common nail through the edge of the stud.

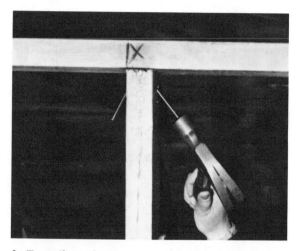

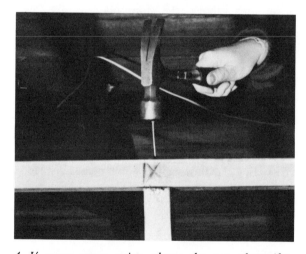

3. Toenail an 8-penny common nail into three or four sides of the top edge of the stud so that the 2×4 is securely fastened to the top plate.

4. If open space exists above the top plate (between the ceiling beams, for example, as shown here), drive in two 10-penny common nails through the top plate directly into the end of the stud. This is easier than toenailing.

5. Here is a row of studs as they appear, every 16", along the shoe.

6. These are the same studs shown fastened to their top plate overhead.

15, "How to Install Doors."

When you have completed this procedure, you will have framed out your room. Now you're ready to call in an electrician to install the wiring and a plumber to install the pipes and perhaps heating ducts. If you have a building permit, now is the time to call in the building inspector for an inspection. This must be done before the wall framing is covered by insulation or walls.

CONVERTING AN ATTIC

It's very common nowadays to expand the living area of a house by converting an open attic into one or more bedrooms and a bathroom. (Essentially, this is the kind of area we are working with in this demonstration.) If this is what you are doing, you'll probably encounter some situations here that will be particular to the way attics are framed; the rafters joining the ceiling beams create their own specific set of circumstances.

If you plan to arrange the living space to include the addition of a bathroom, try to place the bathroom directly over a bathroom on a lower floor so that the plumbing will be accessible and easier and less costly to hook up.

If you are planning more than one room—as we did in our demonstration—allow for a central hall. The hall needn't be too wide, but should not be any more narrow than 3'. Be certain that there is room for a door to swing open into the hall.

Speaking of doors, you must not overlook the ceiling height. Be sure to allow for doors where you have the greatest height. In Chapter 18, "How to Install Special Doors and Windows," we describe how to hang a door that is angled properly into the configuration of the attic ceiling, but this is acceptable only for closet doors, not for entrances.

Before you convert the attic, consult with your building inspector about the regulations governing the structure of the attic area. The floor beams should be strong enough to withstand the added weight of the room and activity.

If your attic is like ours, subflooring already exists. If not, you will have to install subflooring before you begin to partition. Follow the instructions for the installation of subflooring in Chapter 9, "Flooring over Concrete." This explains all you need to know about nailing subflooring to the floor beams.

KNEE WALLS

In an attic the roof rafters are generally supported by a short wall called a *knee wall*. If a

7. *The entire wall is partitioned: the studs are plumb, fastened securely to the shoe and top plate. Onto these studs the walls will be fastened.*

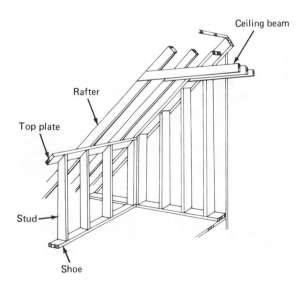

1. *This is the construction of a knee wall. Attach the shoe to the floor and the top plate to the rafters, and insert studs in between, angled to fit.*

2. After installing the shoe, insert a cat between the rafters at the point just over the knee wall.

3. Insert a cat at the point where the rafters are joined to the ceiling beams. Nail the cat so that it extends slightly beyond the edge of the rafters and place it so that its bottom surface is parallel to the floor and flush with the other ceiling beams in the room.

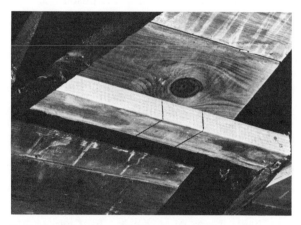

6. Mark the other cat in the same way, placing the 2×4 on the shoe and making it plumb.

7. Both cats are now marked in the same way.

10. Insert another cat between the ceiling beams. Mark this cat in the same way you marked the others by standing a 2×4 on the shoe and holding a level to it.

11. Attach a 2×4 to the cats, in the same line. Notice that by angling the cut of the first top plate there is more room for attaching the second to the same cat.

4. Rest a 2×4 on the shoe and, holding a level alongside its edge, mark on the cat where the 2×4 lines up when it is plumb.

5. The mark is clear, indicating the edge of the 2×4 in its position plumb to the shoe.

8. Measure from the knee wall to the midway point on the second cat, and cut a 2×4 to this distance. Cut the 2×4 at a 45-degree angle with the circular saw.

9. Anchor the 2×4 to the two cats, between the two marks made earlier, the angled end attached to the second cat.

12. Now mark the 2×4's for the studs every 16″, as you did earlier. Draw crosses on the shoe and on the top plate wherever the 2×4 indicates it is plumb above and below.

13. Mark off the top plates and insert studs between the shoe and plates, angling them to fit properly.

knee wall doesn't exist in your attic, you should construct one so you'll have a surface on which you can hang a wall. The method of making a knee wall is not much different from partitioning, as we described it earlier. Studs are attached to a shoe that is nailed to the floor and to a top plate that is nailed to the rafters. The only significant difference here is that the rafters are not parallel to the floor; they are at an angle. The studs must be cut at the same angle so that they can be nailed into the top plate.

How high do you want the knee wall to be? The more into the center of the room you place the knee wall, the higher it will be. Our knee walls are 5'; most are 4'. Walk over to one end of the attic, and measure up from the floor 4' to the nearest rafter. Do the same with the rafter at the other end of the attic. If your attic is quite large, mark off one or two other rafters in the middle of the room 4' from the floor. Connect these points with a chalk line, and attach the top plate to the rafters—with 10-penny common nails—along this chalk line.

After the top plate is nailed to the rafters, locate the shoe in relation to it. Go to the extreme end of the top plate and hold a length of a straight 2×4 up against it, placing the 4' level alongside the 2×4 to locate where it should stand in order to be plumb. Mark this point on the floor. Do the same at the other end of the top plate and pop a line on the floor, connecting these two points. Lay the shoe alongside this chalk line. Be sure it is on the correct side.

Now insert the studs—16" on center—between the shoe and the top plate. Here you'll cut each stud at an angle where it will be joined to the top plate. It's simplest to make a pattern to size. It's easy to establish the angle. Hold the 2×4 alongside one of the rafters and scribe the angle of the rafter along the edge of the 2×4. Then establish the height of the 2×4 when installed to the top plate. Use this pattern to cut all the studs along the knee wall.

PARTITIONING ALONG AN ANGLED CEILING

In an attic a knee wall rises to the rafters and the rafters connect with the ceiling beams, giving you a nice angle for a ceiling. You can retain this angle by installing cats between the rafters and the ceiling beams, as we described earlier. First lay the shoe, as before. Between the rafters above the shoe insert the first cat. This is placed so that its bottom surface is flush with the edges of the

rafters and it is inserted just above the knee wall. Between the same rafters insert a second cat, this one just at the point where the rafters intersect with the ceiling beams. Nail the second cat to the rafter at the same angle as the ceiling beam, parallel with the floor, the edge extending beyond the rafter just enough to provide a nailing surface.

Now mark these cats for the top plates. Place a 2×4 on the shoe and hold a level up against it. Mark the cats where the 2×4 is plumb. You will nail the top plate to these cats, between the marks.

When you cut the 2×4, angle the end slightly, and measure it so that it extends from the knee wall to the midway point on the second cat. The next top plate will share the cat as a nailing surface and the angle gives it more room to fit. Join the top plate to these two cats with 10-penny common nails.

Insert a cat between the next set of ceiling beams and mark it with a 2×4 in the same way as earlier, indicating where it is plumb over the shoe. Nail a top plate between these marks so that it continues the line made by the first top plate. They share the nailing surface at the point where the rafters intersect with the ceiling beam. You now have a top plate that follows the line of the rafters and continues onto the ceiling beams.

After the top plates are nailed into the cats, install the studs in the same way as previously, 16" on center. Rest the 2×4 against the shoe and against the top plate, and mark it where it is plumb, every 16". Trace the angle of the 2×4 by holding it plumb against the angled top plate. Then cut the 2×4 down to the proper length (you'll have to measure each stud individually), toenail it to the shoe, and anchor it to the top plate as you did earlier. The angle in the ceiling has now been retained.

FRAMING A BASEMENT WALL

To finish a basement, it's best to frame it out first with studs, rather than attach anything to the masonry walls directly. Although we discuss dampness more extensively elsewhere in the book, you'd be wise to consider this first before finishing the basement. Assuming that your basement is suitable for finishing, frame it out first with studs. Nail a shoe to the concrete floor by driving in tempered-steel cut nails. Above this attach a top plate to the ceiling beams. Insert studs between the top plate and shoe in the way described earlier. This will give you a regular surface, dry and solid, for hanging new wallboard.

Now the entire room in the attic has been partitioned off. The doorway has been framed according to the methods described in Chapter 15, "How to Install Doors."

Here is the arrangement for installing studs against a masonry wall. The wallboards are anchored to these studs after insulation is inserted.

CHAPTER 5

Insulation

Before you go any further, consider what you want to hide behind the walls. Now is the time to install the wiring, or perhaps the pipes for heating or plumbing. Discuss these matters with an electrician and plumber, and attend to them before you proceed. Once you have the necessary installations made, followed by the inspections such work may require, your next step is the insulation.

WHY BOTHER WITH INSULATION?

Authoritative tests have shown that heating an uninsulated house during cold weather is 50 per cent less efficient than heating an insulated home. This means that half of the heat produced by a heating system in an uninsulated house is actually wasted, which means that half of the money spent on fuel is wasted, too. Uninsulated houses are also subject to drafts, unequal temperatures, vapor condensation, and many other uncomfortable or unhealthy conditions.

Insulation is also desirable for *warmer* climates because it retards the inflow of heat, particularly through roof and wall surfaces exposed to direct rays of the sun. An insulated wall can provide more than four times the heat resistance of an uninsulated wall. Simply stated, insulation functions like the furry coat of an animal: it helps to retain the desired heat in the winter and to resist the unwanted heat in the summer.

UNDERSTANDING WHERE HEAT IS LOST

Just how much heat is lost in any house depends largely on the type of construction, style, amount of insulation, and other features of the house. In an uninsulated two-story house with a basement, for example, the total heat loss would probably be distributed in this way:

Walls: 33 per cent
Window glass and doors: 30 per cent
Ceilings and roof: 22 per cent
Air leakage (infiltration): 15 per cent
Floors: negligible
Total heat loss: 100 per cent

(Obviously, this 100 per cent does not mean that you are *losing* all the heat, but represents lost heat that must be constantly replenished, so that at any time your heating system is only 50 per cent effective. In other words, your heating system must work twice as hard.)

Naturally, houses of different styles will vary in their heat loss characteristics. A single-story house, for example, contains less wall area and a proportionately larger ceiling area, so that the greater loss would occur through the ceiling. Similarly, greater heat loss through floors would occur in houses erected over concrete slabs or unheated crawl spaces.

Windows and doors are generally sources of greater heat loss than either walls or ceilings. For this reason, weather stripping around doors is used, reducing air infiltration by more than half. In colder sections of the country, heat losses through glass surfaces can be reduced by half or more with double-glaze windows or storm sash and storm doors.

WATER VAPOR

Water vapor, as you probably remember from your science classes in school, always moves from a warmer to a colder region, appearing in the form of dew or frost when it reaches a surface cold enough to cause it to condense. You may wonder what this has to do with your home. It's simple. Moisture is continually being released into the atmosphere of the house from cooking, bathing, breathing, and plants, and in numerous other ways. Unless prevented, the moisture, or water vapor, will slowly move into and through the walls. In cold weather, the water vapor makes its way outward and will eventually meet a cold layer near the outside, at which point condensation will occur. This condensation will eventually damage the sheathing or siding of your home, causing paint to peel and wood to rot, or producing efflorescence on a brick surface. Insulation provides a vapor barrier to prevent this flow of moisture through the walls.

NOW CONSIDER ALL THE REASONS

Insulating your home is a measure you take for reasons of economy and comfort. Here's how it all adds up:

•Insulation reduces the cost of heating your home by enabling you to use a smaller heating system. Likewise, it reduces the cost of cooling your home by enabling you to use a smaller system, or no system at all.

•Insulation will pay for itself by the amount of fuel you save. Since it reduces waste, it reduces fuel consumption.

•Insulation reduces the amount of power needed to operate the heating or cooling system in your home. These systems will operate more efficiently.

•Insulation helps protect against vermin. (Loose fill insulation, in particular, helps keep away unwanted animals.)

•Insulation reduces the traffic of water vapor through your walls, preventing the rotting and peeling of exterior surfaces.

•Insulation controls noise by interrupting the transmission of sound through the home.

•Insulation retards the speed of fire.

•Insulation makes your home safer, more comfortable for living.

Have we convinced you?

WHAT IS INSULATION?

Any building material will resist the flow of heat to some extent, wood being the best of the insulating construction materials, better, at least, than the denser materials, concrete or metal. But none of the building materials retard heat movement to any great extent. Insulation can be achieved efficiently only with a substance that can effectively resist the flow of heat through its bulk. Insulating materials are lightweight and contain a high percentage of air spaces or voids. Some natural substances—such as cork, fur, cotton, wool, and straw—have been used as insulating materials for quite some time, but are obviously inappropriate for modern construction. Synthetic ma-

terials have been developed to perform the same function, designed to retard heat movement by breaking up air spaces into tiny pockets. For example, a modern fiber glass blanket only 6″ thick blocks the flow of heat as effectively as 8′ of solid brick wall.

TYPES OF INSULATION

There are many manufacturers of insulation, but the varieties may be grouped into a few basic types. Almost all insulation employs a basic few materials, fiber glass and rock wool accounting for more than 90 per cent of all insulation sold in the United States.

Blanket and Bat: Blankets are flexible rolls made from mineral or glass fiber. Bats are the same except that they are produced in uniform lengths, usually about 4′ or 8′. This form of insulation is available in several widths, lengths, and thicknesses and is encased in either plain kraft paper or aluminum foil. Blankets and bats usually have thin marginal strips along their edges, called flanges, for stapling. Blankets are best for long runs of unobstructed space. A blanket or bat 3½″ thick fits neatly between 2×4's and costs considerably less than 6″ blankets.

Loose Fill: Sold in packs, this insulation is bulky and normally manufactured from vermiculite or fiber glass. We do not recommend that you try installing this yourself, since a costly forced-air blower is needed for the job. Loose fill is desirable for a low attic or other above-ceiling space, but it is difficult to install fully into walls.

Foam: This is another form of synthetic, a plastic foam that flows around obstructions to fill a space completely, then hardens to a rigid mass. Foam made of urea formaldehyde, for example, provides excellent fire resistance and high insulation efficiency, so is especially good for exterior walls. It does require professional installation, however. Likewise, urethane provides excellent insulation efficiency, but must be installed professionally.

Boards and Slabs: These are rigid boards produced in large units, generally from a lightweight plastic foam. Boards can be purchased in 4′ or more widths, 8′ or more lengths, and ½″ and 1″ thicknesses. Slabs are generally composed of small rigid units that are 1″ or more thick and up to 24″×28″ long. Slabs are especially made for use in connection with flat or nearly flat roofs. Because plastic boards and slabs are flammable, they should be covered with a fire-retardant material, such as gypsum wallboard.

1. For the walls, you will probably use blanket insulation. Because this measurement is fairly uniform throughout the room you are insulating, you can cut strips of the blanket insulation in uniform lengths. First measure the distance from the floor to the ceiling.

HOW INSULATION WORKS

Because insulation is a poor conductor of heat, it will resist the heat flow when placed in walls, floors, and ceilings. It is not necessary to install the same amount of insulation in all of these areas, however, because the efficiency of insulation reaches a point of diminishing return. The first inch of insulation thickness is the most effective, and each successive layer of the same thickness is less and less effective. For this reason, the materials are manufactured in the thicknesses and for the purposes they can be most efficiently used for.

We mentioned earlier that insulation is also an effective vapor barrier. Most blanket and bat insulation has a wrapper of an impervious material, such as asphalt-impregnated kraft paper or aluminum foil. (Foil also reflects back what little radiant heat comes through the walls, so it serves an additional function.) Where no vapor barrier is provided on insulation, sheets of polyethylene film stapled to studs after installing bats will keep walls dry.

The water vapor insulation must face the warm side during the colder weeks of the year. For example, insulation in the attic is placed with the barrier side down—toward the ceiling of the rooms below—and insulation in the floor is placed with the barrier up—toward the living area.

WHERE AND HOW TO INSULATE

Your ceiling, which is very vulnerable to heat loss, may be the easiest to insulate if you have an accessible attic. Other important areas are outside walls, dormers, walls facing unheated areas (pantries, walk-in closets, and so on), and floors over basements or crawl spaces. You'll have to open up the walls to add most insulation and should probably wait until you are ready for general remodeling.

Assuming that you *are* renovating your home, you will probably insulate with blanket and bat insulation. For exterior walls, 3½″-thick insulation is recommended; for ceilings, 6″-thick. (See also Chapter 9, "Flooring over Concrete," for this particular situation in insulating a basement floor.)

First measure the areas to be insulated, in order to determine just how much material to purchase and in what width. If the studs or ceiling beams are 24″ on center, you will want 23″ insulation; if 16″ on center, order 15″ insulation.

Although it looks as harmless as cotton candy, the fiber glass in the insulation is very nasty to handle. Try to avoid skin contact wherever possi-

2. Lay the end of your ruler against the wall and mark off the measurement on the floor. Allow an extra 4″ to 6″.

3. The mark on the floor is clearly visible. If this is a finished floor—rather than a subfloor, as shown here —you may prefer to protect the surface by covering it with a scrap of wood. You can cut against the wood rather than damage the floor.

4. Place the end of the insulation at the wall and unroll a length to extend over the chalk mark, the fiber glass face down. With one hand, press the insulation firmly against the floor—making it compact— and with the other hand cut into the back of the insulation and through the fiber glass, using a sharp knife.

5. Slice the insulation across its width, following the chalk mark as a guide.

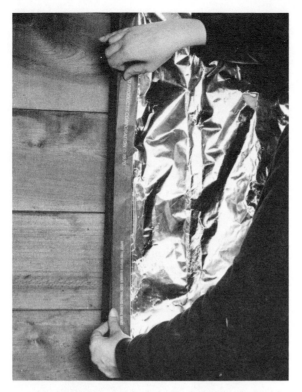

6. The flanges along the edges of the insulation are attached to the studs or ceiling beams. Attach the first flange with staples about 8″ apart. Grasp the free flange and expand the blanket to full width.

7. The next strip of insulation is placed alongside the first. For best protection, staple the flange of the next strip over the previous one. This overlapping will form a continuous vapor barrier.

10. The insulation in the ceiling is installed in precisely the same way. A thicker insulation (6″ here) will be used. Wear a mask or some head protection. The fiber glass spilling over the sides can easily irritate the skin and eyes.

11. Bat insulation has been used for the ceiling, strips 4″ long and 23″ wide. The insulation in the walls here is foil-faced, kraft-faced in the ceiling.

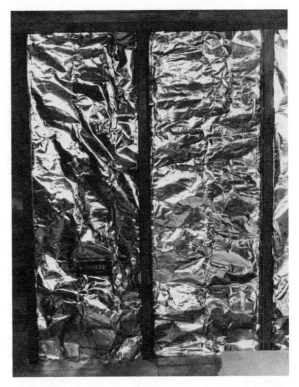

8. *If you intend to hang wallboard or paneling on the studs, attach the flanges of the insulation to the inside faces of the studs, rather than along the outside edge. Although side stapling requires more care to avoid gaps along the edge, this method leaves a smooth surface on the studs to which you can attach the wallboards.*

9. *Insulate between each pair of studs along the walls in this manner.*

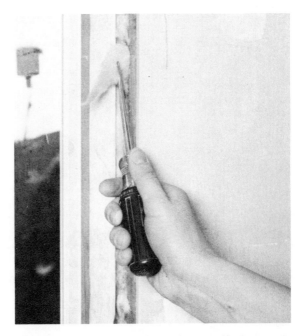

12. *When you encounter an outlet or switch box, simply cut around the fixture with the utility knife and insert the insulation snugly in position.*

13. *For crevices around windows and doors, rip off loose pieces of insulation and tuck them into the spaces. Use any utensil that will force the material into even the smallest crevices.*

ble. After you insulate, you will probably feel as though there were thousands of tiny scratches all over your body. Use gloves, and wear long sleeves. You might even consider a mask.

If you are insulating an entire room or floor, you will most likely require many strips of insulation in equal lengths. To facilitate the process of measuring each strip, mark off the length you desire in chalk on the floor. By laying the insulation on the floor and using the chalk mark as your guide, you can avoid measuring off each length with a ruler. Allow an extra 4″ to 6″ for each strip to permit sealing at the ends.

Place the insulation on the floor, the foil or kraft paper facing you. Press down on the insulation tightly against the floor (for a more compact cutting surface) and slice through the material with a utility knife. It will separate easily.

Blanket insulation has flanges that can be stapled directly onto the studs or ceiling beams. These flanges may be pulled tightly over the edges of the studs, a means of providing the best protection and the greatest effectiveness to the vapor barrier function of the wrapper. Attach the first flange with staples about 8″ apart. Grasp the free flange firmly and expand the blanket to full width, stapling it carefully to avoid any gaps. The next flange will then overlap when stapled, forming a continuous vapor barrier.

Place the blanket insulation between the studs in this way only if you do *not* intend to hang walls over the insulation. If you are attaching wallboard to the studs or ceiling beams, you will find it difficult to obtain a smooth joint in the walls over the stapled flanges. Instead, staple the flanges on the *inside* faces of the studs, rather than on the outside edge. Side stapling requires more care, so staple carefully at 6″ intervals to prevent gaps at the edge of the blanket.

Whenever you come to an outlet or switch box, simply cut the foil or kraft blanket around the fixture with the utility knife and place the insulation snugly in position. For crevices around windows and doors, rip off loose pieces of insulation and tuck them into the spaces.

A standard staple gun is easy for controlling the precise placement of the staples. However, we found that our hands tired quickly from squeezing the compression stapler, so we preferred the stapling hammer for this operation. Since insulating is not a pleasant activity, the stapling hammer made the entire operation go much more rapidly.

CHAPTER 6

Installing Gypsum Wallboard

Gypsum wallboard is known by a variety of names, including gypsum board, plaster board, and drywall. The most familiar name is *Sheetrock,* which happens to be a trademark of the United States Gypsum Company. Regardless of what you call it, today gypsum board is the number one material for building new walls and for rebuilding old ones. No other material even approaches gypsum board in terms of appearance, economy, and ease of handling. It goes up quickly, is very inexpensive, and does not cause moisture problems like plaster. Gypsum board requires little maintenance and produces a smooth, durable surface. It also retards fire and noise.

Gypsum board is not a finished wall surface (although you can purchase a vinyl-surfaced panel), but provides a base for paint, wallpaper, and tile. It is normally applied directly to studs and ceiling beams, but can also be hung over furring strips on masonry walls and crumbling walls that you would prefer not to rip out. In some cases, it is nailed directly over old walls to provide a new surface.

As building materials go, gypsum board is very uniform in quality, regardless of manufacturer. There are no hidden defects; it is visibly good or broken.

Gypsum board is inexpensive, the cost varying with the thickness. Remember, however, to add the cost of nails, sealing compound, and tape, as well as the decorative materials—such as paint, wallpaper, or tile—to your estimate.

Initially, when we installed gypsum board for the first time, we went to great efforts to obtain a neat appearance. We soon discovered that the art of paneling with this material comes later—in spackling with joint compound—not in the actual hanging of the Sheetrock. The procedures described in this chapter assume optimum conditions and results. But keep the thought somewhere in the back of your mind that nearly all of your mistakes can be concealed with careful taping and spackling later. The real craftsmanship lies in the spackling, not in the way you've nailed the sheets to the studs and ceiling beams.

TYPES OF GYPSUM BOARD

All gypsum boards are manufactured by mixing plaster of Paris with water and additives and by spreading this mix to form a smooth, dense, fire- and sound-resistant core that is sandwiched between two layers of strong paper. The boards are 4' wide and 6' to 16' long. (We used 4'×8' sheets only, the larger sizes being too unwieldy for us to manage.) The standard thicknesses are ¼", ⅜", ½", and ⅝". Building codes may insist on certain thicknesses to be used for specific purposes, so check your local building codes before selecting the panels. The ¼" sheets have a tendency to bow and do not insulate sound very well, so they are normally used for resurfacing existing walls. The ⅜" panels are generally used for multi-ply construction of walls and in single thicknesses for top-story ceilings. The ½" panel is the thickness most frequently used for walls and ceilings. The ⅝" panels are required by

Materials for hanging wallboard: gypsum sheets, nails, corner bead, hammer, utility knife, rasp, ruler.

codes in some large cities because of their greater ability to resist fire and to control noise. (They are available in a size no larger than 4'×8' for reasons that are obvious when you try to lift a sheet!)

Regular gypsum board has a gray liner paper on the back. On the facing side and edges, this wallboard has a smooth, heavy paper covering, usually in off-white, that can accept paint. The edges are slightly tapered, beveled, or squared, and the ends are not tapered or covered with paper. If you ask your lumberyard for a number of, let's say, 4'×8'×½'' Sheetrock boards, this is what you will receive. But in addition to these standard boards, there are a variety of other types designed for special purposes:

Superior-fire-rated Boards: Improved by the addition of glass fiber reinforcement and other materials, these sheets are known for having greater fire resistance than standard boards and are usually available only in ½'' and ⅝'' thicknesses.

Special-edged Boards: These are sold under various trademarks. They differ from standard boards because their edges are tapered as well as beveled or rounded. These boards are used primarily when walls are framed badly or exposed to high humidity, conditions that may cause excessive warping. The joints are filled with a high-strength compound before being taped and spackled in the conventional manner.

Insulating Gypsum Boards: These have aluminum foil laminated to the back surface to provide thermal insulation and to act as a vapor barrier. They are to be used only on the inside surfaces of exterior walls.

Backer Boards: These are low-cost panels, with gray liner paper on all surfaces and edges, to be used as a base layer where several plies of Sheetrock are being installed for extra fire resistance, sound insulation, and strength.

Water-resistant Boards: With a water-resistant gypsum core and water-repellant facings, these boards serve as the base for tile walls in bathrooms or other high-moisture areas.

Prefinished Boards: These boards—normally vinyl-faced—provide a strong wall covering on the front with an attractive durable finish.

Most wallboard is installed on framing constructed of 2×4 studs spaced at 16'' intervals between centers. However, some homes may have studs spaced at 20'' or 24'' intervals. If studs are spaced more than 16'' apart, wallboard panels of at least ½'' thickness are required. All the procedures for installing wallboard in this book are based upon the installation of 4'×8' panels on wood framing with studs spaced at 16'' intervals, and ceiling beams of 24'' intervals. It is also assumed that rough wiring, plumbing, and insulation have already been installed.

ESTIMATING YOUR NEEDS

To establish just how much Sheetrock to order, first measure the total length of the walls to be covered and multiply this figure by the height. If you are figuring close, then deduct the area of the windows and doors. But don't feel that you must calculate very precisely. It would be safer to figure generously, rather than the reverse, because the actual monetary saving here is minimal, and you may create more headaches for yourself in terms of added efforts later with patches and extra spackling if you order too few sheets. In estimating our needs, we calculated the walls and ceilings only, and used the scraps for closets and pantries.

The number of panels you order is determined by dividing the total square footage of the walls and ceilings by the area of a single panel. Professionals normally work with the largest sheets possible and hang the panels horizontally to reduce the number of joints to be filled and taped. However, we found it far easier to work in sheets of 4'×8', hanging the panels vertically. We preferred to tape more seams than struggle with the added weight of the larger sheets. (A ½''-thick panel weighs about 2 pounds per square foot!)

OTHER MATERIALS YOU'LL NEED

When you order gypsum board, you'll also want to order the materials for spackling—tape and joint compound—as well. Read the next chapter to determine your quantities for these materials. Additionally you'll be needing the following items:

Nails: Special nails are designed for the purpose of hanging drywall. If the board is applied directly to the studs, use annular nails, which have ring-grooved shanks to provide exceptional holding power. If you are installing the gypsum board over an existing wall, use cement-coated nails. Refer to this chart to estimate the size and quantities of nails:

Wallboard Thickness	Size of Nail (Cement-coated)	Size of Nail (Annular)	Quantity per 1000 Square Feet
¼'' or ⅜''	1⅝''–1⅞''	1¼''–1⅜''	5¼ lbs.
½''	1⅝''–2¼''	1¼''–1⅜''	5¼ lbs.
⅝''	1⅞''–2¼''	1⅜''	6¾ lbs.

Corner Beads: These are metal strips to be attached to all the outside corners. (Count how many corners of this kind you will be covering before you call in your order.) These are usually available in 8' lengths, which are cut down to size with tin snips.

Hammer: A standard hammer can serve perfectly well for hanging gypsum board, though you should try to avoid breaking the paper surface of the wall with the head of the hammer. Crown-headed hammers designed for hanging Sheetrock are also manufactured, designed with a slightly rounded face—called a bell face—that "dimples" the board when you drive in the nail.

Utility Knife: This is a vital and very inexpensive tool you will need for cutting the gypsum board. Be sure to have many extra blades on hand, because they dull quickly as they cut into the particles of plaster sandwiched between the paper.

Wood Rasp: A rasp for filing wood will be handy for smoothing down ragged edges or for reducing the dimension of your board the fraction that may be necessary for it to fit snugly.

Awl: A sharply pointed instrument, such as an awl, will be useful when you want to indicate the placement of a cut on both sides of the sheet.

Miscellaneous Tools: An 8' ruler, a pencil, a stepladder, screwdrivers for removing electric plates, and two pieces of wood to make a lever for hanging walls.

PREPARING FOR WORK

When the gypsum boards are delivered, be sure they are piled in a dry place where they won't be subjected to abuse. They are easily damaged. For long-term storage, the boards should be stacked flat; but if you expect to use them soon, you can set them horizontally on edge. Stand them as straight as possible to avoid any chance of warping. Because panels are heavy, be sure not to stack so many sheets in one place that you will be putting too much stress on the floor joists. (If panels are stacked flat, the pile can serve as a work surface for measuring and cutting panels.)

If you are hanging new walls directly onto studs, you need to make no special preparations, providing that you have followed our instructions for partitioning in Chapter 4. It is particularly important that each edge of the gypsum board be anchored to a firm support, so check for nailers. Can the corners be anchored? Have you allowed for a nailing surface at the corners where the walls and ceiling meet?

If you intend to rip out old wall surfaces and apply Sheetrock directly to the framing, pry the door and window casings loose and rip out the baseboards and moldings before removing the old walls. Hammer down protruding nails and replace any unsound or badly warped studs.

Old walls to be resurfaced must be made level and reasonably smooth. Knock out areas which bulge outward; level large areas that bulge inward by gluing short, thin wood strips across the center. Electric boxes should be moved outward to allow for the extra wall thickness added.

CUTTING SHEETROCK

It's very satisfying to hang whole sheets of 4'×8' panels at one stretch because the work goes rapidly and the results are handsome. But we discovered that almost every sheet needed to be adjusted in size in order to accommodate the particular dimensions of our room, to account for window and door openings, and to permit exposure of electric boxes and switches. Fortunately, gypsum board is easy to handle, and these cutting operations do not require much time or practice.

Gypsum board is cut with a utility knife rather than a saw. You first mark your line with a pencil and then score the line with the sharp blade of a utility knife. Only medium pressure is necessary, but make sure to cut completely through the paper into the gypsum core. Don't try to go too fast, because the knife easily veers off into unwanted regions. You can use a straightedge as a guide for scoring (in fact, a 4' T square is made especially for this purpose), but we found that the straightedge was hardly necessary. By simply following the pencil line with a free hand, our cuts came sufficiently clean and even.

After you have scored the line with your knife, slide the gypsum sheet over the edge so that the scored line extends beyond the panels stacked below. Fold the Sheetrock downward, snapping the gypsum core, and then slice the paper on the back of the fold, following the crease made by folding back the board. With this method of cutting, the edge will always be slightly rough, so cut the sheet ¼" shorter than the actual space you wish to fill. This will allow for rough ends of pieces to fit together.

MAKING CUTOUTS

Whenever you hang walls, you have to make cutouts in the gypsum to allow for the exposure of

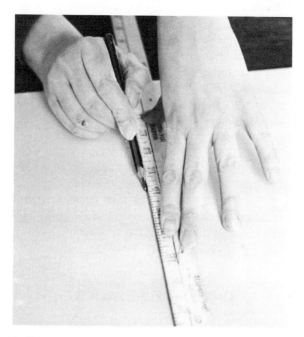

1. To cut gypsum wallboard, first measure off the panel and make a pencil line where the sheet is to be cut.

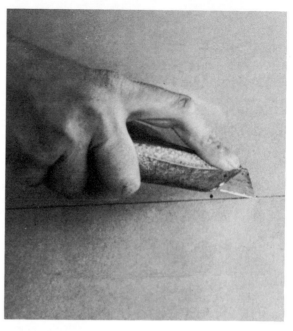

2. Score the pencil line with the sharp blade of a utility knife. Press through the paper into the gypsum core.

3. Snap the gypsum sheet against the scored line, bending it backwards.

4. With the knife, slice through the paper along the crease made by bending back the gypsum board. Allow an extra ¼" space for the rough edge. File the rough edge of the gypsum if lumps of plaster interfere with fitting the board into place.

electrical boxes, switches, and so on. Making these openings is also a simple procedure. First, locate one corner of the box: measure off from the ceiling (don't measure from the floor because the wallboard will hang about 1″ above the floor line). Then measure the distance from the last installed panel to where the edge of the box will fall. These two dimensions should enable you to locate one corner of the box. Draw the box on the face of the panel. We traced an actual electric box so that we didn't need to measure the opening each time: as long as we had the location of one corner, we could quickly draw the opening from our template. Allow an extra ⅛″ on each side of the box for good measure.

Now punch holes through the panel at the four corners of the box. You do this by placing the point of the awl in the corner and tapping it with your hammer until the point punctures the gypsum, emerging on the other side. With your utility knife, score the lines you have marked in pencil, from hole to hole, from corner to corner. Turn over the gypsum board and score the sheet on the reverse side as well, from one puncture to the next. The shape of the box should now be etched on both sides of the gypsum board. Turn over the panel, so that the face of the sheet faces you, and knock out the piece by tapping it with the hammer. Tap until you punch out the opening. If the edges of the opening are rough, file them lightly with the rasp. If the opening needs to be enlarged, slice the edges with your utility knife.

NAILING GYPSUM BOARD

Nails should be driven into the gypsum board and slightly countersunk, forming a "dimple" around the nailhead, without breaking the paper or crushing the gypsum core. This depression, which should not be more than $\frac{1}{32}$″ deep, is later filled with joint compound when the seams are taped.

The standard method of nailing gypsum wallboard is to space the nails 6″ to 8″ apart all around the edges and up and down the intermediate studs or ceiling beams. Drive the nails ⅜″ to ½″ from all edges, countersinking them as just described. As you drive each nail, exert pressure on the panel to ensure that it is drawn up tight to the framing. When driving the nail, be sure to hold the nail perpendicular to the panel, not at an angle.

For ceilings, we advise double nailing. Here nails are driven around the edges of the panel as in standard nailing; but on the intermediate ceiling beams they are inserted in pairs. The distance between the center of one pair and the center of

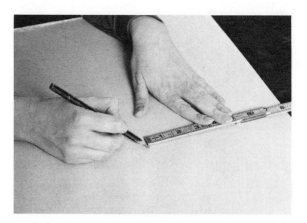

1. To make a cutout, first locate one corner of the opening. Mark this corner on the face of the sheet.

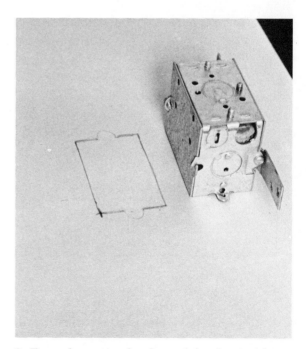

2. Use a pattern to draw the shape of the cutout. Here we have used the electrical box itself, placing it in the corner marked on the sheet.

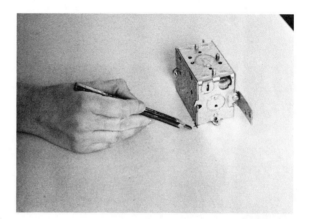

3. Trace the rectangular shape of the electrical box.

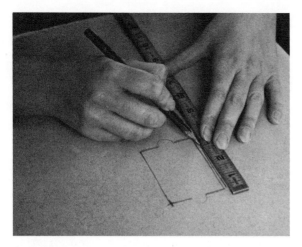

4. *Enlarge the size of the opening about ⅛″ all the way around.*

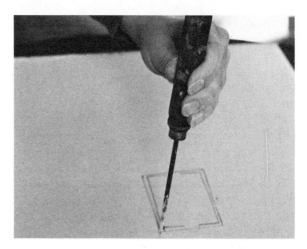

5. *Puncture a hole at each corner by tapping an awl through the sheet.*

8. *Now score these lines from corner to corner with the utility knife.*

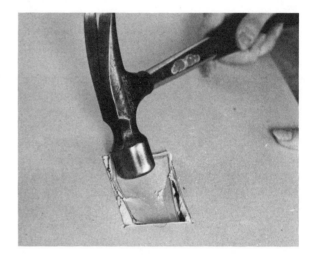

9. *Turn the sheet back to the facing side and tap the hammer around the area within the scored lines.*

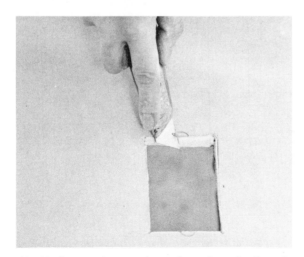

12. *If the opening needs to be enlarged, slice the edges with the knife. Allow for the configurations of the box.*

13. *The notches in the cutout are carved with the knife, just enough to permit entry of the outlet through the opening.*

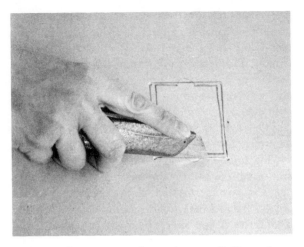

6. *Score the gypsum along the pencil lines, from corner to corner.*

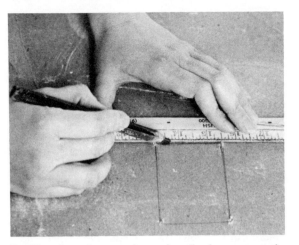

7. *Flip the sheet and mark off the rectangular shape by drawing the lines from punctured corner to punctured corner.*

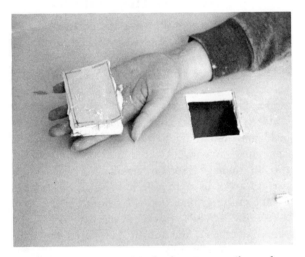

10. *Continue to tap with the hammer until you have punched out the opening. It should come through in one piece, like this.*

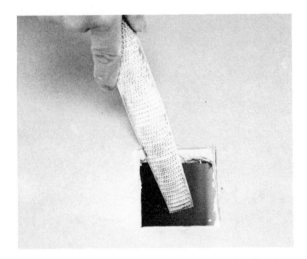

11. *If the edges of the opening are rough, file them with the rasp.*

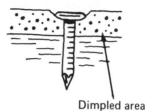

1. Drive the nails into the gypsum so that they are countersunk below the surface, the paper facing "dimpled" by about 1/32".

the next pair down is about 12". The nails in each pair are 2" apart. The idea behind this method is to prevent nail-popping, a common affliction in gypsum that occurs when nails loosen in the ceiling beams and pop headfirst through the wallboard surface, causing unsightly blisters and holes.

The edges of adjoining gypsum panels should be snug, but not jammed together. With panels having tapered edges, some carpenters prefer to butt a cut edge next to a tapered edge; some prefer the reverse. After you've spackled a few joints, you'll determine your own preference. Don't fret if the space between panels is larger than you anticipated. The seams are easily concealed with tape and compound.

INSTALLING THE CEILING

If you are hanging both walls and ceilings, always start with the ceiling. The walls placed below will give added support to the panels above.

Unless you are both a trained weight lifter and an acrobat, you will not be able to hang ceilings alone. The boards are extremely unwieldy and it is nearly impossible to hold them in place overhead and nail them to the ceiling beams at the same time. We even found the job difficult for two to manage. So we arranged a little work party: four of us were able to hang all the ceilings for the entire ground floor of a house in less than a full day. While three people supported the panels overhead, the fourth hammered the nails until the boards were secure.

Before submitting yourself to the arduous task of lifting the boards overhead, be certain that your sheet is the correct dimension. Measure from the corner to the 4' or 8' point and deter-

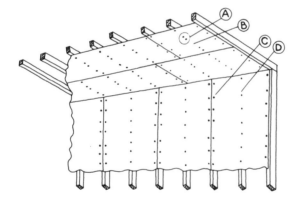

2. Here is how the nails should be placed in the walls and on the ceiling. (A) double nailing 2" apart. (B) pairs of nails 12" apart. (C) 3/8" from edge. (D) nails 6"–8" apart.

3. Several hands are needed to lift the sheets overhead and place them in position against the ceiling beams. As the ceiling panel is held in position, the nails are driven into the beams. Press the sheet into the nailing surface for a close fit. Double nailing is recommended for the ceiling.

mine where the edge of the gypsum board will be attached. Don't assume that the room is square. In fact, a room can be as much as 2″ out of square, shaped like a parallelogram. So before you trim pieces to fit, measure at various points along the last installed piece so that you can trim the last sheet to the exact angle needed.

In general it will work out better if you run the boards at right angles to the ceiling beams, butting the ends on the ceiling beams so that they are anchored firmly, not hanging in mid-air. Figure the layout of the sheets for the fewest seams to tape later. Working overhead is not comfortable, so try to minimize those later efforts. (Remember also that joints made by cut edges of gypsum are harder to tape than those made by two tapered edges. The tapered edges are depressed to accept the tape and joint compound.)

When nailing gypsum board to the ceiling, you will need something to stand on. Select ladders or sawhorses that are stable and relative to your height. A professional "Sheetrocker" has a sawhorse built to his size so that his head will be 3″ from the ceiling.

Before starting the job, mark on the exposed wall where the ceiling beams will fall. As you nail the ceiling panels in place, you can refer to these marks and know where the ceiling beams should be. If—and this always happens overhead—you should hammer a nail "into space," without making contact with a beam, be sure to remove the nail before you forget where it is. (We found it easier to circle these nailheads with a pencil mark, removing them later.) If these floating nails are not removed, they will probably pop out long after the ceiling is spackled and painted, so get rid of them while they're on your mind.

Start with a corner and lift the sheet into position. While the sheet is being held against the ceiling beams, butted tightly in the corner, drive in a few nails in all the edges to hold it temporarily. After the first few nails are in, nail all the way across one ceiling beam and continue this way. Nail the ends of each panel in place last. You'll have to work fast because the gypsum board is heavy and it can pull through the nails and come down. Butt the second panel against the first with the beveled edges meeting.

HANGING WALLS

Once the ceilings are in position, you can proceed with the walls. This is a far simpler procedure and can even be done if you are alone, since it is less physically demanding.

Again, plan your strategy to leave the least amount of taping later. A good place to butt

4. To hang the walls, cut the sheet of gypsum about 1″ short. On the floor near the wall place a piece of wood on a block of 2×4, in a seesaw-like position, like this.

5. Rest the gypsum board on the front end of the wood and step on the back end so that the sheet is driven upward, tightly butting against the ceiling.

6. With the lever pressing the sheet of gypsum against the ceiling, your hands are free for nailing.

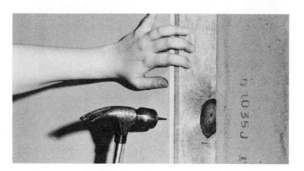

7. As you drive in the nails, press the board against the studs for a close fit.

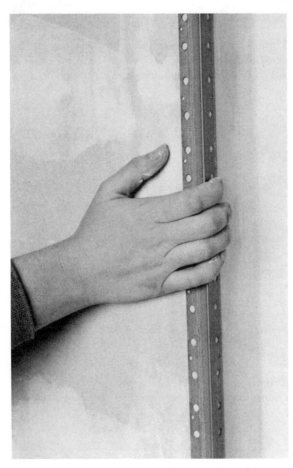

1. Outside corners are susceptible to chipping and disfiguration. Corner beads will protect these corners.

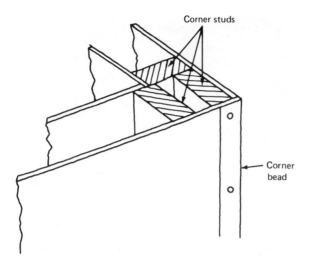

2. Snip off a section of the metal to the desired length.

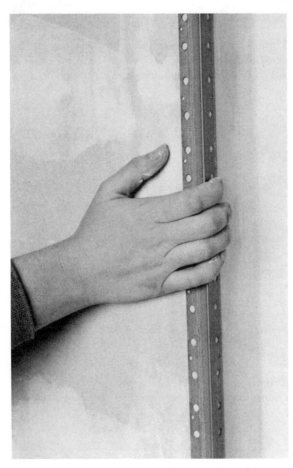

3. Press the corner bead snugly against the corner.

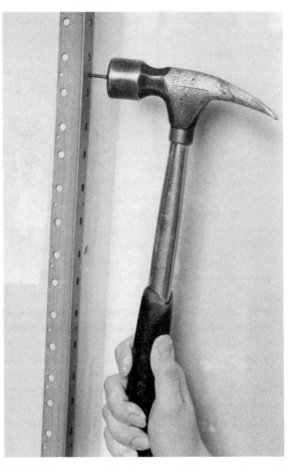

4. Nail the corner bead on each flange at least 6" apart.

panels is next to or above a window or door. This reduces the amount of taping, by giving you a short joint rather than a long one. Before starting on the walls, mark the stud locations on the ceiling. As mentioned earlier, most professionals would rather hang the panels horizontally to reduce the number of seams, but we found it far easier to hang the walls vertically because we could use the lever device described below.

Install the first wall panel at the corner. You can then work from this either in both directions or in one direction all the way around the room. Measure off the width at the top near the ceiling and at the bottom close to the floor. If it is more than ⅜″ off at the top or bottom, the edge of the panel should be trimmed so that it butts into the corner.

After you have measured for the width, measure the height. Cut your panel about 1″ shorter than the actual distance between floor and ceiling. A panel that is too short is easier to work with, and the gap at the bottom can be concealed with baseboard trim.

On the floor, just below the section of the wall you are about to hang, place a block of wood parallel to the wall, and another piece of wood, a strip of steel, or a wrecking bar over this block in a direction perpendicular to the wall, in a seesaw-like position (the same principle as any lever and fulcrum). Now lift the gypsum board and lower the bottom edge of the sheet onto the front end of this lever, near the wall. Position the sheet to the left and to the right so that both vertical edges are leaning directly on the centers of the studs. Now step on the back end of the lever and the sheet will lunge upward, butting tightly against the ceiling panel. While you are holding the sheet in position with the lever, your hands are free for nailing. With the sheet attached to the studs, step off the lever and complete the nailing.

Drive in nails about every 7″, down into each partition and all along the edges. If any nails fail to make contact with the framing, pull them out immediately, before you forget.

The width of the first panel and all succeeding panels depends on the spacing of your studs. Vertical edges must bear on studs from floor to ceiling. If the studs are spaced 16″ on center (as ours were), the panels will fit over them neatly and should not require cutting. Cutting can also be avoided in cases where the stud spaces measure 24″ on center.

After all the gypsum panels are installed, attach metal corner beads to the outside corners. Any outside corner is susceptible to chipping and the beading protects this edge, also providing a neat, squared-off corner for spackling. Do not join short sections of corner beads. Install them in a single, unjointed length, if possible. Cut the corner bead to the correct length with tin snips. Press the corner bead tightly against the corner and nail in drywall nails at 6″ intervals, on both sides of the flange, directly opposite each other.

INSTALLING A DOUBLE LAYER OF PANELS

Multi-ply construction is used in the home primarily to reduce the transmission of sound from room to room or to deaden the sound of water racing through pipes in a wall. It also improves fire safety.

Ideally, the sheets in the two layers of gypsum panels should be at right angles to each other, but this is not imperative. However, you should install the top layer so that the joints offset the joints in the bottom layer by one stud space or more.

After nailing up the first layer, apply the top layer either with nails or with an adhesive recommended by the manufacturer of the gypsum board. Nailing is easier. Just be sure to use nails long enough to penetrate the studs. However, gluing makes a tighter, more sound-resistant wall. The method of gluing depends on the adhesive, so read the manufacturer's instructions before applying it.

After gluing, tilt the face panel up against the wall and secure it with a few nails. Then go over the entire panel with a rubber mallet or with a board and carpenter's hammer and impact it tight to the base layer.

GYPSUM OVER EXISTING WALLS

First find the studs and mark their location on the ceiling. This is necessary because the nails used to secure the gypsum board should be driven through the old wall surface into the studs.

The actual installation of the gypsum is similar to installing it directly over studs. Don't make the mistake of thinking that, because an old wall surface is sound, the vertical edges of the gypsum panels need not fall over studs. Unless they are nailed into studs, there will be some play in them, and the taped joints may crack open.

If you are like we were, you will probably look at your walls and ceilings with some degree of dismay, feeling pessimistic about the final results. Torn edges, bad seams, unattractive spaces and nails seem to glare mercilessly down at you. But fear not, the miracle substance called joint compound will come to the rescue and you'll soon forget how unsightly these walls and ceilings once looked!

CHAPTER 7

Spackling with Joint Compound

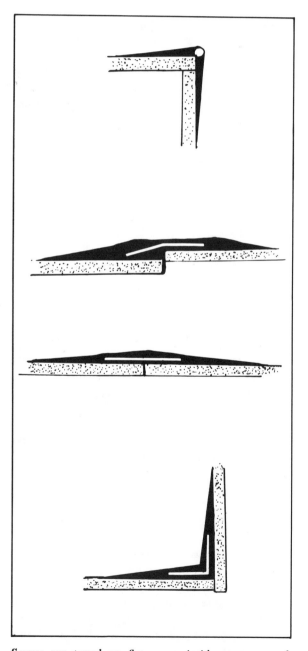

Seams are taped on flat areas, inside corners, and over recessed joints. A corner bead is used for an outside corner.

Until now, every procedure demonstrated in this section of the book—partitioning, insulating, and installing wallboard—has described work that will eventually be concealed. The closer you come to visible surfaces, the more painstaking your efforts must be. Be prepared for the unavoidable fact that all finishing procedures—whether they include spackling, painting, and wallpapering, or installing molding and casing around windows and doors—demand patience. Any sloppiness or carelessness will be clearly evident here and, regardless of how skillful your construction below the surface may be, your efforts will be judged on the way in which you finish these surfaces now. So regard spackling as a real test of your craftsmanship: this attitude will go a long way in determining the final results.

The most common error made in spackling is that of trying to achieve in one or two heavy coats what should be accomplished in four or five paper-thin coats. Rule number one: don't rush. Allow yourself at least four sessions of spackling, not fewer, and you'll see your efforts develop slowly but surely. Also remember that the more carefully you apply tape and joint compound in the first place, the less sanding and cleanup you will have later on.

Before beginning to work, inspect your room to be sure you are ready to tape and spackle. In major home renovation, spackling is done after the walls have been installed, but before the installation of final flooring and moldings.

Spackling can be very messy. Globs of wet compound inevitably splash onto the floor, and sanding creates a white powder everywhere. So cover your floors if they are finished and cover furniture or, better yet, remove the furniture from the room altogether.

If wallboards have been installed on both sides of a partition, be especially careful to check for panels that may have been loosened by hammering. Push firmly against all panels to determine whether there is movement toward the studs or beams. Drive in nails as required.

MATERIALS YOU WILL NEED

Spackling requires very few materials, but ones designed specifically for the these procedures.

Joint Compound: Joint compound is a marvelous substance to work with: it washes off easily, has no offensive odor, and responds instantly to any kind of manipulation. However, be sure to read the warnings posted by the manufacturer of the material. Inhaling the powder created by sanding can be harmful to your health. (In fact, you can now purchase a joint compound that does not contain the harmful ingredient asbestos.)

There are two types of compound available on the market: the dry version that you mix yourself and the ready-mixed. We strongly advise against the first type. Following the advice of an economy-minded friend, we tried mixing our own compound and disliked the entire experience. The mixing process was laborious and time-consuming. Because storage is difficult, you must mix only as much as is needed for the day. Ready-mixed compound, on the other hand, arrives in the proper consistency and keeps longer than the kind you mix yourself. It also handles better than the self-made mixture. We found that the monetary saving was hardly worth the negative features; ready-mixed compound is inexpensive enough.

One word of caution: don't store the joint compound in an unheated room. If the mixture freezes, it becomes unusable.

Tape: 2″-wide paper tape is designed specifically for concealing joints. It is generally available in 250′ rolls. Two kinds of tape are currently on the market. One has a rough texture and perforations that are so small they're practically invisible. (This is the kind we used in our demonstrations.) The other has much larger holes. Some prefer the latter variation because it is quite thin, but we found it more difficult to handle. The compound had a tendency to ooze through the holes, creating little bumps that required sanding after they had dried.

A special tape reinforced with a thin ribbon of metal may also be used. This is made primarily for reinforcing corners of less or more than 90 degrees. Frankly, we never found this tape particularly useful. Once we learned to work with the conventional paper tape, we never used any other.

Use the following chart to estimate compound and tape:

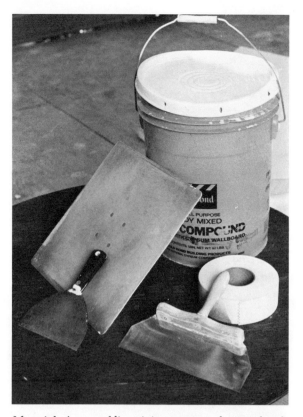

Materials for spackling: joint compound, tape, hawk, knives.

Open the can of joint compound and stir to the consistency of very thick mayonnaise. Add a little water if necessary.

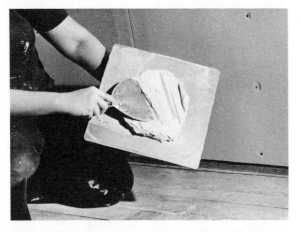

1. Scoop up a portion of joint compound with the knife and drop it onto the center of the hawk. Collect a supply about the size of a grapefruit.

2. Use the edge of the hawk for scraping off excess compound from the knife. This keeps the blade edge clean and free of unwanted compound.

Surface Area	Ready-mixed Compound	Tape
200 square feet	1 gallon	120 feet
400 square feet	2 gallons	180 feet
600 square feet	3 gallons	250 feet
800 square feet	4 gallons	310 feet
1,000 square feet	5 gallons	370 feet

Hawk: A hawk is like an artist's palette: it is 14″ square, usually made of aluminum or stainless steel, mounted on a wooden handle. On this flat surface you carry a supply of joint compound while you're working.

Knives: Specifically designed for applying joint compound, spackling knives look somewhat like over-sized putty knives. They are also called scrapers. You can do the entire job with only one knife, 4″ to 6″ wide, or you may prefer to add another knife as well, using the smaller one for the first coats and the larger knife—10″ to 12″ wide—for the finish coats. Don't settle for a scraper that is too narrow, however. It will create extra work for you because it applies compound in stripes rather than sheets. A 4″ scraper is the smallest size you should use. A corner knife, made for spackling inside corners, is also available, but not essential. For our work we used only two knives: one 6″ and the other 10″.

Corner Beads: These have already been described in the last chapter. Beads are long steel strips folded lengthwise to form a right angle and perforated along the sides. Cut them to the height of the wall and nail them over the corners to protect against damage and to provide a straight and square edge for joint compound.

FILLING DENTS

First we begin with the holes and dents in the walls and ceilings. Then we will describe the taping of seams to the flat areas, and finally the corner seams. Each is a progressively more difficult procedure.

The temperature of the room should be maintained at 55 degrees or higher from the time work starts until the last application of joint compound has dried. The room should also be ventilated sufficiently to eliminate the moisture given off by the joint compound.

Open the can of joint compound. The water may have separated, so stir the mixture with a stick until it is even and smooth, about the consistency of very thick mayonnaise. If it is too soupy, it will be difficult to control, and large globs will slide onto the floor. To thicken the compound, let it sit awhile, until the air evaporates some of the moisture. If the compound is too thick, it will not apply smoothly. Loosen the mixture by adding water and stirring strongly. A little water will go a long way, so add only a few drops at a time until you obtain the desired consistency.

Always keep the inside edges of the container clean. If a thin layer of joint compound dries and becomes mixed into the rest of the compound, it will produce lumps. Likewise, your tools must be clean and free of dried particles. Wash them carefully with tap water after each session of spackling.

With your knife, pick up a few globs of compound and drop them onto the hawk, until you have a supply about the size of a grapefruit. Centralize the pile in the middle portion of the hawk.

Scoop up a portion of the joint compound on your knife and, holding the knife at about a 45-degree angle to the wall, fill a sunken area around a nailhead, the dimpled well created by the head of the hammer. Butter this depression with the edge of the blade pressed firmly against the wall surface, depositing the compound into the dent as you move the knife across the surface. Return to the same dimpled area again, this time scraping in the opposite direction, and remove any excess compound you left behind the first time. This is a simple one-two motion—first in one direction, second in the opposite direction—and should go rapidly. Do the same with several dents along the wall until you've established your rhythm. One-two, one-two.

A nail that protrudes above the surface of the wall will be obvious to you as you scrape your knife over the head. The metallic sound will alert you immediately and the compound will not conceal the dark head. Drive in these nails whenever you discover them and refill the depressions with compound.

Wait for the first coat to dry (overnight). Apply several more coats in the same way until you have obliterated any sign of a depression. Three or four coats of compound are usually necessary.

TAPING THE FLAT JOINTS

Depressions are filled with compound. Seams require tape. First practice with the flat joints, before attempting the corners. After you have gathered a supply of compound on your hawk, scoop up a portion with the 6″ knife. Holding the knife at a 45-degree angle to the wall, spread a generous amount over the seam, a ribbon about 4″

3. First fill the dents in the walls and ceilings. With the first stroke, deposit the compound in the sunken areas. With the second stroke, scrape away excess compound (see diagram).

1. Now for the flat seams. With the knife, apply a generous amount of compound over the joint, starting at the top.

2. Spread the compound down the length of the seam in a ribbon about 6" wide. Don't leave any bare spots on the wall.

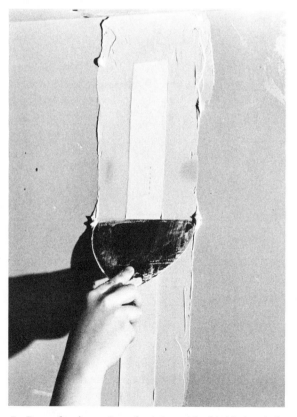

5. Press firmly against the joint with the blade of the knife and imbed the tape in the compound.

6. Return to the same area and scrape away excess compound. Return to the seam a third time with a slight "skim coat" of fresh compound.

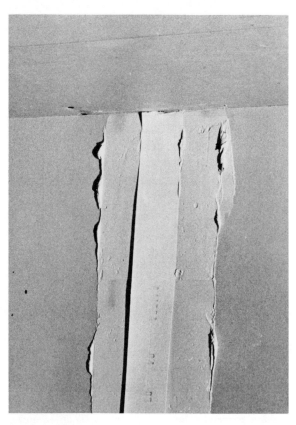

3. Tear off a piece of tape the length of the seam. Place one end of the tape over the center of the joint and gently lay it into the wet compound.

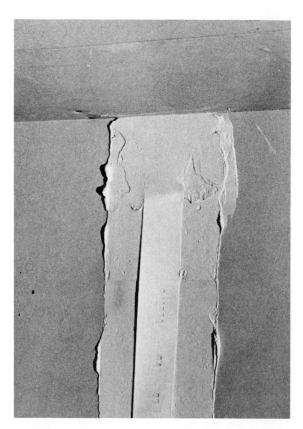

4. Anchor the top edge of the tape more securely by slapping on a bit more compound over the tape.

7. The first coat is always the roughest. After the compound dries, sand the seam lightly with a medium-grade paper.

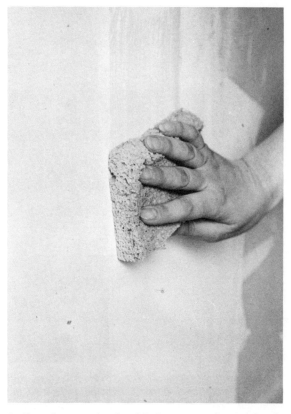

8. Rough areas in the dried compound can also be smoothed down with a damp sponge. Use this carefully; it's easy to remove too much compound.

9. Over the first coat of compound apply three additional coats, waiting for each to dry before applying the next. Each coat is slightly wider than the previous one. Use more pressure with the knife with each coat, scraping away excess compound and feathering out the edges to blend into the wall surface.

10. On the final coat, scrape the compound in a direction perpendicular to the tape to fill in whatever depressions you have missed earlier. Use the wider knife for the last coat and widen the ribbon to about 18".

11. After the last coat is dry, check for areas that may need additional work. A light held close to the wall will create a beam raking across the surface, which will highlight the irregularities. Sandpaper the rough areas you find, or return with fresh compound to fill in depressions the light may reveal.

or 6" wide and about ⅛" thick. Apply the compound down the full length of the joint; it doesn't have to be evenly applied, but every spot of the wallboard must be covered. Bare spots will create air pockets, which will produce bubbles under your tape.

Tear off a piece of paper tape to the proper length of the seam. Center the tape over the joint and gently lay it into the compound. Attach the top edge of the tape with a little extra compound to anchor it more securely. Pressing firmly against the joint with the blade of your knife, imbed the tape in the compound. Return to the joint a second time, scraping away the excess compound. Return this excess to the hawk, scraping the side of your knife against the edge of the hawk to remove most of the wet compound from the blade. Be sure to remove any lumps of compound from the wall as you scrape downward against the joint. Concentrate on stretching the tape slightly with the knife as you go, pressing against the seam firmly and evenly. However, don't press down on it so hard that you force all the compound out from beneath the tape. If this happens, the tape will pull loose from the joint when it is dry.

If wrinkles occur on the tape, pull it loose to a point behind the wrinkles and start over again. If the tape veers away from the joint, lift it and reposition it, or tear the tape in two and start a new strip just below the torn strip. (Do not overlap the tape. This will only create two thicknesses, which will appear as a bump on the wall surface.) Now return to the joint once more and cover the tape with a skim coat of joint compound. This coat should be sufficiently thin for the tape to be visible through it. Complete one joint before going on to the next; otherwise the joint compound will begin to dry and become hard to work.

Allow the first coat to dry thoroughly before proceeding further. This should take about 24 hours, depending on the heat and humidity of your room. (The edges dry first, and when the color is uniform, the compound is dry.) With a medium-grade sandpaper, sand the areas where you find irregularities and encrustations of joint compound. If you should scrape over any of these dried particles with the joint compound, you will create an unsightly washboard-like surface, so sanding down the rough spots is essential.

Over the first coat of joint compound apply three additional layers, waiting for each coat to dry before proceeding to the next. Thinner coats obviously take less time to dry, so that you can conceivably do two coats in one day. Each coat is slightly wider than the previous one. The first coat, in which the tape has been imbedded, is about 4″ or 6″ wide; the next, about 10″ wide; the next, about 14″ wide; and the final coat, about 18″ wide. Each layer must be carefully feathered or blended in; use more pressure on the knife with each coat. The first two coats fill in the tapered edges and go beyond them slightly; the final coats are really for smoothness. Collectively, all coats should be about $\frac{1}{16}$″ thick and level with the surrounding wall area.

The object is to apply each coat so smoothly and evenly that sanding is unnecessary. No doubt as you work you will develop your own system, as we did. Some prefer to apply the compound with the larger 10″ or 12″ knife, for example. We found this tiring, reserving the large knife for the last coat only. We applied all the other coats with the 6″ knife. We applied a generous amount of compound over the taped seam. Then we scraped off the compound in strokes parallel to the tape: first along the outside left edge of the compound; then along the right edge; and finally down the center of the seam, leaving no excess behind. Fi-

nally, on the last layer, we used our large knife.

For the last coat, scrape the compound in a direction perpendicular to the seam, rather than parallel to it. By scraping in this direction you will more effectively feather the edges into the wall so that it will be impossible to detect where the wall ends and the joint begins. The last coat will also fill in the final pits and irregularities in the surface.

After the last coat is dry, check for any areas you may have overlooked. If you hold a light close to the wall, its beam raking across the surface, the shadows will highlight the irregularities in the surface. Sandpaper lightly or run a damp sponge over rough areas. If the light shows up any depressions or scratches, smear a bit more compound into them with your knife. Rubbing your hand over the wall, you should be barely conscious of the hump formed by the joint compound along the seam.

INSIDE CORNERS

Tape is placed along all the inside corners. Amateurs frequently avoid taping the corners between ceilings and walls, using molding instead to conceal these joints. However, cracks often form between the molding and wallboard, unattractive spaces that must be filled with paint. Taped seams, on the other hand, are square and neat, worth the extra effort of spackling. The procedure for taping all corners is precisely the same.

The same tape is used for inside corners as for flat joints. You'll notice that the tape has a slight crease running lengthwise down its center, making it easy to fold. Tear off the length necessary for the seam, and fold the tape along this scored line.

Apply joint compound to both sides of the corner. You can do this by stroking in dabs of compound with the 6″ knife, then spreading the compound downward with the knife, producing a continuous bed of joint compound down the length of the wall. Pick up the folded tape and, starting from one end, gently poke it into the wet compound with the blade of the knife. Now imbed the tape in the compound, in much the same way that you pressed the tape into the flat seams. Start from the end of the paper and press downward along one side of the corner. Then do the same along the other side of the corner. Do not pull the tape away from the corner as you work, but concentrate on maintaining a straight and even line with the tape in the corner. As you bring the knife in a downward motion along the corner, rest the side of the blade against the opposite wall, using it as a guide.

1. *For taping an inside corner, first tear off a piece of tape the length of the corner or to a length you feel you can best manage. Fold the tape down the center along the crease.*

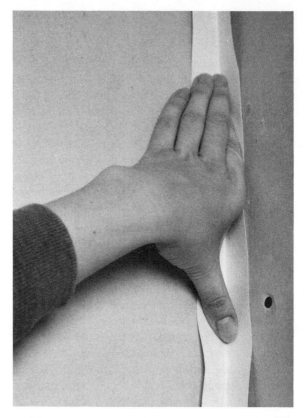

2. *The folded tape will fit into the inside corner like this.*

5. *Now imbed the tape in the compound, starting at the top. Bring the knife downward, resting the side of the blade against the opposite wall.*

6. *Now repeat this on the other side, pressing the tape into the compound without pulling it away from the corner.*

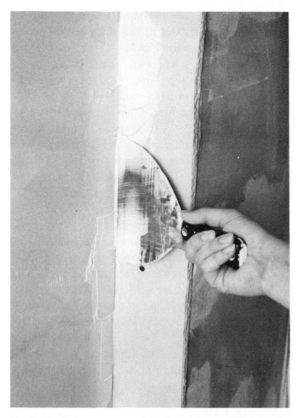

3. Apply joint compound to both sides of the corner by stroking in dabs of compound with the 6" knife.

4. Starting at one end, gently lay the tape into the wet compound, poking it into the corner with the edge of the blade.

7. The corner will bulge if too much compound remains beneath the tape. Squeeze out the excess compound by forcing it from beneath the tape with the knife. Pull the blade away from the corner without pulling the tape away. This takes practice.

8. After the corner is dry, app'y wet compound to one side only, stroking it in without depositing any compound on the opposite wall.

9. Clean off the blade against the hawk. Smooth out the wet compound. Bring the blade downward, resting its edge squarely against the corner, and continue to stroke the wet compound repeatedly until the corner is neat and even, yet conceals the edges of the tape.

10. After the first side of the corner is dry, return to the opposite side and repeat the process. (You may find dried particles of compound in the corner deposited from the previous coat, so sand them off first before applying the compound to the second side.) With both sides spackled, the corner should be even and square. If not, repeat the process until the corner is perfect.

You may find that the tape, although adhering to the wall, bulges out at the sides because there is too much compound below. This is common. The object here is to remove most of the excess compound without pulling the tape away from the corner. With practice you will be able to do this readily, but at first it may seem frustrating. Keep practicing. Press the edge of the blade into the corner and firmly pull the blade away from the corner, squeezing compound out from below the tape. The tape should remain fixed in position as you remove the compound from beneath it. Do the same to both sides of the tape. The layer of compound should be only about $\frac{1}{16}''$ thick, so that you should not feel any bulge bellying out from the corner below the tape.

Corners require practice, so don't be too hard on yourself during your early efforts. At first your highest priority is getting the tape into position. If your tape is fixed tightly in the corner and the line is relatively even—with no bulges from excess compound—you can afford to overlook the particles of compound you may have left behind. You can always sandpaper away these particles later. As your work improves, you will have less to sand and the work will go more rapidly.

Unlike flat seams, corners need only one coat to cover the tape after it dries. Each wall of each corner, however, must be spackled separately. In other words, you must wait for one side to dry before you apply joint compound to the other side of the corner. (With a corner knife you can do both sides simultaneously, but the corner knife leaves a bead of compound beyond its reach on each wall that has to be removed with the 6″ knife. In the end, the effort seemed to us greater than applying compound to one corner at a time.)

In applying the coat to the other side, try to avoid depositing any compound on the opposite wall in the corner. Wipe your knife frequently so that the exposed sides and edges are free of excess compound. Carefully place the compound all the way into the corner, without permitting it to ooze onto the opposite wall. After you have applied a ribbon of compound down the wall—about 4″ wide—return to the same section and smooth out the wet compound. Hold the knife parallel to the corner so that its edge (which has been wiped clean) rests against the opposite wall of the corner. Stroke the compound downward, the edge of the knife resting against the wall, and wipe away excess compound onto the hawk as it accumulates on the knife. Return to the seam and continue to do this until the compound is smooth and even, fully concealing the tape. You may have to stroke the same section with the blade several times before you obtain a smooth surface.

You may have to add compound to build up the surface if a depression is so deep that you pass over it with your knife. Patience here is a vital aspect of the job.

Don't be surprised if the corner takes longer to dry than the seams on the flat areas. The compound is generally heavier in the corner than on the flat. When the corner is dry, run down the entire length of the seam with a piece of sandpaper, just to be certain that you have picked off any particles of dried compound. Now apply the joint compound to the second side of the corner in the same way as to the first, stroking the compound until you have a neat and even corner.

Professionals don't return to a corner once they have applied a coat to each side of the corner, but we weren't so lucky. After the corners were dry we frequently found it necessary to sandpaper sections here and there and to fill occasional holes and pits with joint compound.

OUTSIDE CORNERS

If inside corners along the walls and ceilings can be frustrating until you've gotten the knack, outside corners are exactly the opposite: they are instantly rewarding and require very little practice.

Because they are vulnerable to damage, outside corners are protected with metal corner beads. Since corner beads are normally attached at the time the wallboards are installed, we described this procedure in the last chapter.

When the corner bead is attached to the wall, a slight depression is formed on each side of the corner, which is filled with compound. The corner, therefore, is actually built up to the metal edge with compound to form a squared-off corner.

Apply a generous amount of compound in horizontal strokes, perpendicular to the corner, dabs extending from the corner edge onto the wall by 3″ or 4″. As soon as you have filled in the depression along the entire length of the corner, scrape off the excess compound. Hold the knife at a 45-degree angle to the wall, one side of the blade extending beyond the corner and the other side scraping the wall surface. As you run the blade downward, scoop up the excess compound and square off one side of the corner right up to the metal tip of the corner bead. Repeat the same procedure with the other side of the corner.

The layer of compound on both corners is quite thick, so you will have to wait several hours before it is dry. The corner edge may appear exposed as a metal line running down the corner, but this will be covered with paint or wallpaper. As it dries, the compound may shrink, causing

1. *After corner beads have been nailed to outside corners (see Chapter 6), dab on a generous supply of wet compound. Stroke the blade outward toward the corner, creating a ribbon about 4″ wide.*

2. *Now scrape off the excess compound by stroking in the opposite direction, downward, the edge of the blade extending beyond the corner.*

3. Repeat the same procedure on the opposite corner.

4. After the compound is dry (this may take quite some time, because the layer of compound over a corner is thick), repeat the process again. Continue to do this until the corner is square and even. A coat of paint will conceal the metal edge running down the corner.

cracks to form on the surface. Fill in these cracks with a second coat of compound.

You may find that the second coat—applied exactly like the first—is sufficient. Or you may have to return another time to obtain a perfectly squared-off corner.

BUBBLES AND BLISTERS

If you are taping an entire room or home, you are bound to encounter certain irregularities here and there that normally go unmentioned in instruction manuals on spackling. For example, you might apply compound to a flat seam and unknowingly leave a bare patch on the wall, which creates an air pocket beneath the tape. These pockets surface later as bubbles or blisters bulging from beneath the tape. Generally, bubbles appear after the first coat of compound is dry, just after the taping. But bubbles can also appear later. In fact, we encountered bubbles that surfaced only after the wall was painted!

Bubbles are easily repaired. Using your utility knife, simply slice away the area of tape surrounding the bubble. Cut well beyond the bubble so that you are certain to remove the patch creating the air pocket. Fill the patch with compound, just as you would any other depression in the wall. Apply as many coats of compound as needed to raise the surface to the same level as the wall. You will recognize this point when you can no longer detect the patch in the dry compound.

OTHER IRREGULARITIES

Joint compound can conceal a whole host of irregularities, providing you are patient in handling the material. For example, in an old home it is common to find inconsistencies in the framing. Because a stud or ceiling beam is out of position, a wallboard attached to it may recede or protude. We encountered some panels that actually recessed by ⅝″ because a stud was out of line. To conceal this irregularity we applied a thick layer of compound to the recessed edge, settled the tape over the seam, and scraped away the excess compound from the protruding panel. In other words, the tape was imbedded in a thin layer of compound on one side of the seam, a thick layer on the other. In later coats we feathered out the joint to 18″ on the recessed panel so that it was optically impossible to detect the seam or to tell where the panel was recessed.

Here's another situation commonly encountered that can be remedied with joint compound:

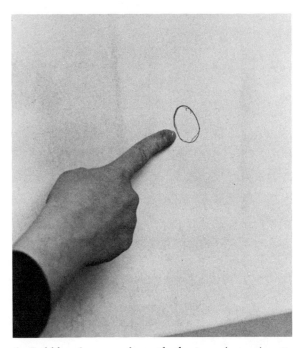

1. Bubbles do occur beneath the tape from time to time, regardless of how careful you are. You will not see them until after the compound is dry, and they may not even appear until after the wall has actually been painted. The photograph couldn't adequately show the bubble bulging from beneath the tape, so we circled the area where it occurred.

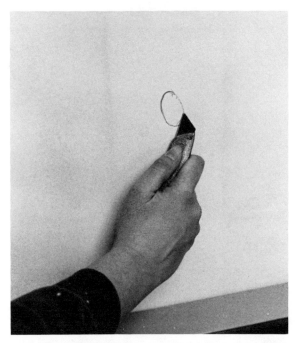

2. With a utility knife, cut through the tape, encircling the bubble completely.

3. Remove the tape from the wall.

4. Fill in the depression with compound, just as you would any dent in the wall. Reapply the compound until you have raised the affected area to the same level as the surrounding wall surface.

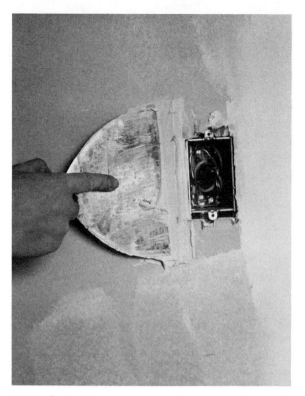

1. *It may happen that the opening for a wall outlet is too large. Position a plate over the electrical box to see if it will conceal all four edges of the opening in the wall. If the cutout extends beyond the plate, you must reduce the size of the opening.*

2. *Apply a generous amount of compound over the edge, up to the outlet.*

4. *Cover the tape with more compound to anchor it securely.*

5. *Without shifting the tape, scrape away the excess compound.*

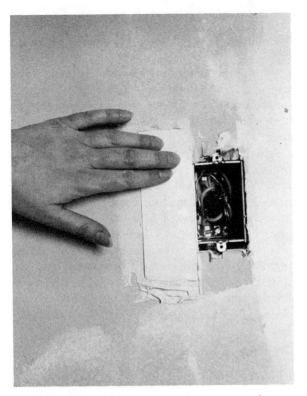

3. Settle a piece of tape into the wet compound.

an opening around an electrical outlet is too large. You can judge this yourself by placing an electrical plate over the outlet. If the opening is too large, it will extend beyond the plate. The size of the opening can be reduced with tape and joint compound. Apply tape to the wallboard so that one edge is attached to the wall, the other extending up to the electrical box. A few coats of compound applied over the tape will produce a sufficiently rigid surface. After all, this portion of a wall receives little abuse because it is protected by the electrical plate attached to the box.

Joint compound can also be sculptured into a curved shape. In an attic ceiling, for example, you may want the ceiling to curve at the point where the beams intersect. You can achieve this by applying several layers of compound over the seam, as shown in the demonstration photographs, shaping the curve with the knife into the wet compound, and later with a wet sponge into the dry compound. With careful work, you can create a uniformly curved surface.

6. The tape is fastened securely. Apply additional layers of compound as you would to any flat seam to conceal the edges of the tape.

1. In an attic ceiling you may have a seam that is angled, like this one.

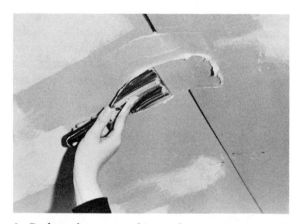

2. Rather than tape this angle, you can actually sculpture a curved surface by applying compound directly over the seam.

3. Several coats of compound applied in this way can create an attractive curved surface. Between coats, smooth the surface with a medium grade of sandpaper or with a damp sponge. Return to the seam several times until the curve is regular and all pits and depressions are filled.

FINISHING TOUCHES

The more time you devote to spackling, the faster and more proficient you will become. Develop good working habits right from the outset and you will certainly progress. Remember, there are no short cuts here. Don't try to accomplish in one coat what would be better achieved in three or four.

After you've completed the spackling you can proceed with the finishing touches. Apply a primer coat to the walls and then paint or paper over the primer. At any stage you may discover bubbles, or areas you've missed with compound. You can always return to these sections, applying compound over a painted surface, and then repainting. After you have painted or papered you can install the final flooring, trim the room with baseboards and casings around the windows and doors, and install plates on all the electrical outlets.

CHAPTER 8

Wood Paneling with Boards

There's nothing more inviting than walls that have been paneled with boards. The rich texture of natural wood, the warm and mellow color, and the random imperfections intrinsic to the material have made it an ideal treatment for dining rooms, living rooms, and dens, rooms that suggest a mood of quiet stability. Paneled walls also provide the perfect rustic touch to a country house. And your painting worries are over!

This chapter will show you how to install solid board panels on your walls, a job you'll find rewarding and far less difficult than you might have imagined.

TYPES OF WOOD PANELING

Solid wood paneling is available in an attractive range of hardwoods and softwoods and can also be bought tinted. The boards are produced in rough and smooth finishes, in clear or knotty grains. The boards generally have tongue-and-groove edges and most are also beveled along the corner of the edges. Other edges are also common: squared-off, lapped, or specially milled.

The thickness of boards for interior use commonly varies from ½″ to ⅞″ and the boards are obtainable in almost any length. The width of the boards ranges from 3″ to 12″, and they can be installed either in random or in uniform widths.

Softwood paneling ready for immediate application is available in almost all lumberyards. The boards are graded either knotty or clear and have a smooth finish. Boards with rough-sawn textures and tinted "barnboards" are also available in softwood paneling. Other woods—birch, oak, or cherry—are less readily available because they must be milled specially for paneling. You can probably purchase these directly from a lumber mill or order them specially through a lumberyard.

Old lumber salvaged from demolished buildings makes exquisite paneling, but a good deal of preparation will probably be required before you can use it. Edges may have to be milled and nails removed, but the final results may be well worth the effort.

ORDERING AND PREPARING THE BOARDS

To establish how much lumber you should order, measure the height and length of the walls you are paneling. Also calculate the area of the door and window openings, dimensions that will be deducted later from the total. You should add something for waste and trimming if the wall height is exactly the length of the boards—8′, 10′, 12′, 14′, or 16′. Little, if any, extra is required if the wall height is less than these figures.

Give these dimensions—the height and length of the walls and the area of the window and door openings—to your dealer so that he can work out the amount of lumber you'll need for the job. He's better able to calculate this than you are. Because of the variables in paneling—the nominal versus the actual size of the lumber, and the amount of space lost from the joints—your dealer will be the best judge in establishing the amount of materials you'll need for the job.

The boards will be packaged as bundles or sold as loose boards. If they are sold as loose boards, examine them before taking them home. If you leave the selection entirely up to the lumberyard, you are likely to find a few boards with large knots, splits, warps, or other defects. Selecting the boards individually, as you would select fruit in a fruit market, will guarantee you a better choice of lumber.

It's also advisable to select all the wood, including the moldings and other trim, in the same kind of wood you are using for the paneling. Left natural, woods of different types will age differently; different woods will accept finishes differently as well.

Have the lumber delivered at least 48 hours in advance of its installation. For a minimum of two days, store the lumber where you will be working, so that the boards can adapt to the atmospheric conditions of the room. If you plan to finish the wall with paint or opaque stain, prime the knots with a stain killer, then apply a priming coat of the selected color to the entire surface and to the edges. The edges should be colored in advance so that the open joints will not be exposed after installation. If you are paneling a basement wall, you might apply shellac, primer, or aluminum paint to the undersides of the boards as a precaution against possible dampness.

OTHER MATERIALS

Paneling is a relatively simple procedure and does not require many other materials and tools. If you are furring out the walls (see below), you'll need strips of 1×3 or 1×4 pine. Furring strips are spaced about every 2'. Calculate the amount of wood according to the area you intend to panel.

For nailing the paneling to the walls you'll use 4-penny finishing nails along the edge of a tongue-and-groove or lapped board and 6-penny finishing nails into the face of all boards.

The tools you need include hammer, 4' level, compass, circular saw, plane, and ruler.

PREPARING A WALL FOR PANELING

You may be lucky enough to be paneling over a smooth, even, and sound wall, in which case virtually no preparation for paneling is necessary. Simply remove the baseboards and casing around doors and windows. It's unlikely that you will want to use the same moldings again after you've paneled—since they probably won't match the paneling—but you can use the pieces for patterns when you cut down the new molding. So remove them carefully, prying them gently away from the walls and extracting the nails.

The chances are, however, that the existing wall is old and uneven. You can panel over any old surface by first nailing lengths of 1" wood called *furring strips* to the wall. Furring strips are used to correct badly damaged or uneven walls and to provide a fastening surface for the boards. Obviously furring strips will increase the wall

thickness by an additional 1". Therefore it will be necessary to move electrical switches and outlets the same distance. Door and window frames will also require change. In general, furring strips must be installed around all door openings, window openings, and other openings to provide a fastening surface for panels and wall-mounted fixtures.

First locate the studs behind the wall, starting at one corner and working from there. Using your fist or hammer, firmly tap the wall. If the sound is hollow, continue to tap along the wall until you hear a solid sound. This is the stud behind the wall surface. The next one will be located to the left or right at an interval of 16", 20", or 24". Mark each stud across the length of the wall.

Nail the furring strips to the wall at each stud. Where you see a gap between the wall and the strip, insert a shim of shingle between it and the wall. (Shingles are wedge-shaped, so that they will fit into the space needed if you slide them from their paper-thin edges to their thicker sides.) More than one shingle may be necessary for shimming if the wall is badly bowed. Drive a nail through the furring strip and the shim into the wall and continue to do this until the inside surface of the strip is even from one side of the wall to the other. There should be no visible gaps between the strips and the wall surface.

If you are paneling to a masonry wall in a basement, anchor furring strips to the walls with adhesive designed for this purpose or 8-penny cut nails. As an added precaution against dampness, staple polyethylene sheets over the furring strips. If your basement is excessively damp, you should also apply asphalt asbestos coating to the walls. (As already mentioned, you can also prime the back of the paneling with primer, aluminum paint, or shellac, as an additional precaution against dampness.)

PANELING TO STUDS

You are better off paneling directly onto studs than onto furring strips. Even if you have an old wall, it would be better to strip it down to the studs rather than build it up with furring strips. Once you are down to the studs you can do one of two things. You can nail furring strips horizontally to the studs—one at the base, one at the top, and two more equally spaced in between. Or you can nail two or more rows of 2×4 blocks *between* the studs. Although this last procedure is more time-consuming than the first, you avoid increasing the thickness of the wall. (This is the method we used in our demonstration.)

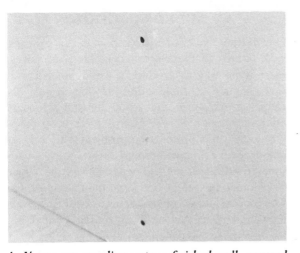

1. If you are paneling onto a finished wall, proceed by furring out the wall. First locate the studs behind the wall, and draw a line wherever they occur. (On this wall, nails indicate the stud below.)

2. Nail furring strips across the wall. If the wall bows inward, you'll see a gap beneath the furring strip.

3. Shim out the gap with shingles until the furring strip makes contact with the entire surface of the wall from one end to the other. Secure the shims by nailing them through the furring strip and into the wall.

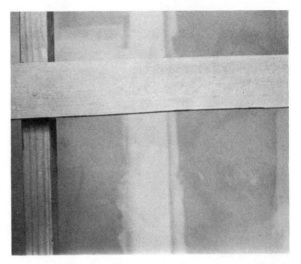

4. If you are paneling over studs, you can nail furring strips onto the studs and attach the paneling to the furring strips.

5. The ideal method of paneling is this way: onto studs, with nailers placed between the studs.

6. We were paneling on both sides of the studs, so we placed our nailers this way so that we had a surface on which to attach the paneling from both sides.

1. If you are starting the wall from an inside corner, proceed this way. Tack the first board into the corner as close to the corner as possible in a plumb line.

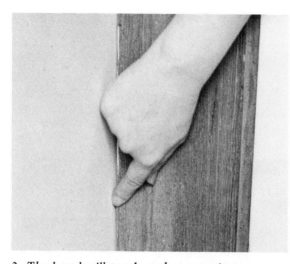

2. The board will touch at the corner in some parts and there will be gaps in others. Look for the widest gap along the edge.

3. Place the point of a compass or scribe against the wall and the pencil along the edge of the board where the widest gap occurs. With the scribe open to this point, trace the entire length of the board, holding the instrument against the corner wall, following its contour and marking the board with the pencil. Cut along this line and the board will fit tightly into the corner on one side and be plumb.

AN ADDED SUGGESTION

One further piece of advice if you are paneling with boards that are squared off at their edges: there is no way to produce a wood-paneled wall that does not ultimately develop open joints, because shrinkage in the wood inevitably occurs after installation. If the boards have been properly joined, this presents no problem with tongue-and-groove or lapped boards. But boards with squared-off edges tend to separate and the larger cracks look obviously open and may admit drafts. To conceal these open seams, cover the wall framing with a layer of black building paper before installing the paneling.

INSTALLING THE BOARDS

First establish the length of the boards. Measure the wall from ceiling to floor and reduce this measurement by ¼″ so that the boards will not be too snug. You want the boards snug at the ceiling, but the gap at the floor can be covered with baseboard. (If you are installing paneling in the basement, where dampness is a problem, allow a ¼″ gap at the top *and* bottom of the panel. Gaps will allow the air to circulate. Special ceiling molding with slits is available to cover the gap at the ceiling and to permit air circulation.) Cut down the board and see if it is a good measurement for the entire wall. If it is, you can avoid measuring each board individually and simply use this as a pattern for cutting all the next boards.

If the boards are of uniform width, you want to be sure that they are installed in such a way that you don't end up with a sliver at the second corner. Measure the wall and divide it by the uniform width of the boards. If there is only a small dimension left over from this calculation, you will probably be left with this undesirable sliver. Rip this small piece from the first board, rather than the last, or adjust the placement of the boards so that those at opposite ends of the wall are more or less equal in width.

Begin installing the panels at the corner and work across the wall. Cut the first board to the correct height. Rest it against the wall and push the grooved side into the corner. The first panel must be installed so that its inside edge fits tightly against the corner and its outside edge is plumb. As you hold the board against the wall and into the corner, check it with the 4′ level to see if it is plumb. If it is plumb, you're ready to begin. If it is not, shift the position of the board to where the level indicates it would be plumb. If there is only a tiny crack along the corner edge, you can attach the board as it is. But if there is a wide, uneven crack, you'll have to rip it to fit.

4. Cut down the board to the correct length—¼″ shorter than the distance from the floor to ceiling— and lift it so that it butts up against the ceiling. With 4-penny finishing nails driven into the nailer, stud, or furring strip, anchor the board along one edge.

5. Face-nail as little as possible, using 6-penny finishing nails and driving them into the nailer, stud, or furring strip.

6. If you are going to butt the boards at an outside corner, chisel or plane the edge of the board so that it is flush with the surface of the stud all along its edge.

7. We butted the outside corner so that the lapped edge formed an attractive line down the corner. You can also miter these corners by planing the two edges at 45-degree angles.

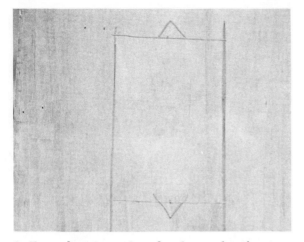

8. To make an opening, first locate the placement and size of the cutout by measuring from the ceiling and from the side of the paneling. Draw the cutout on the underside of the paneling. (*This is an opening for an electrical outlet.*)

9. It's easiest to cut out the opening with a saber saw. To begin the cut, lean the saw forward, placing the point of the blade on the pencil line. Turn on the saw and the blade, rubbing against the surface of the wood, will penetrate and begin the cut. Continue to saw along the pencil line with the saw upright.

10. The opening is made into the paneling. If necessary, it can be enlarged with a file or knife.

To rip the board accurately, you will have to "scribe" as follows: attach it to the wall temporarily with one nail and pivot the board into a plumb line. Open a compass (or scribe) slightly wider than the widest point in the gap. Hold one leg against the corner and the other leg on the board and draw them down from the ceiling to the floor. If you do this carefully, you will mark on the board a line that conforms exactly to the vertical contours of the corner. Trim the edge of the board to this line with a saw so that it will butt tightly into the corner. Boards at all other inside corners are handled in the same way. At outside corners, butt the joints or, if you have the patience, plane their edges at 45-degree angles so that they are mitered. This makes a more attractive joint.

Avoid nailing through the face of the panel as much as possible, especially in the middle of the board. You probably won't be able to avoid it altogether, however. Boards in corners must be face-nailed; boards more than 6″ wide require some face nailing to prevent warping. If the wall is to be painted or finished with a dark or opaque stain or paint, face nailing isn't unsightly. On a wall with a transparent finish, try to drive the nails diagonally through the edges of the boards rather than along the face.

With a lapped or tongue-and-groove board, drive a 4-penny finishing nail at a 45-degree angle through the tongue and a 6-penny finishing nail through the face of the board if it is wider than 6″. If you are working with squared-off boards, you will have to face-nail, the number of nails depending on the width of the board. (If the board is 6″ wide or less, two nails are sufficient; greater widths require three nails.)

Countersink all face nails. On a painted or dark-stained wall, cover the heads with wood putty or spackle. For light walls, use plastic wood that is colored to match the wood.

Our barnboard paneling was particularly simple: the point was to preserve the rustic appearance. We could do just about anything without harming the appearance of the wood in any way. We face-nailed wherever we pleased, and made no attempt to conceal the nailheads. (In fact, it's even possible to purchase specially made nails that are manufactured to resemble old barn nails. The end result is very convincing.)

OPENINGS AND OBSTRUCTIONS

When you encounter an electrical outlet in the wall, you'll have to locate its position accurately on the board. Do this in the same way you would on wallboard, measuring from the ceiling down to the top of the box, and from the end of the panel. (If the opening is too small, you can enlarge it with a utility knife or file.) Draw the contour of the electrical outlet on the underside of the board and cut out the shape with a saw. (A saber saw is the easiest tool to use here, but you can also use a keyhole saw.)

Whenever you encounter an obstruction with an irregular edge—such as a fireplace—handle it in the same way as you did when you scribed the first board in the corner. Cut the board to the correct length and stand it alongside the obstruction. Plumb it and tack the board into place. Scribe the line just as you did earlier, then cut along this line with a saw and fit it into place.

11. Paneling can be left untrimmed around the ceiling.

MOLDINGS

We made our moldings from the materials used in the paneling. We trimmed along the edge of the board and used the lap as a corner molding, tacked into place with a 4-penny finishing nail. We ripped a board for the baseboards and nailed that into place. When the molding turns a corner, simply miter it as you would any trim (see Chapter 20) or you can notch it—as we did—to make a fancier turn.

You can also rip the boards for casing around doors and windows. In the case of barnboard, you attach the molding around three sides of the door without mitering the corners. Simply butt them for a more rustic appearance.

12. We preferred to nail trim around the paneling at the ceiling. We ripped a piece from the barnboard paneling and nailed it along the top edge of the wall.

OTHER METHODS OF PANELING WITH BOARDS

In addition to the traditional method of paneling as just described, there are other methods of joining boards that may appeal to you.

Batten and Board: Square-edged boards can simply butt against each other, but they can also be installed vertically about 1″ apart. The joints are covered with 1×2 strips of wood (battens) of the same wood. The reverse—board and batten —can also be constructed; here the battens are placed behind the boards rather than in front of them.

Board and Board: This is the same as batten and board, except that boards are used instead of battens. In other words, the boards are spaced about 2″ apart and another board is nailed over this gap. All boards are the same width, usually about 8″.

13. Around the corner the trim has been mitered and notched and nailed into place.

14. *At the floor there will be a gap between the base of the paneling and the flooring.*

15. *The gap is concealed with baseboard. This baseboard was created by ripping a piece of a board 2¼″ from its edge.*

16. *The baseboard was mitered and notched to make the turn at the outside corner.*

Horizontal Paneling: With square-edged or bevel-edged boards, the panels can be nailed directly to the studs in a framed wall, horizontally, with no cross-blocking or furring necessary. Over a masonry wall, furring strips are applied vertically 2′ to 3′ apart. All outside corners must be made by mitering the ends of the adjoining boards so that the porous, coarse end grain is concealed.

Diagonal Paneling: Rather than install the boards horizontally or vertically, you can install them diagonally, usually at a 45-degree angle. The angle may also be dictated by the pitch of the roof or the angle of a stairway. The boards are nailed directly to the studs, but some blocking be-tween studs may be required in corners. Furring strips over a masonry wall can be applied vertically or horizontally. Place the boards at the corners so that the diagonal pattern is not interrupted.

Herringbone Paneling: Here the wall is divided vertically into two or more equal sections, and the boards in adjoining sections come together to form a *V* or inverted *V*. Because the effect is busy, use boards that are not shaped in any way along the edges. No furring is necessary. The boards are nailed directly to the studs. Some blocking between the studs may be needed behind the shortest boards.

17. The paneled wall is complete.

18. The paneled wall was integrated in design with three steps, which were rebuilt at the same time (see Chapter 14, "Rebuilding Old Steps").

CHAPTER 9

Flooring over Concrete

In the interior of a wood-framed home, you're unlikely to encounter much masonry, unless you're renovating a basement or converting a garage. In this case, your plans may have to include methods of handling concrete floors and walls. In Chapters 4 and 6 we've already given you some hints about how to attach walls directly to masonry, and here we will consider the flooring.

In a room designed for frequent use, you must allow for some kind of floor covering over the concrete. Bare concrete floors tend to be unattractive and uncomfortable because they are damp and lack resilience underfoot. There are, however, a number of ways to cover concrete floors, depending on the conditions currently existing in the room and your plans for the finished room.

FIRST CONSIDERATIONS

You can either use the concrete as a subfloor—flooring directly on the concrete itself—or you can construct an entirely new subfloor *over* the concrete. Which one of these you choose will depend on a number of factors:

Level: Place your 4′ level on various places across the surface of the floor. If the floor is absolutely level, you can lay your flooring directly on the concrete without having to make any structural alterations. But the chances are that the floor will swoop and dip in several places, particularly if the floor is angled for drainage. Obviously, you cannot place a floor in direct contact with a floor that is not level. Correct this level in

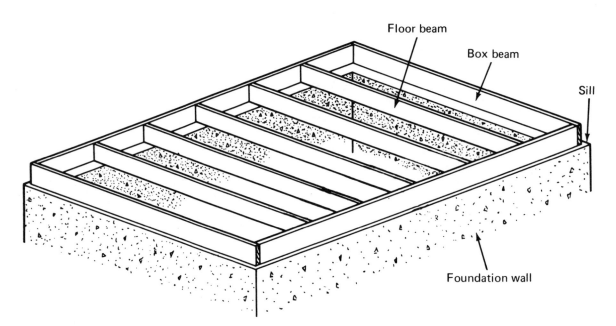

Diagram of the framing for a conventional ground floor: foundation wall; sill; floor beams; box beams. Over these beams are nailed subflooring and finished flooring.

one of two ways: re-cement the entire floor, making it level by following the instructions given in any good book on masonry; or build up the level of the floor with so-called *sleepers,* pieces of lumber laid (or nailed) into the valleys of the floor, creating a surface area that is at the same level throughout. Of course, if you would prefer not to adjust the irregularities on the concrete floor, you can avoid this by suspending an entirely new subfloor over the concrete, as we will describe in our demonstration.

Dampness: Concrete floors tend to "sweat," producing moisture by the condensation created when warm air comes into contact with cold air. This moisture can rot out and eventually destroy a new floor laid over it. Dampness can be prevented from seeping through the new floor if a moisture barrier is installed between the concrete and the new floor covering, by means of sheets of polyethylene stretched across the total area of the concrete floor. Again, however, if the floor is excessively damp, you might be better off suspending a floor between the concrete and the framing, placing two moisture barriers sandwiched with a good insulation in between them.

Heat or Cold: If you have any questions about how effectively you will be able to heat the room after the renovation is complete, don't install flooring directly over concrete. Heat loss through concrete floors is far greater than through insulated floors. A concrete floor covered by a moisture barrier and insulation tends to create a more comfortable room in general.

Ceiling Height: If the ceilings in the room are lower than 8′, you may be better off laying a floor directly over the concrete, rather than reducing the ceiling height any more than necessary. On the other hand, you may well want to reduce the ceiling height if it is greater than 8′, and a raised flooring could be the solution.

Room Function: The purpose your new room is designed to serve may also determine the floor construction. If the room is to withstand a great deal of traffic, you might consider a new floor. A concrete base tends to be fatiguing because it lacks resilience underfoot and is not nearly so comfortable for walking and standing as flooring over a wood subfloor.

FLOORING DIRECTLY ON CONCRETE

Laying a floor directly over concrete differs little from laying a floor over any other surface. The procedures are still identical. What is different is the way in which the concrete subflooring is prepared to accept the new floor. First, as we mentioned, the concrete floor must be level or made level with sleepers or by re-cementing. Second, a moisture barrier may have to be inserted between the concrete and the flooring if dampness is excessive. And third, a nailing surface must be placed on the concrete if the new flooring is to be wood. Installing these nailers is described in Chapter 11 in the section called "Laying Hardwood on a Concrete Floor." If you intend to lay resilient flooring—vinyl or linoleum, for example—on concrete, simply follow the same procedures described in Chapter 12 on resilient tile flooring. Ceramic tile floors over concrete are described in Chapter 13.

SUSPENDING A SUBFLOOR OVER CONCRETE

After we studied the condition of our concrete floor, we decided to install an entirely new subfloor suspended over it. It seemed to us that new flooring would reduce the problems of dampness, would provide better insulation, and would be simpler, in the long run, to install. Oddly enough, although our situation seems very common in home renovating, we have never seen the procedure described anywhere, so we decided to detail the steps carefully in this book, knowing that it would be valuable to others encountering a similar situation.

BASIC FLOOR CONSTRUCTION

When your home was built, it was framed out according to basic principles of home construction already described in Chapter 3. By building a new subfloor you are actually reframing one entire section of the building according to the same principles. First consider how a floor is constructed. We will assume that the concrete floor is on the first, lowest floor in the house, in the basement or the garage. (If not, some of the following may not apply.) Generally, the floor will be constructed with the following features:

Foundation Wall: All around the base of the wall you will see the foundation wall of your home, generally constructed with cement blocks or poured concrete.

Sill: The top side of the foundation wall is the sill. The sill can be the top side of the concrete itself (such as ours in the demonstration), or a sill may be constructed with lumber that has been attached to the top side of the concrete foundation wall.

Girders: Depending on the size of the floor area, one or more girders may have to be installed; these bear solidly on the foundation walls at both ends. Although usually solid, wooden girders are often built up from two or more lengths of 2″-thick dimension lumber spiked together.

Floor Beams: Also called *floor joists,* floor beams distribute a floor's load to the main bearing supports of a floor. Made from 2″-thick lumber, beams vary in width from 6″ to 12″, depending on the load they carry, the length of the span, and the spacing between them. Local building codes determine the exact size and spacing used for specific loads and spans.

Floor beams are normally installed 16″ from each other, but sometimes they are spaced with 20″ or 24″ intervals between them. The wood used for beams should be strong, stiff (to minimize vibration), free from warp, and able to hold nails firmly. Although most softwood framing lumbers are acceptable, be sure to check with codes governing framing size and grade.

Box Beams: Also called *rim joists,* these box beams rest on two sides of the foundation wall, perpendicular to the floor beams. The floor beams are joined to the box beams.

Subflooring: Nailed over the beams, and below the finished flooring, subflooring is of two general types: plywood or board. Generally speaking, ⅝″ plywood sheets are used when beams are spaced 16″ on center, ¾″ sheets are used when beams are spaced 24″ on center.

MATERIALS YOU WILL NEED

Your greatest expense here will be in lumber and insulation.

Floor Beam Lumber: You'll need lumber in 2″ thicknesses for beams, but the width of the lumber will depend mostly on the distance between the concrete and the subfloor. In our demonstration we built the subfloor about 10″ above the concrete floor, so we used 2×6 lumber. Lumber even larger can also be used. The number and size of the lengths will, of course, depend on the area you are covering. If you are covering a floor 16′ wide, for example, you will need two 8′ lengths for one beam, running from one side of the wall to the other. If your room is 20′ wide and you are installing beams every 16″, you'll

need 15 beams. To this number, add the number of beams you will need along the sides of the room. It will help you to draw a plan of the floor, laying out the position of beams on paper, before ordering the lumber.

Girder Beam: Down the middle of your room, if your room is wider than 12′ (check your building codes), you'll need a center beam for added support. Use the widest possible 2″ lumber you can, if space allows, and order two lengths of this lumber in the same size because you will spike them together. We used 2×8 lumber for the center beam, running the distance of the room (20′).

Subflooring: For easy installation, lay the subfloor in plywood sheets. We suggest interior plywood, ⅝″, in 4′×8′ sheets. Estimate the amount of square footage in the room and divide this number by the square footage of a single sheet. (Our room was 400 square feet, divided by 32 square feet, so we ordered 13 sheets of plywood.)

Moisture Barrier: For a moisture barrier, you will stretch sheets of polyethylene across the concrete floor. This plastic is available in rolls and is relatively inexpensive. One roll will probably be more than enough for your needs.

Insulation: Over the moisture barrier you will install bats of insulation, the thickness depending on the amount of space between the concrete floor and the subfloor. Since we had a 10″ space, we were able to install 6″ insulation, the ideal size for this purpose. Again, establish the amount of insulation you need on the basis of the square footage to be covered. Order insulation in 15″ widths.

Nails: To nail beams and girders, use 10-penny common nails. To nail subfloor to beams, use 8-penny coated box nails.

Water Level: There are several kinds of water levels, but we found one particularly good. This is the Hydrolevel, manufactured by Mayes Brothers Tool Manufacturing in Tennessee. It is available at most hardware or building supply stores or can be specially ordered through a local distributor.

Other Tools: Chalk line, level, hammer, 8′ ruler, staple gun, pencil, assorted blocks of wood.

ESTABLISHING THE FLOOR LINE

First determine where to install the beams. How far from the concrete floor will you install your new floor? One wall will probably dictate how high the new floor should be placed, because of an entrance or a stairway, or for some other reason. Our floor line was easy to establish because the original concrete floor was 10″ lower than the floor in the next room, and by raising the floor 10″ we would construct the new floor flush with the floor in the adjoining room. First we measured the distance from the surface of the concrete floor to the surface of the floor in the next room. We knew we would be laying a hardwood floor over the subfloor, so we subtracted ¾″ from the distance. We also subtracted another ⅝″ for the subflooring. Now we had the location for the floor beam. We marked this point on the wall.

Working in reverse, we figured that if we laid the subfloor over the beams and the oak flooring over the subfloor, our finished floor would be exactly flush with the floor in the next room.

Or you may establish your floor line based on the ceiling height. If you can spare the height, raise the floor line at least 6″, but if this means that the ceiling will be much less than 8′, you might have to reduce this distance to 4″. Mark on the wall the point where you want the top of the beam to fall.

MARKING OFF THE LEVEL LINE

Regardless of what method you use to calculate the distance between the concrete floor and the new floor, your first challenge will be to plot out the placement of the beams so that they are level from one side of the room to the other. If these beams are not level, the subfloor laid over them will not be level either. You already know that the concrete floor is not level, so you can't mark off the beams by measuring from the concrete floor. Another system must be devised.

In former times it was necessary to sight the level line on four walls with a specialized instrument used by surveyors, or to use string and line levels. A recently developed instrument called a Hydrolevel makes this procedure far simpler for the amateur to accomplish. This kind of water level consists of a round plastic container that houses a long, flexible tube and a reservoir into which about two cups of water are poured. Place a low table or bench in the center of the room, so that you have a flat surface fairly close to the concrete floor. Now set the container on the table or bench and take out the long plastic tube. Pour some water into the container and add a little food coloring to make the liquid more visible. With a siphon action, the water will trickle down into the tube.

1. On a low table or bench in the center of the room, place the Hydrolevel. Extract the tube from the container and pour water into the well, adding food coloring for greater visibility. Siphon the water into the tube.

2. Hold the tube against a stud on an outside wall. No matter where you place it, the water level in the tube will rise only to the level in the reservoir now standing in the center of the room. (Water seeks its own level.) The food coloring in the liquid makes this point more visible. Mark the stud where the water level has risen in the tube.

3. Bring the water level over to the two adjacent studs and mark off on each the point where the water level has risen in the tube. Mark these points clearly on the three studs; they all represent the same height.

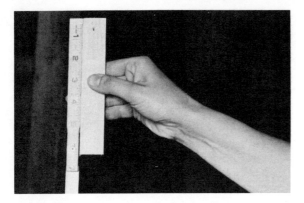

4. *You now have a fixed height, but it probably doesn't correspond to the floor line you had in mind. Measure the distance between the point marked with the Hydrolevel and the point where you want to install the subfloor. Our mark made with the level was exactly 6¼" higher than where we wanted to install the subfloor. We sawed down a piece of wood to 6¼" and used it as a pattern or guide.*

5. *We placed the piece of wood on our water level mark and made a new mark, exactly 6¼" below the first one.*

7. *With a chalk line placed precisely over the three new marks, extend the line across the entire wall of the room, from the first stud to the last on the wall. You now have a level line on one entire wall. Repeat the same procedure on the other walls in the room, using the level and the piece of wood just as you did for the first wall.*

8. *First the two box beams will be attached to the walls. Here we used 2×6 lumber. Two box beams should butt over the center of the stud—rather than at the spaces in between—so mark this point off on the lumber before cutting it down.*

10. *Attach the box beam to the stud with three 10-penny common nails. Position the board so that its top edge touches the mark made by the chalk line earlier.*

11. *Butt the next piece of lumber over the stud, as shown. Nail into the stud with three 10-penny common nails.*

6. We made new marks on all three studs, each 6¼″ below the first marks. Eradicate the earlier marks.

9. The 2×6 lumber has been cut down so that its end falls at the center of the stud.

12. The box beam is now anchored to the wall. The edge of the board touches the chalk marks on each stud. The board is secured to each stud with three 10-penny nails. If you put a level on the top edge of the box beam, you should find that it is perfectly level, regardless of its varying distance from the concrete floor below.

The principle here is simple: water seeks its own level. The liquid inside the tube will flow to the level of the liquid in the container. If you hold the tube in the air, the liquid will climb and climb until it reaches the same level as the liquid standing in the reservoir on the table or bench in the center of the room. No matter where you stand in the room the water in the tube will not go any higher or any lower than that level.

Walk over to the first wall in the room—where you had established the floor line—and hold the tube against one of the studs. With a pencil, mark off exactly the point to where the liquid has risen. (The food coloring in the water will make this more evident.) Now mark off this point on the next stud on the wall, and the next, so that three studs in a row are marked at the same point. Although these lines are level, they probably don't correspond to the height you had established earlier for the floor line. It doesn't matter. From these points you can easily locate where the beams should be placed along the four walls.

Measure the distance—higher or lower—between the mark made from the water level and the mark you made earlier to indicate the point where you wanted the floor beam. In our demonstration our floor line was 6¼″ lower than that marked with the Hydrolevel. (We sawed down a piece of wood to this size—6¼″—and used it as a guide for all four sides of the room.) Now mark off this measurement on all three studs. With the chalk line, continue this line across the entire wall, being sure to place the cord precisely on the marks you have just made.

Follow the same procedure for all four walls: first mark off where the water level has risen in the tube, then mark off the distance between this point and where the beams will fall (use a pattern or guide, as we did, for a constant measure), and continue these marks along the wall with the chalk line. All four lines should meet at the four corners. Now you have your level established.

ATTACHING THE BOX BEAMS

All four walls are now marked, so you know precisely where the beams will be installed against the studs. Because we raised our floor by 10″ we could use 2×6 lumber for all our floor beams, which is ideal. Obviously, if your floor is being raised by only 4″, you must use 2×4 wood instead.

Box beams are installed along the longest walls, the floor beams later toenailed to them at 90-degree angles, parallel to the two shorter walls.

13. *A girder beam is made by spiking two 2×8 boards together, crown sides up. Rather than using one continuous strip of lumber—which would probably twist and warp and provide insufficient support —the beam is constructed with two long and two short pieces of lumber. First we laid out a 16′ board on the floor and then a 4′ board butted to its end. Then we placed a 16′ board on top, spiking it into the two pieces below. Here the piece on top awaits the short piece.*

14. *The 4′ piece of 2×8 has been spiked to the board below. All crown sides are along the same edge.*

15. *Turn the girder beam on its side, crown side up, and rest it on a block of wood so that its top edge touches the mark made earlier with the chalk line.*

16. *Lift the other end of the girder beam to the chalk mark at the opposite wall as well. Support the middle with a block. Now toenail the ends into the two walls.*

17. *The weight of the center beam will probably cause it to sag in the middle. Shore it up with blocks of wood until it is level. The box beams and girder beam should all be level now.*

Install the two box beams on the two longer walls, placing them so that their top edge touches the lines you marked along the studs with the chalk marker. Join the ends of the box beams at the studs for added support, even if this means cutting down the length by a few inches to allow the ends to butt over the studs.

Wherever the beam is in contact with a stud, drive in three 10-penny nails. Also drive in three nails at each end.

GIRDER BEAM

If the room is wider than 12′ (check your building codes), you should also install a central beam down the middle of the room, parallel to the box beams, so that the floor beams will not span too great a length. (Our room was 20′×20′, so we installed this central beam down the middle of the room.)

Our girder beam is constructed from two lengths of 2″-thick dimension lumber spiked together. Since there is no foundation wall down the center of the room, it is possible to construct this girder beam with a larger piece of lumber than those used for the beams elsewhere. (We used 2×8.) If you are installing a girder beam, don't attempt to span a distance greater than 12′ with a single length of 2×8. Pine any longer than this has a tendency to twist and warp and doesn't have sufficient strength to withstand stress. For greater ease in installation and for added strength, therefore, use two shorter lengths rather than one continuous length. (For our floor, spanning 20′, we used two lengths of pine to extend the full distance.)

To construct the girder beam with two short and two long pieces, follow this procedure: first lay one long piece, flat side down, on the floor, and one short piece—cut to the proper length— touching end to end. Now place the second long piece over the lumber on the floor, setting it over the shorter end so that the butted beam is resting against the longer piece on top. The object here is to avoid butting the short pieces at the same place on each side. Rather, these seams should be staggered, not lined up. Spike all the lumber together with 10-penny nails, their crowns all on the same side. (Follow the pattern for nailing that we described in Chapter 1, "Some Tips on Nailing into Wood.")

Now turn the girder beam on end and line its end up with the mark on the central stud. The beam is heavy and awkward to maneuver, so rest it on a block of wood while you adjust the other end. Attach the ends to both walls by toenailing into the sides and top with 10-penny nails.

The girder beam may sag in the middle because of the weight, so support it with blocks of wood, leveling it at the same time with the 4′ level. Shim up this support with slivers of wood until your level indicates that the girder beam is level from one end to the other.

INSTALLING FLOOR BEAMS

With the box and girder beams installed, you have the frame on which to nail the beams. The beams will be toenailed perpendicular to the box and girder beams, every 16″ and along both walls. First mark off where these beams will be attached, just as if you were marking off for studs in partitioning as described in Chapter 4.

Start from one corner, marking the box beam at the wall where you will nail the first floor beam. The next mark will be 15¼″ from the wall. (This is important: the first measurement of 15¼″ allows you to rest one edge of a 4′×8′ sheet of subflooring on the beam flush against the wall, while the other end will fall on the center of the floor beam, not short of it.) Then continue to mark the rest of the box beam every 16″, indicating with a cross which side of the line the floor beam will be nailed. Now mark off the second box beam and both sides of the girder beam.

Measure the distance between the box beam and the girder beam at the first mark and cut down the floor beam to precisely this measurement. Nail the beam against the wall, toenailing it to the box beam at the top and sides, toenailing it to the girder beam, and driving three nails into every stud it touches against the wall just as you did with the box beam earlier. Now pick up the next board for the floor beam and cut it to size. Before nailing it to the box beam, check the board for the crown side along the edge (see Chapter 2).

In construction where any kind of bearing weight is to be placed on the lumber, always arrange it so the crown side faces the stress. As the weight is pressed against the lumber, the crown will resist the weight, adding strength to the support. In the floor beam, for example, the crown side should face the subfloor.

Attach this beam at the point you've marked, one end toenailed into the box beam, the other end toenailed into the girder beam, and the crown on top. Be certain that the joints where the beams are toenailed are all flush at the top.

If you notice that the crown arches higher than the level line of the floor, don't be alarmed. As the floor is used, the weight pressing down on the beams, these curved pieces of lumber will settle and straighten.

18. Mark off the placement of the second beam, 15¼" from the wall. (The first beam will be flush against the wall.) This is important: the first measurement of 15¼" allows you to rest one edge of the 4'×8' sheet of subflooring on the beam flush against the wall so that the other end will fall on the center of the floor beam, not short of it.

19. The floor beams will be toenailed perpendicular to the box beams. Mark off the box beam every 16", indicating which side of the line the floor beam will be secured. Do the same with the second box beam.

22. The distance between the box beam and the girder beam will determine the length of the floor beam. Cut the lumber down to this precise size.

23. Anchor the first beam at the corner, crown side up, securing its sides against the studs at the marks indicated earlier with the chalk line.

26. To each floor beam attach three legs—one at each end and one in the middle. Use scraps of lumber here. One end of the leg touches the floor, the other end is no higher than the top edge of the beam. Anchor the legs to the side of the beam with three 10-penny nails.

27. For sections of the floor where added support may be required because extra weight is anticipated (such as a fireplace), toenail the legs beneath the beam rather than alongside it. Several may be necessary.

20. *Mark off the girder beam on both sides in the same way, 16″ on center.*

21. *Measure the distance between the box beam and the girder beam.*

24. *Toenail the floor beam to the box beam, driving two 8-penny nails into each side and one into the top edge. Be sure the top edges are flush. Attach the other end to the center beam, also flush at the top.*

25. *Now begin to roll out a sheet of polyethylene moisture barrier and lay it over the concrete floor. If possible, staple the edges of the plastic to the wall or to the beams so that there are no openings through which the dampness can seep. If stapling is impossible, use tape. Unroll the plastic a section at a time.*

28. *Roll out additional sections of polyethylene as you work. Continue to install the floor beams from one side to another with legs on each beam until you have completed them all.*

29. *Now staple insulation over the beams, fiber glass facing down. Attach each bat of insulation at the flange, forming a continuous vapor barrier toward the living area. Six-inch insulation was used here.*

30. Lay down the first sheet of plywood subfloor. (The first sheet may have to be cut down in order for its edge to fall along the center of a beam.) Draw lines across the sheet where the beams are located below. Drive in 8-penny coated box nails every 8″, anchoring the plywood to every beam.

31. The seams of the subfloor must meet at the center of a beam for required support; 4′ × 8′ plywood sheets will fall naturally onto beams that have been spaced 16″ on center.

32. Alternate the joints so that the seams are staggered across the floor, as shown here. This means using a half sheet as a starter in every alternate row.

MOISTURE BARRIER

Before too many floor beams are installed, bear in mind that you will be laying down sheets of polyethylene directly onto the concrete floor. The plastic is very slippery underfoot and shifts easily, so avoid laying out too much at one time. It will only be a nuisance and could be hazardous. It's also awkward to work in large quantities, polyethylene being exceptionally difficult to control. Here's how we worked with it: from the large roll we made a smaller roll, with just enough plastic to cover one strip of floor from one wall to the next. We stapled the end of the strip to the wall and gradually unrolled the polyethylene in 5′ sections, attaching the foundation wall as we progressed. We attached a few floor beams, unrolled another 5′ of plastic, attached the legs to the beams (see below), then continued in this way down the row until the beams and legs were all nailed. Overlap sections of polyethylene by 2″ or 3″ and avoid stretching or puncturing the sheet. Simply lay it loosely over the concrete and anchor the sides to the side walls wherever possible.

Note: If termites are a problem in your area, it is recommended that you lay the plastic into mastic. An adhesive is a deterrent to termites, we are told.

ATTACHING LEGS TO THE BEAMS

For additional support to your floor, we recommend that you attach legs to each floor beam. Here is a perfect opportunity for you to use the assorted fragments of wood you've probably accumulated during your renovating. The wood blocks can be 2×4's, 2×6's, 2×8's, whatever you happen to have on hand.

These blocks are nailed—with three 10-penny common nails—up against the side of the beam, the end touching the floor. The length should be sufficient for the maximum amount of nailing surface, but should not extend beyond the top edge of the beam. Attach three legs to each beam— one at each end and one in the middle.

If a crown seems to be particularly exaggerated, rising well above the other beams, attach the middle leg so that its bottom end is an inch or so above the floor. As the crown settles, the leg will eventually touch the floor.

You may have planned that certain sections of the finished floor will support particularly heavy loads, a fireplace, for example. Wherever you anticipate these loads, place the leg under the *bottom* edge of the beam—rather than at its side— toenailing it through the beam into the block.

33. *You may have a stairwell, like this, or some similar structure in your room. We removed the steps first, then installed box beams beneath it, notching the lumber to permit exposure of a heating pipe.*

34. *We simply proceeded as normal, placing the beams where we were able to circumvent the stairway supports. We attached legs as elsewhere.*

35. *We patched the subflooring below the stairwell, using remnants from other sheets.*

36. *We replaced the stairway, having removed the lower rungs to allow for the raised floor. (Later this stairway was rebuilt entirely; see Chapter 14.)*

Depending on the weight you intend to support, you'd be wise to attach several legs in this way, side by side, along the beam. These legs will give the extra support you need to withstand the unusually heavy load.

INSULATION

The amount of space you have between the subfloor and the concrete floor will dictate the thickness of the insulation you can use. Six-inch insulation is ideal, but anything less would also be better than none at all.

Installing insulation between the floor beams is no different from installing it in the walls or ceilings (see Chapter 5). Place the insulation with the vapor barrier facing the living area, the fiber glass toward the concrete floor. Staple the flanges of the insulation to the top edges of the floor beams, forming a continuous vapor barrier.

SUBFLOORING

The plywood subflooring is now nailed to the beams. The first sheet is laid into the corner, the sheet cut, perhaps, in order to permit the edge to lie along the center of a floor beam. But successive sheets should line up correctly over the beams, without cutting the plywood, as long as they have been installed 16″ on center. All joints must butt against each other, but they must be resting on a beam below.

Draw lines across the top surface of the plywood, guides for where the beams are located beneath the sheet. Drive in 8-penny coated box nails approximately every 8″. If you happen to drive in a nail in the wrong location, missing the beam below, pull it out immediately before you forget.

In laying out the sheets of plywood over the beams, stagger the joints to avoid a continuous seam running from one side of the room to the other. This avoids putting too much stress on individual floor beams and also prevents splitting the floor beams from too many nails penetrating along the edges. Start every other row with a half sheet.

Continue to attach the floors to the beams in this way until you've covered the entire area. This is a standard subfloor. Now you are likely to complete the room by returning to Chapter 4—partitioning, then wiring, insulating, hanging walls and ceilings, and so on. All these must be completed before you finish the floors. For finished floors, you can lay down underlayment and carpet or tile, or you can install a hardwood floor directly over the subfloor. All these are described in the following chapters.

CHAPTER 10

Underlayment

Selecting a floor for any given room is a matter of personal preference, a choice determined by the function of the room, the amount of money you are willing to spend, and your own personal taste. In this book we have tried to anticipate the variety of choices open to you and to incorporate all these options in our discussion of flooring. In the following chapters we will describe how to lay a hardwood floor and how to tile your floor with resilient and ceramic tiles. Of these procedures, only hardwood can be applied directly to a subfloor. If you intend to install wall-to-wall carpeting, tile, or linoleum, you must install underlayment first.

Underlayment serves several functions. Nailed to a subfloor, it strengthens the flooring. For example, if you have ½" plywood subfloor, an additional layer will prevent the final floor from giving way underfoot. Underlayment provides a more stable surface. Underlayment creates a surface smooth and even enough to accept tiles. Underlayment also raises the floor to a height that may be desirable if you are flooring a nearby room, perhaps.

MATERIALS FOR UNDERLAYMENT

Just what kind of material you use for underlayment depends largely on what kind of finished flooring you have in mind and how much you want to raise the floor level.

Until recently floor underlayment was almost exclusively plywood. Plywood is still popular. For this purpose ¼" or ⅜" panels are used. We recommend plywood if you want a smooth surface without raising the floor more than a fraction of an inch. For example, if you intend to refloor a kitchen with vinyl asbestos tile, you may find plywood desirable. You can simply nail ¼" sheets of plywood underlayment directly onto the old tile and tile over an entirely new surface. (One precaution here: hammering into plywood creates dents in the surface. These must be filled with wood putty before tiling.)

If, however, you want to raise the floor line by more than ¼"—to equalize it with an adjoining room, perhaps—we suggest using hardboard. The generic term *hardboard* refers to any material made from a softwood pulp that is forced into sheets under heat and pressure. Hardboard is available in a variety of forms, but the kind of hardboard most commonly used for underlaying is *particle board* (also called *chipboard* and *flakeboard*).

Particle board is inexpensive and is normally sold in sheets of 4'×8' in thicknesses of ½" and ⅝". It is heavy and tough and provides an excellent underlayment. There is a difference of opinion regarding the suitability of particle board as underlayment for tiles. At least one major tile manufacturer will not guarantee work done on particle board. Most carpenters, however, maintain that particle board is a superior underlayment. Unlike plywood, it will not dent easily from the blows of the hammer. It has other advantages as well. Particle board is less expensive than plywood. Hardboards have improved greatly over the years and no longer create the problems formerly associated with them. They are durable and tough, not as subject to "flaking" as they once were. Properly sealed, they should not expand and contract as readily as they once did.

With particle board, standard woodworking tools may be used. Store the panels flat, taking care to protect the corners and edges from damage. Also avoid damaging the surface; once the

1. Only hardwood can be applied directly to a subfloor. In all other cases underlayment must be installed. Carpeting and tiles are placed over underlayment.

2. Lay down the first sheet of particle board (or plywood, depending on which you have chosen for underlayment) opposite to the direction of the subflooring. If a space exists below the gypsum wallboard, slip the board into it. The baseboard will conceal any other irregularities around the edges.

3. Locate the position of the floor beams below the subflooring and extend this line—in pencil—onto the sheet of underlayment. Drive 8-penny coated box nails every 8″ or 10″ along these lines so that the underlayment is attached to the floor beams themselves.

4. Drive 8-penny coated box nails every 8″ or 10″ around the perimeter of the sheets as well. Butt the next sheet alongside the first, but stagger the rows so that the seams are interrupted. Start every other row with a half sheet.

5. Continue to draw the pencil lines across the next sheets of underlayment so that you are certain to drive the nails directly into the floor beams below.

smooth top crust is broken, sandpapering will not restore the original surface.

Regardless of whether you are working with plywood or particle board, use 8-penny coated box nails. Their greater holding power is designed for flooring because coated nails reduce the possibility of squeaking floors underfoot and do not work their way up through the floor.

The procedure described in this chapter refers primarily to working with particle board. Underlayment in plywood is precisely the same procedure as that for laying a plywood subfloor, described in the previous chapter.

PREPARATION

If you are doing major renovation in your home, delay the installation of underlayment until the walls and ceilings are hung and painted or papered. By waiting until this point you will protect the floor from soiling and will make your later work much easier. The only room in which the underlayment is installed earlier is the bathroom, where it is placed in position before installation of the bathtub. Otherwise the underlayment should be installed after everything else is completed.

Before laying down the sheets, check your subfloor for irregularities. Drive in any raised nails that may have emerged; fasten loose boards; replace or repair warped floorboards. Sweep the floor and scrape it, if necessary, to remove all spackle, concrete, or plaster particles.

INSTALLING THE SHEETS

Place the first sheet on the floor at the corner of the room in a direction opposite to that of the subfloor. If you followed our suggestions for hanging wallboard (Chapter 6), there should be a space, about 1″ wide, at the base of the wall. Slip the board into this space. If there is no space, place the board as close to the wall as possible. Baseboard will conceal the irregular spaces around the edges.

With the first sheet laid in position, determine the location of the floor beams below. You can sight these by finding the row of nails in the subfloor alongside the particle board you've just laid. Extend this row by marking a line in pencil across the width of the sheet. With 8-penny coated box nails, anchor the sheet to the floor. Drive the nails into the pencil lines—every 8″ or 10″—so that you are anchoring the boards to the floor beams themselves. Also hammer in nails around the perimeter of the board, every 8″ or 10″. Nailing thoroughly will prevent the board from shifting underfoot, and the rosin-coated box nails reduce

squeaking and will not work back up. By installing the underlayment securely around the edge, you avoid any chance of spring (or "whip") in the middle.

Continue to lay the sheets on the floor, staggering their seams. Start every other row with a half sheet so that the seams are alternated. Cut the boards where obstructions occur. In small enclosures—closets, for example—you will have to cut the board into two pieces in order to fit the flooring into the small space.

Don't fret over small gaps that occur here and there. A space greater than ¼″ should be filled with wood putty, but do not fill spaces any smaller than that. They will only creak as the floor shifts slightly underfoot.

TIPS ON WORKING WITH PARTICLE BOARD

Although your woodcutting tools are appropriate for working with particle board, there are some unusual features with this substance worth noting.

Nailing: Driving coated nails into any surface is difficult, but into the tough particle board it can be particularly frustrating. When the hammer strikes a coated nail even slightly off balance, these nails will fold up very easily, especially when driven into a hard substance like particle board. And the hammer tends to slide on the face of the head because the coating is slippery. If you hold the hammer loosely, you will probably be more successful. The head of the hammer settles more squarely onto the head of the nail, improving your chances of a clean hit.

Removing a crippled box nail can also be frustrating. Ripping the bent nail from the particle board by tugging at its head with the claw of a hammer only severs the head from the nail shank. You'll get better results if you extract the nail by gripping its shank—rather than the head—with the claw of the hammer. The metal in the nail is relatively soft, so that you can force it into the corner of the hammer claw. We used two hammers for this operation. With one hammer we drove the claw opening of the other hammer onto the nail shank (see photo). Lean the hammer sideways and the nail will pull out easily.

Cutting: For cutting particle board, use a fine-toothed blade in a circular saw, and always cut on the underside to minimize chipping of the face side. The saw will have a tendency to veer off the line as you work unless you raise the blade, as shown in Chapter 1. Also support both ends of the sheet on its underside with sawhorses at both ends to prevent binding.

6. Coated nails bend easily when they are driven into the tough particle board.

7. To extract a bent coated nail from the floor, drive the claw of the hammer onto the nail shank. We used two hammers in this way, getting a tight grip on the soft metal nail shank.

8. Lean the hammer sideways. The nail will easily pull out.

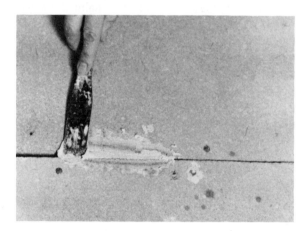

9. With wood putty, fill holes or gaps greater than ¼″.

10. Sand down dried and rough wood putty with medium paper before you tile the surface.

CHAPTER 11

Installing a Hardwood Floor

Regardless of the ever-rising costs of hardwood, its popularity for flooring has hardly diminished. It remains a preferred material for floors in living areas of the house, serviceable, durable, and, when properly maintained, the most elegant of all surfaces.

Hardwood flooring is most generally oak—the wood we have shown in our demonstration—but hardwood flooring can also be installed with maple (gymnasium floors are generally maple), beech, birch, and walnut (for decorative effects, usually). Softwoods may also be used for wood flooring, particularly fir and pine. But we will devote our discussions to oak in particular, since this is what you will most likely be using in your home.

TYPES OF OAK FLOORING

There are three general styles of oak flooring: plank, block, and strip. Each comes in varying lengths, widths, and thicknesses. Only the procedures for installing strip flooring are described in this chapter because it is the most popular, the one you are most likely to use, the most economical.

Plank Flooring: Usually selected for a rustic appearance, plank flooring is rather wide, the sides squared off. The planks are often bored and plugged at ends to give the effect of the wooden pegs once used to fasten down such planks. Widths range from 3″ to 9″. If you're using different widths, these can be applied randomly. Thicknesses and methods of joining are the same as for strip flooring; their joints are butted.

Block Flooring: Blocks come in square and rectangular units, often in the familiar "parquet" style. Usually made from three or four short strips of flooring glued together or joined with splines, blocks are most commonly $2\frac{5}{32}$″ thick. The square or rectangular dimensions of the blocks are determined by the size of strips they are made from.

Strip Flooring: This consists of flooring pieces cut into narrow strips and available in several different thicknesses and widths. Strip flooring is laid in random lengths, the end joints being scattered, not clustered. Most strip flooring is tongue-and-groove. A special machine at the flooring mill cuts a tongue on one side and end, and a groove on the other side and end. The tongue and groove allow the flooring pieces to join snugly. Another feature of modern strip flooring is the undercut. This appears on the bottom of each piece: grooves hollowed out to provide better resiliency underfoot. The undercut enables the board to lie flat, even though the subfloor surface may contain slight irregularities.

Despite its extensive use, strip flooring retains individuality in character because of its handsome grain. No two oak floors are exactly alike. Most strip floors are composed of pieces of uniform widths, but interesting effects can also be achieved using random or mixed widths. Interesting patterns, in either case, can be obtained by using pieces selected for variations in color, mineral streaks, or other natural irregularities.

The grading of hardwood flooring is based primarily on appearance, because all regular grades of oak flooring possess adequate strength, durability, and resistance to wear. Chiefly considered are such characteristics as knots, streaks, pinworm holes, amount of sapwood, variation in grain, and variation in color. The most commonly used grades of oak are—in descending order— clear (uniform color, vertical grain); select (some vertical grain, some flat; some variation in color); No. 1 common (greater variation in color and flat grain); No. 2 common (even greater variation in grain and color). For general-purpose flooring, No. 1 common is the most attractive.

1. *Strip flooring contains a groove along one edge and around one end.*

2. *On the opposite edge and end is a protrusion called a tongue. The tongue of one strip fits into the groove of its neighboring strip.*

3. *Along the underside of strip flooring run hollowed-out grooves, an undercut to provide better resilience underfoot.*

Standard thickness and width of oak flooring are $2\frac{5}{32}'' \times 2\frac{1}{4}''$. This is called, in the vernacular, 1×3 oak flooring. Other widths and thicknesses are also available in certain parts of the country, but 1×3 is standard. For our demonstration we used 1×3 No. 1 common oak flooring.

Boards can be purchased finished or unfinished, the finished naturally being more expensive. Although it sounds tempting to order the finished variety—because you think you can avoid the final step of sanding and finishing—in fact we found this deceptive. It's virtually impossible to install a floor without somehow marring the surface before you've completed the operation. At best, the finished floor will need touching up, a time-consuming procedure that can be more tedious than finishing the entire floor.

OTHER MATERIALS YOU WILL NEED

Only a minimum number of materials are needed for laying a hardwood floor. They are as follows:

Nails: Because of its density, hardwood must be installed with nails designed to penetrate the wood without splintering or collapsing from the blow of the hammer. Consequently, two kinds of nails are available for this purpose: cut nails (made of tempered steel and used for all hard substances, including cement) and tempered-steel thread flooring nails (designed with a thread that grips the wood securely as it penetrates it). We used cut nails, but the thread nails are probably easier to use. Either nail should be 8-penny.

Rosin Paper: So-called red rosin paper is laid beneath the hardwood to prevent noise caused by the expansion and contraction of the floor. If the finished floor moves a little, it presses against the paper instead of the subfloor, and this reduces squeaking. Rosin paper also protects the interior of the house from dust, cold, and moisture that might otherwise seep through the floor seams. The paper is inexpensive and comes in large rolls. Calculate your needs based on the square footage of the area you are flooring.

Hammer: In nearly all our renovating work we tended to use the 20-ounce hammer, but there is a special hammer for flooring that you can buy. It weighs 32 ounces and usually has a crosshatched grid on the face of the head so it won't slip off the nails. Since driving into hardwood takes a pretty hefty slam with the hammer, there's no question that this specially designed tool can save you some muscle. But bear in mind one important fact before you run out to buy it: the cross-hatched head on such a heavy hammer can put you out of commission for quite some time if you should accidentally strike your finger!

Flat Bar: This is an instrument of great value for this particular job. Also called a pry bar or, by the trade name, a Wonder Bar, this inexpensive tool is as indispensable as a tire tool. It will help you to force the hardwood strips into tight contact with the grooves and ends.

Nail Set: You will set every nail as you work. For tempered-steel nails you'll need a special soft nail set because a conventional one will splinter and break when used on the tough nails. This is easily damaged. We didn't use any nail set for the steel nails. We preferred to use 10-penny common nails for setting the cut nails, throwing away the nails as soon as they became too battered for the job. This method of setting the nails is described later.

Miscellaneous Tools: In addition to these specialized tools, you'll also need a saw, a ruler, and a pencil.

IS YOUR TIMING CORRECT?

Don't rush into this job unless you are certain that this is the correct time for flooring. Finish flooring should be nearly the last operation in remodeling the house. Your wiring, heating, plumbing, and insulation should all have been completely installed; the walls and ceilings already hung; and the spackling, painting, and papering completed. The reason for this is obvious: the finished floor should not be used as a working surface for other operations.

Do not install flooring in a room where moisture may be a problem. First check for *visible* signs of moisture. Are there any leaks in the plumbing, radiators, roof, and walls? Does rain come through the openings of the windows and doors? Correct these conditions before the floor is installed.

Other forms of moisture may be more difficult to detect, because they may not be visible. For example, in your locality there may be excessive atmospheric humidity. If so, be certain to leave extra expansion space at the walls where the hardwood flooring begins and ends. (Allow at least ¾″ between the face of the wall and the adjacent flooring strips.) Other conditions may also create excess moisture that may not seem so obvious at first. If recently installed plaster walls or concrete floors seem damp to the touch, you are

not ready to install flooring. Wait for this moisture to evaporate before you begin. Likewise, if the framing has been recently installed, check for green lumber. Moisture in new wood must be completely released before you install the new floor.

OTHER PREPARATIONS

A hardwood floor is nailed directly onto a subfloor. No underlayment is necessary. However, sound subflooring under the finish flooring is absolutely essential. If hardwood flooring is to be laid over old wood floors, inspect the floors first for irregularities. Check to be sure each board in the subflooring is face-nailed at every floor beam with two nails. All the butt joints in the subflooring should rest on floor beams. Also examine the subfloors for loose boards or defects. Raised nails should be driven down and loose or warped boards corrected or replaced. Sweep the subfloor thoroughly and, if necessary, scrape it to remove all spackle, concrete, or plaster particles that may have dried on the surface. If the subflooring is loose, cupped, or humped up in places, drive 8- or 10-penny common nails into the bad spots to flatten them. If you can't get it perfectly flat, you can take down the high spots later when you sand the finished floor. Remove baseboards and door casings before you begin.

ESTIMATING YOUR NEEDS

Boards are generally sold in bundles containing strips of hardwood in varying lengths. Make a detailed diagram of the floor to be covered (graph paper is handy for this purpose). Measure all the dimensions and write them down on the diagram. Take it to your lumberyard; the dealer will help you determine the amount of flooring and nails you need for the job.

If you happen to be a consumer who would rather make these calculations yourself, use this method of figuring. First determine the actual area in square feet and add one third to that figure for waste. Divide this total by 3. Each bundle is marked with its nominal length. Buy enough bundles so that the total of their nominal lengths is equal to the above number. For example, if the area is 20′×15′, or 300 square feet, adding one third equals 400 square feet: divided by 3, equals approximately 133. The total lengths of the bundles you buy should equal 133, give or take a foot or two.

After you purchase the materials, store the boards in the room in which they will be installed

1. This subflooring is of the older variety: planks nailed into the floor beams every 24".

2. Before laying down the hardwood floor, you must be certain the subfloor is anchored tightly to the beams. Drive in protruding nails wherever they occur.

3. Scrape away any lumps of hardened spackle, plaster, or cement that may have dried on the surface of the subfloor.

4. Sweep the floor to remove any loose particles and dust.

5. Plan your strategy by first measuring the room to establish if it is square. Measure the distance from one corner to its opposite along one wall; then measure the distance along the opposite wall from one corner to the other. If the difference between these measurements is more than 2", the room is very much out of square. If so, rip both the first and the last board so that they share the difference between them. If the room is less than 2" out of square, it is sufficient to rip only the last board you lay.

6. Lay down the first strip of red rosin paper from wall to wall in the direction you intend to install the strip flooring. With a soft pencil, mark off the location of the floor beams below.

for at least five days. They must be allowed to adjust to the room temperature and moisture before installation. Stack the boards loosely to allow the air to circulate freely around each piece of wood. The room should be at least 70° F. when you begin to lay the floor.

THE FIRST STAGE

In what direction will you install the strips? In general, oak flooring lies flatter if it is at right angles to the subfloor boards, but it stays tighter if it is at right angles to the floor beams and nailed to them. (The best results are obtained if the subflooring is installed diagonally and the finished floor at right angles to the floor beams, but this is rarely the case in an older home.) Remember also—in deciding the direction of the flooring—that existing flooring in the next room may determine the choice. Although it may not have been installed in the ideal way, you will still have to continue the new floor in the same direction as the old.

We have laid our oak flooring perpendicular to the floor beams, parallel to the boards on the subfloor.

Measure the floor from one side of the room to the other. If your room is relatively square, the measurement you take from one corner to the other along one wall should be just about the same as it is from one corner to the other of the opposite wall. If there is more than 2″ difference, you'd be wise to rip the first board you lay against the wall. For a 2″ difference, rip the board so that there is a difference of 1″ in the width between one end and the other, so that you will have to rip the last board by only 1″.

Start the job by laying out the red rosin paper over the subflooring. Lay one strip absolutely flat, from wall to wall. (After you nail the boards over this strip, you will put down another strip of paper, overlapping the previous one by 1″ or 2″.) With a crayon or soft pencil, draw lines clearly to mark off the places where the floor beams would be beneath the paper. You can detect these easily enough by locating the nails in the subflooring and continuing the lines onto the paper. The floor beams will probably occur every 16″ or 24″, depending on how the framing was constructed. (Ours were every 24″.) The lines on the paper will guide you when you nail the boards to the floor beams.

Carry the first bundle of oak flooring over to the area in which you will be working. Line up the boards on the floor, side by side, in order of size, from the longest to the shortest. Be certain the tongues are placed in the same direction. In this way you can easily select the length you need, saving time and avoiding waste.

7. *Take the first bundle of strip flooring and lay the boards on the floor in size order. Place all the tongues on one side, all the grooves on the other, so that you have easy access to whatever you will need as you work. This avoids waste.*

Lay the first and longest board parallel to the first wall, and into the corner, the groove side facing the wall. The grooves along the length of the strip and the end of the board should lie about ¼″ away from the wall. (In our demonstration we were obliged to slip the first floorboard beneath the baseboard heating unit.) Face-nail this piece into every floor beam with cut nails or steel thread nails, one nail per floor beam.

Face nailing is driving a nail straight down through the top of the board, unlike *blind nailing,* which is driving a nail at an angle into the tongue of the board, later concealed by the adjacent board. The face nails will be countersunk later, when the floor is finished—the holes filled with wood putty and totally concealed. The first and last rows are face-nailed; the remaining boards are blind-nailed.

Continue with this first row along the wall. With the next board, slip the groove at its end into the tongue at the end of the fastened board so that there is only a minute space between them. The last piece will probably have to be cut down to fit. Select a length of flooring that is closest to this dimension and cut it down with a standard saw. Allow approximately ¼″ space between the last piece and the wall. But you needn't fuss too much over this. It's not necessary to cut ends of boards very accurately or straight, since the wallboard and baseboard molding will conceal the cut ends anyway. In fact, you don't want the flooring tight against the wall, because it will expand and contract according to the atmospheric conditions and a little space avoids any problems of the floor buckling in damp weather. (Incidentally, whenever you cut the last piece in a row, be certain to saw off the tongue end, not the groove end.)

BLIND NAILING

After you have face-nailed the first row of boards to the floor beams, fasten the strips even more securely by anchoring them to the floor at their sides. These nails are toenailed at the sides at an angle so that they are concealed as soon as the next board is placed onto the tongue. Hold the

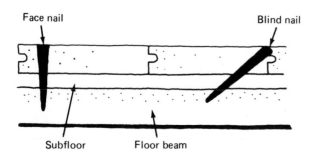

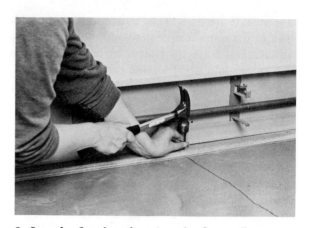

8. Lay the first board against the first wall, grooves along the edge and at the end facing the wall. Here the first board was placed beneath the baseboard because the heating had already been installed in the room. The space between the board and the wall should be even. Face-nail the first board by driving nails into the floor beams through the top of the board (see diagram).

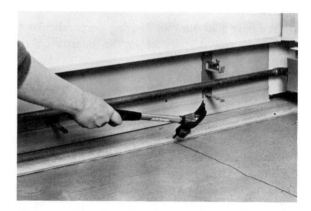

11. Now lay the second row. Insert the groove tightly into the tongue and drive the nail, at a 45-degree angle, above the tongue of the next board, directly into the floor beam below (see diagram).

14. From time to time, you will probably split the tongue of the oak flooring when you drive in the steel nail. Here is such a case.

9. Saw the last piece in this first row to size with the circular saw. Be certain not to saw off the groove end of the piece.

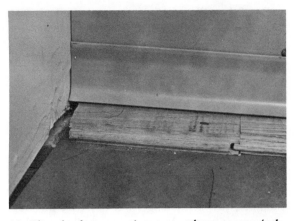

10. Slip the last cut piece onto the tongue of the board, leaving a small space between it and the facing wall. Face-nail this piece into the floor beam.

12. To countersink the nail, lay a 10-penny common nail along the top of the tongue and rest its head on the head of the nail you've just driven into the board.

13. Strike the head of the 10-penny common nail with the hammer so that it forces the other nail more deeply into the flooring. Each time you use the 10-penny nail in this way you will damage its head slightly. When the head is too battered for further use, throw it away and use a new nail for countersinking.

15. With the claw of the hammer, rip away the splinter of wood. Avoid pulling away more tongue than necessary. Countersink the nail.

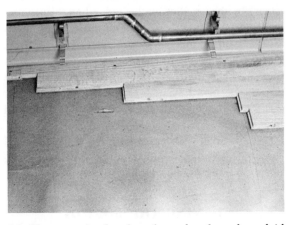

16. Here are the first boards as they have been laid in order of their size.

point of the nail at a 45-degree angle to the board. This angle is important: if you drive the nail too flat, it won't reach far enough into the subfloor. If you drive it too straight on, you'll only break off the tongue. Above all, the angle forces the board tightly against its neighbor.

Start the nail carefully. Once it is anchored into the wood at the correct angle, you can put all your weight into hammering it home. Don't be discouraged if the first few nails give you trouble. It takes practice to do it correctly every time. No doubt you'll mar the surface of the board with the hammer, just at the edge, but don't let this concern you. These nicks are removed when the floor is sanded down later, and you'll never notice these signs of your early learning experience.

After you've driven in the nail so that it is nearly flush with the board, sink in the nail still farther. We used the head of a 10-penny nail for this purpose. Place the nail on its side, resting on the tongue, and put the nailhead directly over the head of the flooring nail you have just driven into the board. Strike the head of the 10-penny nail with your hammer, sinking the flooring nail deep into the board. After you sink a few of these nails, you'll have to throw away the 10-penny nail because its head will become battered from the abuse. Start over with a new one.

No matter how careful you are in toenailing, occasionally you will split the tongue of a board so that it is so badly deformed that you will be unable to bring the next board into close contact. If this happens, simply tear away the split wood with the claw of your hammer, without ripping off any more of the tongue than necessary. As long as there is enough tongue for the next groove to grab, you won't have to worry about occasional sections of tongue being removed.

If nailing fatigues you very much, or if you find you have absolutely no knack for it whatsoever, you can rent a nailing machine designed specifically for laying hardwood floors. The machine is held in one hand against the board and struck with a mallet in the other hand, automatically driving in special nails at the correct angle. Some nailing machines are even power-driven. You will still have to exert some effort in nailing, but the angles will always be true. Your decision should be based on the amount of flooring you want to lay. The more flooring, the more it would make sense to rent the machine.

Finally, don't underestimate the importance of adequate nailing. Insufficient nailing may easily result in loose or squeaky floors later on.

LAYING THE BOARDS

Now that you've managed to learn the art of blind nailing into beams, the hardest part is over.

Each board is tucked into the tongue and groove, attached to the floor beams by cut nails, and so on until you've reached the other wall. Lay all the boards from one bundle side by side, rather than end to end, so that you systematically lay each board in its respective length—from shorter to longer or from longer to shorter—thereby avoiding unnecessary waste in any bundle.

The first few boards will be difficult to install because the nearby wall makes it awkward to swing the hammer properly. As you progress, moving away from the wall, you'll be able to kneel on the new floor, hammering over the nail at a more comfortable angle.

After you have finished the first bundle, open the next bundle, and attach the oak flooring to the boards you have just laid. The tongue and grooves at the ends and along the sides will fit snugly into each other. Tap the board into position with your hammer. The object is to get an absolutely snug fit. You may have to jockey the board somewhat to lock it into position, but there are techniques to help here. If you have a gap at one end, for example, and the loose board is running up to the wall, simply force the board into position by prying it away from the wall with the flat bar, as shown in the demonstration.

With longer boards, you will probably encounter warping, though this never seems to be mentioned in instruction manuals. These warps can be maddening, particularly if you are working over an irregular subfloor. In the demonstration we picture a method of wedging the board into position, straightening out the warp. At the point just above where the warping occurs in the board, tuck the flat bar under the groove, and drive it into the subfloor. Pull the flat bar toward you, forcing the warped board into position. This may take all your strength, depending on the degree of warping in the board. As you pull the board in position with one hand, use your other hand to drive the nail into the floor beam. It should anchor the board into the correct position and eliminate the warp.

To fit flooring around a door frame, you can make a cardboard pattern to fit around the frame. Then use the cardboard as a template and cut the flooring to it.

Continue to lay the boards in this way until you come to the opposite wall. You'll find out that the last three or four rows of boards can't be toenailed: you won't have any room to swing the hammer without hitting the wall. Cut and fit these pieces and put them into place—staggering the joints in the same way that you have until now—without nailing. Most likely the last board will have to be ripped along its length to fit into the remaining space. If the room is out of square, the board should be ripped to fit. Perhaps it is wider

17. Standing farther back, you can see that the boards are anchored firmly to the floor beams below.

18. Continue to lay all the boards in the bundle in the same way. Lay down additional rosin paper as you go, overlapping its edges by 1″ or 2″ and marking off the floor beams on the next sheets as well. When you have installed the first bundle, open the second and lay out the boards.

19. Now install the second bundle of strip flooring onto the ends of the first. Slip the groove at the end onto the tongue at the end of the installed board.

20. Tap the board in lightly with your hammer. If greater force is needed, protect the tongue of the new board with a block of wood, striking the block rather than the board with the hammer. The end groove along the edge of the board should slide onto the tongue along the edge of its neighbor.

21. As you approach the wall, you can pry the loose board onto the end of the installed one so that they make tight contact.

22. Just as the ends should be tightly joined, so should the edges. With longer pieces of board you may encounter warping that prevents close contact between groove and tongue. Notice the gap here between the last board and its neighbor.

23. Just above the place where the gap occurs, drive a flat bar into the subfloor, placing it just below the outside edge of the board.

24. As you pull the flat bar toward you, forcing the groove of the board tightly onto the tongue of its neighbor, use your free hand to hammer the nail into the floor beam. When you remove the flat bar, the board should remain in place.

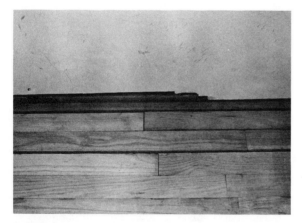

26. The last board has been ripped so that it fits into the small space along the wall. If the room is out of square, the board should be ripped so that it tapers to the size necessary for the proper fit against the wall.

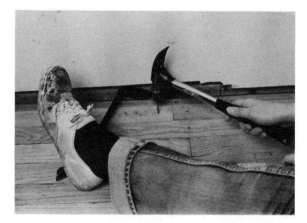

27. Pull the boards of the last four rows into position by prying them together with a flat bar. As you hold the bar, face-nail the boards into the floor beams.

29. The pre-drilled hole should be just the size to facilitate the tight entry of the nail through the wood.

30. Baseboards will conceal spaces and irregularities between the floors and walls.

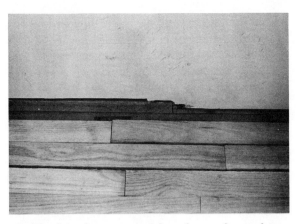

25. *The last three rows of boards are dropped into place. Blind nailing is impossible because the wall is too close for a proper swing.*

28. *You can also face-nail the last pieces with 8-penny common nails, but you will have to pre-drill holes in the hardwood in order for these nails to penetrate without splintering. Be certain not to drill through the subfloor.*

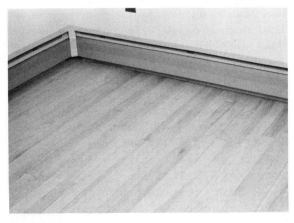

31. *The floor is complete.*

at one end than at the other. (Earlier we mentioned that if the room is less than 2″ out of square, you rip only this last piece. More than 2″, and you should rip both the first and the last boards. Ripping one board by more than 2″ is very difficult.) Drop or slide this last piece into place. With all the pieces in, return to the boards and draw them up snugly by driving a flat bar into the subfloor, as described earlier, and pulling the boards tight. Then drive in cut nails or 8-penny steel thread nails through the flooring, into the floor beams, if possible. If hitting floor beams isn't practical, you'll have to take your chances and drive into whatever there is. You may save yourself time and muscle by pre-drilling for the nails in those pieces. Be sure not to drill through the subfloor. Drill each hole the size that will permit the nail shank to fit snugly. The nails will be countersunk when the floor is finished.

LAYING HARDWOOD ON A CONCRETE FLOOR

In Chapter 9 we described a method of installing a subfloor over a concrete floor. In terms of insulation, this method is superior to applying any flooring to the concrete directly. But you may want to consider laying a hardwood floor directly on the concrete, which is possible if your concrete floor is even and level. This means, of course, that you must prepare the floor first by installing a nailing surface into which you can attach the flooring. These nailers are called *sleepers,* or *screeds.*

Generally, the concrete is sealed first, then a moisture-proof adhesive is applied over the sealer. The sleepers are laid into the adhesive. If the concrete floor is excessively damp, a plastic vapor barrier must be laid as well, two layers of sleepers being installed instead of one.

Specifically, here's how to proceed. First check your floor for moisture. Assuming that it is only slightly damp, you will be laying only one layer of sleepers. First apply an even coat of sealer to the floor, according to the manufacturer's instructions. Allow it to dry, and then apply adhesive over the sealer, also according to the manufacturer's instructions, about ⅛″ thick. Use a notched trowel spreader to apply the mastic, much as you would to prepare a surface for ceramic tiling. First install strips of 2×4's along the entire border of the floor, laying the 4″ side of the wood into the adhesive. Then lay in rows of 2×4's 18″ to 48″ long along the floor with 10″ intervals between each row. Lay the first piece, the 4″ side down in the adhesive, its end touching the border along one wall. As you continue the row, lay each sleeper alongside the previous one, overlapping the end by 4″ or 6″. When they are

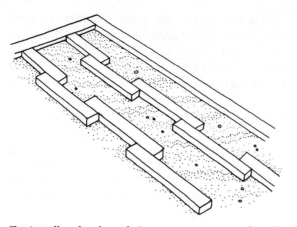

To install a hardwood floor over concrete, first lay sleepers in this arrangement for nailers. The sleepers are placed into a mastic that has been spread evenly across the concrete floor. The hardwood is nailed to the sleepers, as shown earlier.

placed in this way, you have a nailing surface for the hardwood flooring. After the mastic is dry, and the sleepers firmly in place, proceed as you would if you were nailing into floor beams. Be certain that each piece rests on at least two sleepers and that you join the ends of the boards on the sleepers for added support in an area that could be weakened.

If your concrete floor is excessively damp, use 1×4 wood instead of 2×4. Lay down the 1×4's across the floor into the adhesive as just described, then lay a polyethylene moisture barrier over the installed sleepers. Do not stretch the plastic. Lay it loosely over the sleepers. Where two sections of plastic meet, have them overlap by 3″. After the plastic is laid over the sleepers, apply a second set of sleepers exactly over the first set, sandwiching the plastic in between the layers. Be sure that the sleepers are the same length as the first set. Drive in 1½″ cut nails flush with the surface of the sleeper. Center the nails on the sleeper ½″ from the ends. The remaining nails should be placed at 6″ intervals along the sleeper. Proceed as described earlier.

FINISHING THE FLOOR

The final step in installing a new floor is to sand it off and finish it. (Frankly, we preferred to leave this entire operation to a specialist. Renting the equipment and undertaking the job just didn't seem worth the extra effort to us!) The face nails are countersunk and the entire floor is sanded with a big floor sander, in degrees, from very rough sandpaper through the finer sandpapers. Two machines are necessary, an edger and a big sanding machine. You can rent them through a dealer listed in the Yellow Pages. The dealer will certainly give you instructions about using these machines.

Countersink the nails at this point because you may have to set them much lower in some sections than in others, depending on how much floor you'll have to remove in areas that are higher.

Fill the nail holes with wood putty. When the floor is sanded, these holes will blend in completely. You'll also be reassured to see how quickly your errors will vanish, the sander obliterating any signs of your inexperience.

There are several finishes available for the floor: varnish, stain, shellac. The most protective of the finishes is polyurethane, which should be applied according to the instructions on the can.

CHAPTER 12

Resilient Floor Tile

Any description of flooring would be incomplete if it did not include some reference to resilient floors. These floors are called resilient because the material used is fairly soft underfoot, giving or yielding under pressure because it is pliable. These floors are easy to install and to maintain, making them popular for floor coverings in dens, kitchens, basements, and family rooms, and also in bathrooms and entryways, rooms where a good deal of traffic and soilage is expected. Resilient floor coverings come either in sheet form, such as linoleum, or in tile form. In this chapter we discuss the tiles.

TYPES OF RESILIENT FLOOR TILE

There are four basic kinds of resilient floor tile.

Vinyl Tile: Vinyl tiles are the most popular above-grade flooring materials, with good reason. They are softer than other tiles and can be cut easily with scissors, which makes their installation easy. A good vinyl in the right pattern and color is easy to maintain. The original shiny vinyl (in a so-called plate finish) showed scuffs and smudges, but this finish is rarely seen today. Embossing has helped vinyl, and other tile materials, to conceal wear marks. Inlaid patterns and colors extend throughout their entire thickness. Because of this, vinyl tiles are very hard to wear away. Carved, pitted, fissured, or grained effects are available, but smooth floors require less scrubbing. Textures hide seams, floor irregularities, and dents left by furniture, but they also tend to catch dirt.

Vinyl Asbestos Tile: Vinyl asbestos tiles are made by binding asbestos fillers between outside layers of vinyl. They come in various grades and thicknesses and can be installed anywhere. Vinyl asbestos does not require waxing—buffing gives a low sheen. Colors and gloss are less brilliant than in pure vinyl, but this has an advantage: scratches and soil do not show up as readily. Indentations also show less easily in vinyl asbestos than in pure vinyl. Vinyl asbestos will last indefinitely under normal wear and with normal maintenance.

Asphalt Tile: Asphalt tile, being the least expensive, is the most economical of the resilient floor tiles. It is less durable than other types of resilient tiles and has a grainy surface that can be easily penetrated with grease and oil. Asphalt tiles crack easily, are brittle, and are difficult to cut. They also dissolve easily when they come into contact with harsh chemicals like turpentine or benzene. For only a few cents more per tile you can get vinyl asbestos, which has all of asphalt tile's advantages, plus better color (asphalt tiles tend to run only in dark colors), easier care, and grease resistance.

Cork Tile: This is the only natural material among the resilient floorings. Its richness and beauty are an asset to a room. It is soft and warm underfoot and is resistant to sound. When coated with vinyl, it is easy to maintain.

CHOOSING A TILE

Given these various types of tile currently available on the market, what should determine your final choice? The area in which you intend to install the tile, your imagination, and your budget.

Some types of resilient flooring do not lend themselves to below-grade installation. (This term, incidentally, does not refer to the quality—above or below grade—but to the *placement* of the room in the house. A room that is below grade is a room below the ground level of your home. The basement and the family room are the most common below-grade rooms in the house.) Some tiles are not suitable for installation on a concrete slab. When purchasing tile, be certain to consult with your dealer, describing the placement and construction of the room. This may eliminate entire categories of tile.

The variety of designs and patterns in tile is overwhelming. Only a few years ago the selection was small and all tiles looked very much alike. Today it is possible to purchase tiles that are imitation brick, slate, stone, or wood, as well as a variety of decorative patterns. So before you choose a new floor covering, look at the many samples. You'll be astonished by the wide variety of options open to you. The solid colors are somewhat more difficult to maintain. (White and black are especially difficult.) The more textures and variations in the tile, the more effectively it will hide the seams, floor irregularities, scratches, and soil. But remember that textures can also be dirt catchers. Remember, too, that some colors bleach when continuously exposed to sunlight, especially light shades such as pink and yellow.

You will also be astonished by the differences in price among what may appear to be rather similar materials. First bear in mind the sizes of the tiles. Needless to say, the larger the tile, the greater the cost, but you will need many more 9″ tiles than you will 12″ tiles. The larger the tile, the less time it will take to do the job, and there will be fewer seams.

Of all the types of tiles just described, cork tile is the most expensive. A sealer must be applied to it to prevent it from getting soiled, and it is difficult to install.

Vinyl and vinyl asbestos tiles are the most popular tiles today, and even here there are ranges in price. Solid vinyl costs more than vinyl asbestos because the vinyl asbestos has only a veneer of vinyl on top of a cheaper material. The thickness is one factor that affects the cost. Vinyl and vinyl asbestos are available in ⅙″ and ⅛″ thicknesses; the heavier the gauge, the more expensive the tile. (The thicker tiles are also more durable but more awkward to install.)

Self-sticking tile is available, too, which may be more costly but is far simpler to install. A wax-paper backing is pulled off the underside of the tile, and the tile is placed directly onto the floor. (One word of caution: throw away the paper backing as soon as you've pulled it off the tile, depositing it immediately into a waste paper bag. The wax paper is slippery and, if you step on a piece, you can really hurt yourself!

ESTIMATING YOUR NEEDS

To estimate the number of tiles you'll need—in one color only—first measure the length and width of the room in feet. For 12″ tiles, you can arrive at the number easily by multiplying the length times the width to get the number. For 9″ tiles, find the length and width measurements in inches. Multiply the width by the length to arrive at the square inches. Divide this figure by 81 (the area of a 9″ tile) to arrive at the number of tiles you need. In either case, add 10 per cent to your figure for wastage.

In other words, if your room is 10′×13′, it is 18,720 square inches in area. Divide this figure by 81 to arrive at 232. Add 10 per cent for waste and you will order 255 tiles.

If a fireplace or other structure protrudes into a room, measure this obstruction separately and subtract the appropriate number of tiles. Divide irregularly shaped rooms into two or more rectangles, calculate the number of tiles needed for each, then combine the totals.

If you intend to lay tiles of two colors in a checkerboard pattern or in alternate rows, halve the total amount and buy equal quantities of each color. For more complex patterns, shade in the pattern on graph paper—letting each square equal one tile—and count up the number needed of each color.

OTHER MATERIALS YOU WILL NEED

Tiles are adhered to the floor with a mastic that is either brushed on or spread with a notched trowel. Both types are good. Professionals prefer the troweled material because they are accustomed to it, but the brush-on type is better for the amateur because it avoids the risk of applying too much or too little cement. (It is very tempting to apply too much mastic the first time. The thicker mastic—spread with the trowel—will ooze between the seams if too much is applied.)

Different adhesives are used to install different types of tile. For asphalt or vinyl asbestos tile, an emulsion type of mastic is used. This can be spread on an entire floor before installing any tiles. This system means that you don't have to handle glue and tiles at the same time, making the job neater—and it's faster because you lay all the whole tiles before having to cut any.

Another kind of adhesive—for vinyl tile—can be spread only for five or six tiles at a time. Work with an assistant who will spread the adhesive while you place the tiles.

If you are installing tile that is thicker than ⅟₁₆″, we also advise you to purchase a propane torch to heat the tiles before cutting them.

In addition, you should have on hand a ruler, chalk line, sharp utility knife, and rags.

PREPARING THE FLOOR

Resilient floors may be installed on wood, concrete, or underlayment, or on top of other resilient floors. Because a resilient floor is flexible, it will assume the shape of whatever is beneath it, and any irregularities may be visible after the installation of the new floor. Consequently the surface of the old floor must be smooth and clean.

If there are baseboards around the room, remove them before you do anything else if you intend to replace them. (You can tile right up to the baseboards, if you intend to retain them.)

If the floor is wood, check it for protruding nails, loose boards, high or low spots, cracks, or gaps. A wood floor must be firm, even, and clean before you can install resilient tiles. It is unwise to install a resilient floor directly over plank or strip flooring. It would be better to lay an underlayment over these planks or strips before tiling (see Chapter 10).

If the floor is cement, it must be level and clean before resilient floor can be installed. Clean the surface of the floor to remove oil, dirt, and grease, and seal it to provide a good moisture barrier between the concrete and the resilient floor. (Check with your dealer for the type of sealer to use.)

If the floor is resilient, be sure that the material —tile or linoleum—is securely attached to the floor. Check for loose tiles or pieces and for cracks and holes. Remove the old wax with a commercial wax remover. If the old resilient floor is beyond repair, remove it completely. If you do this, be sure to remove, or at least smooth, the old adhesive before applying new mastic over it. Or you can simply install underlayment over the old resilient floor, ¼" hardboard or plywood being sufficiently thick for this purpose. (Read over Chapter 10 if you intend to install underlayment.)

Remove any humps or bulges you see in the floor. The underlayment may have to be removed if a bulge is too great, having expanded or delaminated from humidity. Cut out the bulging underlayment with a circular saw or chop it out with a hammer and chisel. It may fall into place by itself, or you may have to remove it altogether, replacing it with another piece of underlayment in the same thickness. Nail down the patch of underlayment with rosin-coated box nails, spaced about 2" apart at the edges and about 4" apart across the inside of the piece, to be certain that it is anchored tightly and will not buckle.

THE STARTING POINT

Before you install the new floor, carry the cartons of tile into the room in which you will be work-

1. Check the floor first for irregularities, loose boards, and high or low spots. Drive in protruding nails.

2. Clean the surface of the floor to remove oil, dirt, and grease. Finally, sweep it thoroughly to remove loose particles and dust.

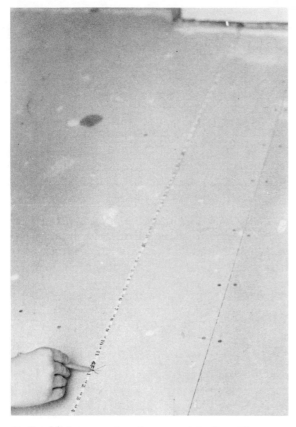

3. Establish two points for a straight line. We measured 4' from the entrance.

4. We took the second measurement 4' from the other end of the wall.

5. Then we measured 5' from one end of the wall at right angles.

6. And measured 5' from the other end of the wall.

ing. Open up the cartons and let the tiles sit for at least 48 hours so that they will adapt to the humidity and temperature of the room. Tiles contract or expand, as natural materials do, according to the weather and conditions in the house. Tiles left in a cold basement or garage until they are used have a tendency to expand on the floor and cause buckling. Likewise, tiles that are installed in a colder room will shrink after installation if they have not adequately adapted to the difference in temperature.

If you've never laid tiles before, you may be tempted to start at one wall and proceed to the opposite side of the room. In fact, this is exactly what *not* to do, because following this method will almost surely create an uneven pattern. You must determine a starting point first, plotting out the tiles so that they will be arranged in an even line and according to an attractively symmetrical pattern.

To arrive at a starting point, establish the center of the room or some other point that is of particular visual importance in the room. For example, the main entrance into a room may be most critical to you, the only point where a perpendicular line is really important. Draw a perpendicular line from the threshold, marking off the midpoint from the door and using a 2' carpenter's square to obtain the perpendicular line. Now pop a line from this point the full length of the room. Intersect this line at right angles with a second chalk line, to form a cross. Your starting point is where the two lines intersect.

It is possible that a certain wall in the room may be the critical line, and you may want all the tiles running along it to be parallel to that wall, even if it is not absolutely square. Take two equal measurements from this wall and pop a line that is parallel to the wall. Do the same with the opposite wall to create a cross with the two intersecting lines.

Now study these lines in terms of what's ahead. If the lines run along a seam of the underlayment, or if they are positioned in such a way that the edge of a row of tiles will run along a seam beneath it, move the line a few inches one way or the other. If the borders in the room will be particularly visible, make certain that your border tiles will be equal in size if you use these lines as your starting point. (For example, you don't want to cut 4″ off the tile on one side of the room and 6″ off the opposite side; therefore moving the line over an inch so that you can cut 5″ off the tile on each side will give you even borders on all sides.) Lay down a row of tiles if you feel uncomfortable about making these calculations mathematically and shift them around on the floor.

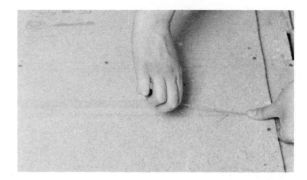
7. *Using the first two marks on the floor as a guide, pop the first line.*

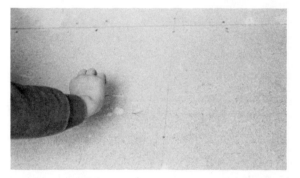
8. *Pop a second line, using the other two marks on the floor as a guide.*

9. *The two lines will intersect, forming a cross. This will be the starting point.*

10. *Place a tile in the angle on the floor where the two chalk lines intersect. The edges of the tile should line up precisely with the lines.*

11. Following the manufacturer's instructions, spread adhesive on the floor. Our mastic was spread over the entire floor, opaque when wet. We knew the adhesive was ready when it became completely transparent.

12. When the mastic is tacky, place the first tile in the angle of the chalk cross. Notice that mastic has been applied over the entire floor, but a bare patch was left so that we had a place to step when we placed the first tiles.

13. Working off the lines, lay the tiles in all directions. While you are kneeling on the tiles, apply mastic to the bare spot on the floor.

After you've firmly established these lines, next check them for the accuracy of their angles. Place a tile in the angle on the floor where the two chalk lines intersect. The edges of the tile should line up with your lines. If they are not precise, you'd better remeasure and make new lines or adjust the existing ones.

LAYING THE TILES

Before opening the can of mastic, read the instructions. There are several kinds of mastic. The kind you spread on with a trowel is somewhat messier, but it has advantages. It spreads very rapidly, and takes far longer to dry thoroughly, so is ideal for exceptionally large surfaces—if you are tiling one entire story of your house, for example. You can spread the adhesive one day, lay the tiles the next. This mastic is opaque, so don't cover your lines with it. Spread the mastic to ¼″ up to the line.

Some mastic dries so quickly that you have to apply it in small areas, dropping in the tiles as you go.

We think our mastic is ideal: you spread it with a brush over the entire floor. It is opaque when applied and transparent when dry. This way you know when it is ready (it is transparent) and you can cover the chalk lines with the mastic and they'll be visible when you're laying the tiles.

Spread the adhesive over the whole floor, but leave yourself one or more patches untouched with the mastic so that you have a place to step across the floor to the starting point. After you've applied a few tiles you can sit on this "island" to apply mastic over the bare patches.

Another reminder about the mastic. The quantity used for vinyl or other resilient tiles, unlike that of ceramic tile adhesive, is critical. In laying ceramic tiles you can apply a little more mastic than is absolutely necessary with no great danger. Ceramic is thick enough for a slight excess not to show. Resilient tile is thinner and mastic will ooze up between the tiles, making for a messy job. Too much mastic will also prevent the tiles from butting tightly together. No matter what the size of the tile, you want the floor to look like one continuous piece when it is completed. So conserve the use of mastic. Never spread more than you are going to lay before you stop the end of the working session. If any adhesive should work its way to the surface, wipe it off instantly with a rag before it dries.

Lay the first tiles along the chalk lines, lining them up exactly. Tiles are not really as square as they should be, so adjust their position until they seem right to you. Some edges may curl slightly, but don't be concerned. In a day or two you can tread the tiles into the mastic for a truly tight fit, or roll them out with a pin or roller.

In your effort to lay the floor neatly, don't lose track of the pattern. Rather than finish one box at a time before opening a new one, mix them up a bit to avoid any slight difference between the tiles from one box to another.

Some tiles have arrows stamped on the back to show where the vertical line of the pattern falls. If a tile must match the pattern of an adjacent neighbor, the arrows will point in one direction. If there is no match from tile to tile, alternate the direction of the arrows. If there is some slight difference in the color or texture, it will not be so noticeable. Read the directions that come with the box of tiles before you plan your strategy.

CUTTING TILES

If your floor did not work out evenly, the border tiles will have to be cut. Each tile is measured and cut individually. You will also have to cut tiles around obstructions in the floor. You can cut tiles as you go or do them all at once at the end.

Marking the Tile: Place a loose tile on top of the last whole tile, the one nearest the border. Be sure the sides are all flush with each other; the two tiles should be in exactly the same place, one on top of the other. Hold another tile on top of these two, this one extended out to touch the wall. Draw a pencil line along the inner edge of the top tile, marking the face of the tile beneath it. Trimming the tile along the pencil line will give you a tile that will fit into the border exactly. Be certain your pencil is sharp so that its line is accurate. And be sure that the tile is facing up, its design matching that of the adjacent tile precisely.

If you are cutting a tile to fit against a door frame, you mark it in the same way. Place and mark the tile as though you were cutting it for a straight border. Then move the tile, without turning it, to the other side of the door frame, and again place it over the nearest fixed tile to it. Draw a line at right angles to intersect the first. This is the guide for cutting.

Treat more complicated shapes, such as thresholds, the same way, but take separate measurements from each surface in both tile positions. If the outline is curved, draw a freehand line between the marks after marking in intersections from the second tile position.

You can also use a paper pattern for more complex configurations. The pattern is traced onto the tile itself. To fit around pipes, a slit is made into the tile and then it is notched.

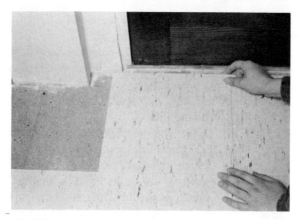

14. *The border tile will have to be notched in order to fit against the configurations of the wall. Place a loose tile on top of the last whole tile nearest the wall. Be sure the sides of both tiles are flush with each other.*

15. *Pick up another tile and lay it on top of the two tiles, but extend this tile so that it touches the wall. Scribe a pencil line along the inner edge of the top tile, marking the face of the tile beneath it.*

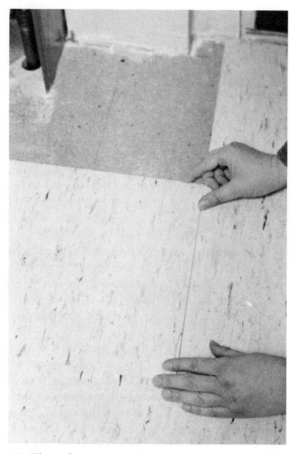

16. *The other side of the notch is marked in the same way. Place the marked tile over the other nearest tile, being sure that it is facing in the correct direction and its edges are flush with the tile below it.*

17. *Place a tile over this and push it to the wall. Mark the lower tile edge as before.*

Although it will make your job easier if you remove all the obstructions you can from the room—cabinets, for example—it is not absolutely necessary. Cutting resilient tile is far easier and more accurate than cutting ceramic tile, so you can insert even the smallest tiles into the tiny spaces with no difficulty.

Cutting the Tile: The key is the way you cut the tile once you have marked it with the sharp pencil. Vinyl tiles that are $\frac{1}{16}$" "press-and-sticks" can be cut easily with scissors or a sharp knife. Thicker vinyl tiles or vinyl asbestos tiles should be warmed before they are cut. Although you may have been told that you can simply score and snap a tile, this is not desirable. A snapped tile will not make a clean line, and it's impossible to cut with accuracy using this method. Warming the tile first will make the job far easier and more effective.

We suggest that you use a propane torch, rather than try to warm the tiles in the oven. A torch can warm only the line you've marked, without your having to contend with the stretching and pulling of a tile that has been completely heated. Hold the underside of the tile over the flame and move the tile continuously up and down the line. Don't stop this movement. Too long over the hot flame and the torch can scorch the tile. When the tile begins to bend slightly from the heat of the flame, it is ready for cutting.

Use the underside of one tile as a cutting surface for all the work ahead. Lay the warm tile on this cutting surface and cut along the pencil line with a sharp utility knife. It should cut like butter. If it is too warm, the tile will pull out of shape from the pressure of the blade; if it is not warm enough, you won't be able to cut easily. Practice will tell you when it is the right temperature.

Incidentally, if a tile should break or be damaged somehow after it is installed, you can use the torch to remove the tile, peeling it back as it is warmed. Warm up the mastic with the torch and lay the new tile in the same place.

Placing the Cut Tile: The tile will stay warm for a few minutes after you've cut it. This makes it both easier and more difficult to work with: easier because you can push the tile into just about any shape to make it fit; more difficult because the tile can stretch and pull if it is handled too much. So drop the tile into position as soon as possible, with a minimum of handling, and push it into place. Use the edge of another tile, if necessary, to force it flat into a small crevice. If you are cutting around a small obstacle, like a pipe, that falls at the edge of the tile, fold back

18. *The tile has been marked for the notch. Always use a sharp pencil so that the line on the face of the tile is accurate.*

19. *A propane torch is handy for warming tiles. It is portable, and its flame enables you to pinpoint the areas to be warmed.*

20. *Place the tile over the torch so that the flame is on the underside of the pencil line. Constantly move the tile up and down the line to prevent scorching. When the tile begins to curl slightly, remove it from the flame.*

21. *Place the warm tile on another tile you've set aside as a cutting surface. Press into the pencil line with the utility knife. The tile should cut easily, like butter, if it has been warmed to the correct degree.*

22. *Fit the tile against the wall, pressing down the still-warm edges into the mastic.*

23. *A tile is marked for a pipe in the same way as for a notch. By holding one tile over another, and scribing a line as you did earlier, take the extreme dimensions of the pipe and draw a circle within these points, as shown here. Warm the tile and cut out the circle with the utility knife.*

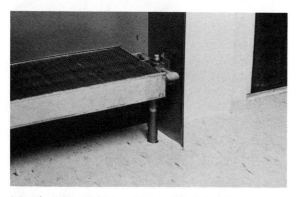

24. *Place the tile in position around the pipe.*

the warm tile along the edges surrounding the obstruction before you put it in place. You can lay it more easily. Once the tile is in position, push back the edges and press them into place against the mastic.

FINISHING UP

After all the tiles are laid, attach the baseboards. You can use vinyl cove molding with a resilient tile floor, an attractive way of completing the job. Sections of vinyl molding are easy to handle and easy to install.

The wall surface along the baseboard areas must be smooth, clean, and dry. Apply vinyl adhesive designed for molding. Your flooring dealer will recommend the type and the tools required for its application. (Adhesive used to install flooring is not advisable.) Follow the manufacturer's instructions for applying the adhesive. Most are applied with a narrow paintbrush or a notched trowel. Apply an even coat of adhesive along the base of the wall, a ribbon just wide enough to adhere to the molding. Allow the adhesive to set according to the manufacturer's instructions.

Begin installing sections of molding at an inside corner. Butt the sections tightly against each other. Press each section firmly against the wall and floor. If the adhesive spreads onto areas not to be covered, have a damp rag handy to wipe off the excess immediately.

At outside corners, stretch the molding tightly around the corner. Press it firmly against the wall and floor. At inside corners, the molding can be cut to fit. Ends of sections can be mitered (see Chapter 19) for a better fit. Use a sharp utility knife or scissors to cut the molding.

Another method can be used at inside corners. Make a cut partway through the back of one section of molding at the location of the corner. The molding is then bent to fit snugly into the corner. Make the cut carefully with a sharp utility knife, without cutting through the front surface.

If you want to put wooden baseboards along the edge of the floor, follow our instructions in Chapter 20, "Baseboards and Corner Moldings."

You can walk on the floor, but don't wash it for three or four days. Give the mastic time to dry thoroughly. Wait two days or so before moving heavy furniture onto the new floor. This extra weight can press the mastic out before it is dry.

Also keep the room warm—a good 75° F. for about two days. The tile will soften from the warmth. Walk around the floor two days later and press this tile into the mastic. The slight upturned edges—if there are any—should settle completely underfoot now.

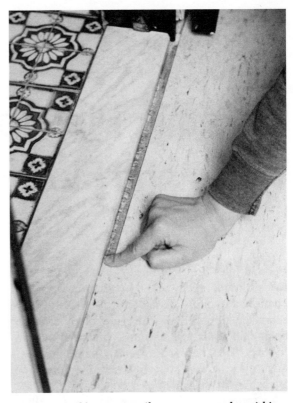

25. It's possible to cut a tile very accurately, within a fraction of an inch. A strip as small as this can be placed alongside a saddle, for example (a saddle is described in the next chapter). While the strip is still warm from the flame, it can be inserted into exactly the position you desire.

26. The small space alongside the saddle is no longer discernible.

CHAPTER 13

Ceramic Tiles for Walls and Floors

Ceramic tiles are very hard-glazed, durable, and easily cleaned. They are non-fading in color and unaffected by moisture and heat. Because of these characteristics, ceramic tiles are often used for floors and walls in bathrooms, kitchens, and entryways. Tiles are also extremely handsome, particularly now that so many varied products are available for selection.

In spite of all the positive reasons for tiling, amateurs are reluctant to try it on their own. The procedure is commonly regarded as difficult, a skill requiring highly specialized labor. Perhaps tiling has this reputation because early procedures were arduous and exacting, when tile was set first on wire lath and wet cement, and when grout required many days and a great deal of care to cure properly. Using modern adhesives and grout has made the task far simpler for the amateur. In fact, we found tiling to be an easily acquired skill, and the results of our efforts were immediately rewarding. We wouldn't hesitate to undertake the job again.

All tiles are installed in the same general way: they are applied to existing floors or walls with adhesive. After the adhesive is dried, grout is used to fill in all the gaps and spaces between the tiles. What you learn in this chapter about applying ceramic tiles may be applied to other materials as well. For example, this procedure is the same as that of laying an imitation slate floor.

ORDERING THE TILE

There are numerous variations of ceramic tile now available on the market. You can discover all the varieties in a library by studying *Sweet's Architectural File* (a collection of books describing most of the building materials on the market today), or you should be able to see a good selection at a dealer's showroom. You'll find that the possibilities are vast, particularly if you include the imported and specialty tiles as well. (While these specialty tiles tend to be very appealing, incidentally, they are also extremely expensive and not as easily handled as standard tiles. If this is your first attempt at tiling, we suggest you start with conventional tiles.)

Although tiles come in fairly standard sizes, those made by one manufacturer are not interchangeable with those made by another. It's best to select all tiles from one manufacturer so that they will match each other in size and thickness.

Loose tiles—which we have used for our demonstration—are sold by the carton. Each carton contains enough tiles to cover a certain area, generally 5 or 8 square feet. Tiles also come in sheets—normally ranging in size from $6'' \times 12''$ to $12'' \times 24''$—attached to a gauze-like paper or web backing. This backing is not to be removed. It keeps the tiles in the correct pattern arrangement while you are laying them, and it helps them adhere to the surface. Some manufacturers still sell their tile with brown paper on the face of the tile. The brown paper is also left in place while laying the tile. There are drawbacks to face-covered tile. First, you won't be able to see if the tiles are defective or incorrectly positioned on the paper until it's too late. Second, removing the paper can be difficult. You have to soak it thoroughly with warm water, loosen it, and then scrub and scrape it off. This is a messy job and one that may well interfere with later grouting.

Tiles come in a variety of shapes and sizes, the square ones normally measuring $4\frac{1}{4}''$, $6''$, or $8''$ square. Additionally, there are hexagonal and oblong tiles, and shapes that are combined to form interesting patterns. All of these are available in a wide variety of colors, patterns, and designs, and in a variety of finishes and textures. (Our demonstration was performed with off-white $4\frac{1}{4}''$-square tiles for the wall and mocha hexagonal tiles for the floor, both having crystalline surfaces.)

Tiles are manufactured for the purposes they are meant to serve. In ordering tile, be sure to tell your dealer exactly how they will be used. Wall tiles generally cannot be used for the floor; nor are tiles designed for tables or countertops suitable for floors.

Tiles are commonly manufactured with spacer lugs protruding from each of their edges. These $\frac{1}{16}''$ spacer lugs enable you to place tiles adjacent to each other—so that they can touch—yet they leave sufficient space in between to accept the grout. If the tiles do not already contain spacers, you will have to use something else to separate the tiles from each other. You can purchase spacers from your dealer or use something like toothpicks for the same function.

If you are covering only one part of a wall—as you might in tiling around a bathtub, for example—you will want to trim the edges of the tile to give the appearance of a deliberate border. For this purpose, *trim tiles,* which are rounded along one edge, are used. Trim tiles are available in a number of forms designed for their specific functions. *Cap strip* or *bullnose tiles* (shown in our demonstration) have one rounded edge and are used to cap a wall or to trim it along the edge. Some trim tiles are the same size as the tiles themselves; some are shaped differently. *Corner tiles* have two adjacent rounded edges and are used to turn corners, as shown in our demonstration. With square tiles, an inside or outside corner can be used for a right or left end of a wall, but with rectangular tiles both right- and left-handed inside and outside corners are required. *Cove tiles* are used on a wall at the base, where it meets the floor, if you intend to tile from the floor up. Cove tiles curve outward at the bottom to eliminate a square, dirt-catching corner at the floor line. They are used only when the floor is tiled as well. Special cove tiles are required to go around inside and outside corners.

In selecting your tile, remember that it will become a permanent fixture in your home. Although you may be stunned by the cost differences between products, be sure you are buying something that will be rewarding in the end. After all, you'll have to live with your choice for quite some time, so don't compromise here. In general, buy top-grade materials. They are easier to work with and the final results will be worth the extra expense.

The quantity of tiles you order will depend, of course, on the amount of area you intend to cover. Since you are buying tiles by the sheet or carton, measure accurately or you might find yourself paying far more than necessary or, at the other extreme, caught short at a very awkward time.

A tile normally contains spacer lugs along its sides and hollowed-out grooves along the base.

With your ruler, measure the length in feet of the area you will tile. Write that figure down. Then measure the width of the area in feet, and write that down. Multiply the width by the length to determine the square feet to be covered. Don't overlook "hidden" areas, such as closets or pantries. In measuring for a wall, establish just how high you intend to go. In bathtubs, for example, the pipe for the shower head comes through the wall at about 6′. Tile should be installed at least 6″ above this. Tiles behind lavatories and toilets and elsewhere in a bathroom are usually 4′ high. Tiling runs over kitchen counters by about 18″. Make whatever adjustments you can to avoid cutting tiles—a few inches either way make a great deal of difference if you have this tolerance—and don't forget to calculate for trim tiles if you are tiling only part of a wall.

If you are tiling a floor, make note of the width of the doorway. A marble saddle across the threshold may be ordered along with the tiles, available in standard doorway sizes.

You'll need extra tiles for waste, of course. (Five per cent is usually sufficient, depending on how much cutting you anticipate.) A reliable dealer will calculate the amount of tile you'll need for the entire job if you give him sufficient information.

TOOLS OF THE TRADE

Your dealer should also furnish you with the necessary materials and tools required for tiling. You'll need adhesive to attach the tiles to the wall or floor surface. Be certain your supplier knows exactly what surface you intend to tile: mastic adhesive is used to install tiles on Sheetrock, vinyl, wood, or concrete; thin-set mortar is used only on cement; and some adhesives dry more quickly than others, depending on their use.

1. The ideal time for tiling a bathroom is after the pipes, walls, and bathtub have been installed, and all painting and wallpapering completed, but before the fixtures have been placed in position. The wall should be smooth, rigid, and even. Here tile will be placed over moisture-resistant Sheetrock.

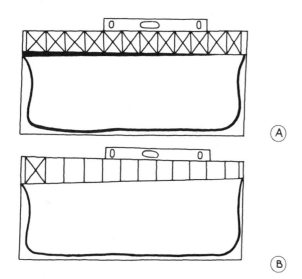

2. Plot your course. First check the level of the bathtub on all three sides and mark off where you will place the tiles on the wall, calculating so that you will cut as few tiles as possible.

3. If the bathtub is not level, use your level to mark off a line on the wall behind the tub where you will place your first row of tiles. If the tub is only slightly out of level, you can mark off a level line from the high point of the tub and later fill in the space at the lower points with grout (A). If this space is too great, measure up the height of one full tile from the low point and cut the bottom row to fit. (The crossed squares here indicate full tiles.)

Your dealer will also advise you about grout, the thin mortar used to fill in the spaces between the tiles. (Five pounds of grout normally covers 100 square feet.) Originally all grout was white or dark gray, but now it is available in a variety of colors, so that you can use it decoratively or to make soiling less apparent. Remember, tile is most attractive when it is featured, and there is no better way to highlight it than by using grout as a contrasting color, such as we have done in the floor of our demonstration.

If your order is large enough, your dealer may throw in a notched trowel spreader free of charge. (At any rate, the cost of this tool is minimal.) You'll need the trowel for spreading the mastic over the surface. The tool should have a wooden handle and serrated edges with two sizes of teeth and it can be re-used over and over, providing it is cleaned after each use with turpentine or mineral spirits.

You will also need a hard rubber trowel for applying grout to the tile, and a tile cutter, which your dealer will most likely rent or lend to you. In addition to these, purchase a pair of tile nippers.

PLANNING AHEAD

This is one job where it's absolutely vital for you to think ahead. "Winging it" after you've begun is not recommended because you are always fighting against the drying times of the various adhesives. So take the time to prepare for tiling.

Ask yourself, first, if this is the right time to tile. Ideally, in a home that is being renovated, tiling should be done just after the bathroom pipes, bathtub, and walls have been installed, but before the toilet, sink, and all fixtures have been put in place. (This was the point at which we tiled our bathroom in the demonstration.) It is also advisable to have already painted and wallpapered before tiling, so that you can, for example, cover the edges of the wallpaper with the tiles, which is far better than trying to wallpaper up to the edges of the tile. (Notice in our demonstration that we have wallpapered first.)

TILING A WALL

Ceramic tiles are inflexible and brittle, so it's impossible to tile over an irregular surface. Your wall surface must be smooth, even, and rigid. If you are working over an existing wall, remove anything that will be in the way—door and window casings, shower curtain rods, and so on. Remove any wallpaper from the surface you intend to tile. Wash off grease and dirt, and scrape off loose paint. If the paint has a high gloss, sand it lightly. Fill holes with spackle, and patch cracks. If the wall is not salvageable, rip it out and rebuild it, using moisture-resistant Sheetrock. Follow the instructions for Sheetrocking in Chapter 6, being sure to place nailers along the edge of the wall making contact with the tub. Leave about ¼″ space between the bottom of the sheet and the top of the tub rim. This space will be covered by the tile. Fill holes and tape seams with joint compound.

Now plot your course. You might start first by planning your strategy with pencil and paper. Plot out your tiles to avoid any more cutting than necessary. You will also want to avoid being left with too many small pieces, especially where they will be highly visible.

Your first—and lowest—row must be level. Ideally, you should be able to rest your first row of whole tiles right along the rim of the bathtub, just as we have done in our demonstration. By being level on all sides, however, our bathtub was exceptional. More commonly bathtubs are not level, so that the first row of tiles rarely sits along the rim of the bathtub. This means establishing a level line for the first row, and marking this line on the wall. As you establish this line, determine your strategy according to what will be easiest and most attractive. If your tub is only slightly out of level, you can mark off a level line from the high point of the tub and later fill in the space at the lower points with grout. If this space is too great, drop the tiles and cut the bottom row to fit. Mark your level line clearly on the wall and place your first row of tiles directly up against it.

Place a drop cloth at the bottom of the tub and take out several tiles from the box. The cloth will provide a more sympathetic cushion for the tiles, preventing them from breaking into pieces and from scratching the tub surface.

Applying the Adhesive

After you have plotted your course, apply the adhesive. Read the manufacturer's instructions about the adhesive before beginning to work, because each type has its own particular characteristics: some are applied over an entire wall and others must be applied a little at a time; some require that you wait until the mastic sets and becomes tacky, others enable you to place the tiles immediately after application.

Open the can and pick up a big glob of mastic with a flat stick (like one used for mixing paint) and slap it down on the surface you are tiling first. Grip the handle of the spreader and press the notched edge into the mastic, holding the trowel at about a 45-degree angle to the wall.

4. Before you begin to tile, place a drop cloth at the base of the tub. The cloth will cushion the tiles, preventing them from breaking and from scratching the porcelain surface.

5. We placed a few rows of trim tiles first. Dip your flat stick into the can of mastic and butter the back of the trim tile. Work carefully to avoid any contact of your fingers with the mastic.

6. The first trim tile (a bullnose) is placed in position. If you are planning to tile the floor later, allow room below this first tile for the floor tile. There should be enough room for it to slip beneath the wall tile. The trim tile is positioned directly against the bathtub with only enough space for grout to be added later.

7. With your flat stick, slap a quantity of mastic directly onto the wall where you are going to place your first rows of tiles.

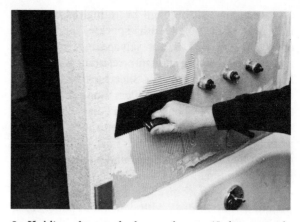

8. Holding the notched trowel at a 45-degree angle to the wall, press into the wet mastic and comb it out in even strokes.

9. Spread the mastic through an area about 3' square, combing evenly to eliminate any globs of mastic, yet leaving no bare patches on the wall.

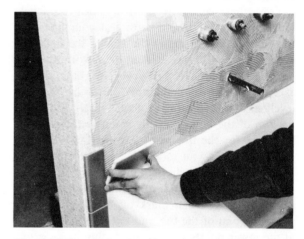

10. Hold the tile by the edges. Rest the bottom edge of the tile on the rim of the bathtub and let the tile fall into the wet mastic without touching the mastic with your fingers.

11. After you have dropped in several tiles along the row, you can shift their position slightly by pressing them into the wet mastic and sliding them to where they are adjacent to each other and on a level line. Our bathtub was level, so we could rest the tiles directly on the rim of the tub. If your level line is marked on the wall, shift the tiles to that position. This first row is most critical, since all the other rows will be placed in relation to it.

Comb out the adhesive in even strokes, without leaving any tiny lumps or globs in the mastic. Excess mastic will only ooze through the tiles and cause you problems later. You can determine the correct amount of mastic in this way: place a tile in the adhesive you have just spread on the wall. If the adhesive oozes out from beneath the tile, you've used too much and should spread it out to a larger area of the wall. Pull the tile free from the mastic and examine the back of it. If the back of the tile is not completely covered, you've used too little adhesive. If it is covered, you've applied the correct amount.

If you have marked guidelines on the wall, avoid covering them with the adhesive. Apply the mastic up to, but not touching, the lines. (The adhesive will spread when you press down on the tile.)

Naturally, you do not want any adhesive to extend beyond the edge of the trim tile. Since it is difficult to spread the adhesive on the wall precisely up to the edge, apply the adhesive directly to the back of the tile instead, as we have done in the demonstration, by "buttering" it with the flat stick.

Cutting Tiles

No matter how well you plan in advance, it is impossible to avoid cutting tiles altogether. The back wall behind the bathtub, for example, never works out as an even number of tiles. (Notice, incidentally, that we took the extra trouble to cut a tile at each end of a row, rather than at one end only. Although it meant cutting twice as many tiles, the symmetry was more attractive than seeing a cut tile at only one end of each row.)

It is possible to cut tiles with an ordinary glass cutter, scoring the tile first, then snapping it as you would a piece of glass. This is not the most efficient way, however. We recommend a commercial tile cutter (which your dealer will lend or rent to you) or a simple tile-cutting tool such as one we have used in our demonstration.

To cut a tile, first establish how much you will need to cut for the tile to fit in place. Allow in your measurement a ⅛″ gap between the tile being cut and the wall or obstruction, the space into which grout will later be applied. First score the tile along the face of the tile. After the line has been etched, you can snap the tile and it will break along the scored line. As you become more familiar with the cutter, you will find that the operation comes more easily.

Some people prefer to place all the whole tiles first, returning later to the cut tiles, but we preferred to cut and place each tile as needed. This method seemed better to us for three reasons.

First, cutting many tiles all in one stretch was very tiring, and we welcomed the interruptions of another activity to ease our aching hands. Second, by cutting as needed, we never worried that the adhesive would dry before we returned to the location. Third, when we cut many tiles at once we tended to confuse the fragments, regardless of how many systems we had established to keep them in order as we accumulated them.

To break off small notches or arches from your tile, use the tile-cutting nippers. These resemble wide toenail clippers. They can be unwieldy, so practice first by cutting a castoff tile before you proceed. The nippers actually crunch off the tile, rather than snip it as you might expect. Moreover, you can't crunch off too much of a tile at one shot because it's impossible to control the place where it might crack or split, so snip away at the tile by taking many small bites rather than attacking your cut all at once. Grip the tile between the jaws of the nippers and hold the edge of the instrument at a slight angle to the tile.

If you can possibly manage it, cut your tiles in another room, or at least far enough from the actual tiling operation so that the little slivers of glass will not scatter into the areas in which you are working. Pieces of glass stuck into the adhesive will surely subvert your efforts to keep the surface smooth.

Don't fret about irregular edges. With the nippers, any small cut is bound to be rather rough. You can smooth the cut edges to some degree with emery paper, a coarse file, or an abrasive stone.

Tiling around the bathtub fixtures requires some ingenuity. When a hole is required in the middle of a tile, to allow for a fixture, cut the tile in two pieces through the center of the hole, then snip out a semicircle in each piece at the point where the fixture will fall. Place one section of the tile to the left and the other to the right of the pipe, pushing together their edges until they touch at the point where you cut them. Once the grout is applied you will barely notice this seam.

Positioning the Tiles

Start with the lowest row, up against the rim of the bathtub. Hold the tile by the edges, being sure that your fingertips do not extend beyond the bottom edge of the tile where they might pick up adhesive from the wall. Although you can remove adhesive from your fingers or from visible surfaces later, take precautions as you work with it. Mastic has a nasty way of adhering to every surface you come in contact with, and if you develop the necessary habits now, you can spare yourself many headaches later.

12. You will need to cut tiles almost immediately. First establish how much needs to be cut from the tile. Allow an extra ⅛″ for the space between the cut edge and the wall or obstruction, a space into which grout will be applied later. Score the face of the tile with your cutter. Apply enough pressure to etch the surface.

13. Grip the tile and apply pressure at the scored line.

16. Start at the corner.

17. Take a small bite out of the tile.

20. Snip a small piece at a time from the cut edge inward. Here a small piece has already been taken and the nippers are positioned for the second bite.

21. Snip away a semicircle in each piece of tile, an arch large enough to clear half the fixture.

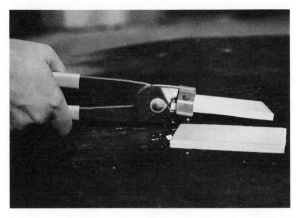

14. Snap the tile along the etched line. It should break precisely where you have scored it.

15. Tile nippers should be held at a slight angle to the tile.

18. For greater cuts, take several small bites rather than one large section.

19. You will need to make a hole in the tile when you reach a fixture. First bisect the tile midway at the point where the hole is needed.

22. When the two pieces of the tiles are re-joined, the seam will go unnoticed.

23. *The first three rows have been placed. Notice the way in which the tiles have been cut to permit exposure of the fixtures. Although the cut edges are irregular, they will be filled with grout and covered with plates later. The tiles in the corner, along the right edge, have also been cut.*

24. *Above the shower head the tiling should run at least an additional 6". The bullnose trim tile extends along the horizontal wall line.*

25. *Apply mastic along the back wall of the bathtub.*

26. *Proceed as earlier, by placing the first row on a level line.*

Lean the bottom edge of the tile on the edge of the tub and let the top edge fall against the adhesive. Once the tile is in contact with the mastic, it will adhere immediately, but its position can still be adjusted by sliding it around in the still-wet substance. Place your first row of tiles in this way, shifting the position of each tile until the spacer lugs touch at the sides and the edge sits on the level line. Sit the next row of tiles directly on the first row, and proceed in the same way.

Remember to retain even spaces between the tiles. If your tiles contain spacer lugs as part of their structure (as ours did), the space should be uniform throughout. Allow the same amount of space each time you position cut tiles, as well, never permitting them to touch any surface. If your tiles do not contain attached spacer lugs, place spacers between each tile, two on each side. You may obtain these spacers from your tile dealer or use toothpicks for this purpose—two or three on each side of the tiles, inserted with the tips touching the wall.

Look over the tiles after they are in place. Any mastic on the surface can be removed with turpentine or mineral spirits before it dries, or with soft steel wool after it dries. Remove any excess mastic that has oozed up in the spaces between the tiles. A thin knife will do the job, but be careful not to move the tiles as you work with the knife.

Applying Grout

After you've placed all the tiles, wait for 24 or 48 hours before proceeding to the next step. The mastic has a tendency to shrink as it dries, so it's advisable not to apply grout until the adhesive has shrunk as much as it's going to.

For applying the grout you'll need the hard rubber trowel and two pails of water—one for mixing the grout and one for clear rinse water to remove excess grout. Also have a sponge on hand for wiping away the excess grout. (For this purpose, a sponge is preferable to a rag because it won't remove the grout from between the tiles.)

Stir the grout into the water, following the manufacturer's instructions, until you obtain an almost pasty consistency. (You may prefer the mixture somewhat more soupy than is recommended by the manufacturer. Although it takes longer to dry, the wetter mixture sinks more readily into the cracks, producing better results in the end.) Pick up a dab of the mixed grout with the rubber trowel and spread it across the surface of the tile, forcing it into the crevices between the tiles with the hard rubber edge. The grout must sink into all these spaces, completely filling them. Now moisten the sponge in the clear rinse water

27. Continue the back wall. Without fixtures, this wall goes very rapidly.

28. Continue with the last wall in the same manner. Notice that the bullnose tile trims off this side as well.

29. The third wall is completed. Notice that the tiles in the corner have been cut on both walls.

30. Special tiles are needed to account for the corners. Notice the bullnose corner tile used here.

31. *In preparing the grout, follow the manufacturer's instructions. Here the white powder is poured into a pail of water.*

32. *Stir the mixture and continue to add the powder until you obtain a pasty consistency.*

35. *Continue to spread the grout across the entire tiled area. Return to the pail for more grout as needed. Don't be concerned about spreading too much grout: it's most important that every crevice is filled.*

36. *After you have spread the grout on one entire wall, rub over the surface with a damp sponge, removing the excess grout. Rinse the sponge frequently in a pail of clear water.*

39. *The grout fills the hole surrounding the shower head as well.*

40. *After the tiling is completed, the bathtub fixtures are placed over the tiles. The holes have been concealed by the plates and the seams are barely evident.*

33. *Pick up a dab of grout with the hard rubber trowel.*

34. *Press the grout into the spaces between the tiles. Do not overlook any gaps.*

37. *To remove any residue of grout, polish the surface with a dry cloth until the sheen returns to the surface of the tiles.*

38. *Now follow the same procedure with another wall. Notice that the grout has filled the large holes surrounding the fixtures. This makes a watertight seal.*

41. *The shower head also conceals the hole and seam made in the tile.*

42. *Dried adhesive still on the surface of the tile is wiped away with a pad of soft steel wool.*

1. *In preparing to tile the floor, first plan your strategy. Since the tiles will be most conspicuous along the base of the bathtub, the floor has been planned here so that a row of whole tiles will run along the edge of the tub. First place a tile at one end of the tub and mark off on the floor the point touched by the edge of the tile.*

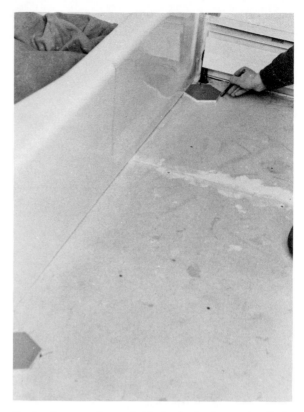

2. *At the opposite end of the bathtub, mark off the point touched by the edge of the tile.*

3. *Place a chalk line over these two points marked on the floor.*

4. *Extend the chalk line even farther, so that it runs the full extent of the room. Here the line extends from one wall to the doorway entrance.*

and immediately wipe the excess grout from the surfaces of the tiles. Rinse out the sponge, and repeat the procedure several times until the surface seems free of the grout. By now the grout has begun to dry. Tool the joints with the narrow end of a rounded toothbrush handle or with some other instrument (we whittled a piece of soft cedar shingle to the size of an Indian arrowhead). This tooling leaves the joints neat and concave. Finally, with a dry cloth, polish the surface of the tiles until they resume their original sheen.

If, after the grout has dried completely, you still find a hazy film covering the surface of the tiles, you can remove it with a mixture of 1 part muriatic acid and 10 parts water. Be certain to wear gloves when using muriatic acid. With a sponge, wash the tiles thoroughly with this solution, then dry the tiles completely with a clean dry cloth.

Years ago grout required several days of curing before it was thoroughly dry, a slow process during which it was necessary to sprinkle water continually over each seam to prevent it from cracking during shrinkage. Modern grouts are not nearly so demanding. You can walk away from the job without any further treatments necessary. Consult the directions on the package to see how much time the manufacturer recommends for drying.

TILING A FLOOR

Basically, the procedures for tiling a floor are the same as those for a wall. There are some steps that require special attention, however, so read this section carefully before attempting the job.

Preparing to Tile the Floor

First consider the floor surface on which you are tiling. You may tile over concrete, vinyl, wood, or other forms of underlayment. Do not tile over a hardwood floor; the surface may warp, causing the tiles to crack. Because the ceramic floor is very rigid, the surface of your floor beneath the tile must also be rigid. Any movement in the floor will cause the grout to crack and chip and may even cause the tiles to break.

The surface must be even, as well as rigid. Any high or low spots will also crack the grout, so make any necessary repairs to your floor before beginning to tile. If the floor is wood, check to be sure it is firm and doesn't move or flex. Check it for protruding nails, loose boards, high or low spots, cracks, and gaps. Remove the residue of old wax. If the floor is concrete, be sure it is

5. *Pop the chalk line so that the mark is clearly evident on the floor.*

6. *Starting at one end of the line—at the doorway, in this case—spread the mastic over an area approximately 3' square. Comb out the adhesive evenly and smoothly with the notched spreader and continue toward, but not onto, the chalk line.*

7. *Place the first tiles so that the edges touch the chalk line. As you press the tile into the wet mastic, the adhesive will spread below the tile, covering the area of the chalk line left bare.*

171

level, clean, and sealed before you tile. Check for high or low spots, cracks or gaps, and moisture. Clean the floor to remove all dirt, oil, and grease. Then seal the floor with concrete sealer, obtainable at any paint supplier.

Before beginning to work, remove any baseboards that may be attached to the walls. Do this carefully so that you won't have to replace them with new ones later. Start from one end of the baseboard and gently ease it away from the wall by prying it loose with a screwdriver or flat bar. After you pry the baseboard away from the wall, mark both the board and the wall with the same number, so that you can line up the nails in precisely the same holes when you put it back into position. Also remove the threshold if one has been installed at the doorway.

Bear in mind that the height of the floor will be raised about ½", so that your door may have to be shortened by about that much in order to clear the tile. (See the section in Chapter 15 entitled "How to Cut Down a Door" for instructions on this procedure.) In preparation, also check the drying times for the mastic and for the grout. You may have to make special arrangements to avoid using the room between the time you begin and the time you complete the tiling.

Where to Begin

Next plot your course for placing the tiles, much as you did when you tiled the wall. In a bathroom, the most conspicuous section of the floor is generally along the base of the bathtub. To make your job easier and more attractive, plan your floor so that you will have to cut as few tiles as possible along this edge. If your floor tiles are square, for example, you will want each square, uncut, to line up against the edge of the bathtub. If your tiles are shaped differently, such as our hexagonal tiles, plan your tiling so that you will have to cut only every other tile.

Place two tiles on the floor against the base of the bathtub, one at each end, and mark with a pencil the points at which the edges of these two tiles lie on the floor. Using these two points, pop a line with a chalk marker, extending the line across the entire length of the floor, from one wall to the opposite. All your tiles will be positioned in relation to this line.

If you don't happen to be tiling the floor of a bathroom, you will have to find some other method of establishing a reference point. Never use a wall as a guide, because the walls of a room are rarely straight or square in relation to each other. Try for some other point of reference. A doorway, for example, can serve this purpose, because you will want the floor to look straight when you enter the room. If the room has more than one doorway, select the doorway most frequently used. First make a line across the center of the doorway entrance. Then, using a carpenter's square, mark a line at a 90-degree angle to the line you have just made across the doorway entrance. Continue that line farther by popping a chalk line across the entire length of the room to the facing wall and proceed as follows.

Laying the Floor Tiles

Start at the extreme end opposite the doorway entrance of the line you have marked across the floor. With the notched trowel, spread the mastic adhesive in a section about 3' square. Apply the adhesive up to the line, but about ¼" away from it, remembering that it will spread when you press the tile into the mastic. Drop the tiles into the adhesive, avoiding any contact between your fingers and the sticky substance, and shift the tiles so that their edges line up directly on the chalk mark. Continue this procedure in 3' sections, working both out and along rather than in one direction only.

When you reach the wall, you will probably have to cut tiles. But you needn't be too fussy here. As long as the space between the cut edge and the wall is not greater than ½", the baseboard will cover up the ragged edges. It is preferable, in fact, to have some space between the tile and the wall, rather than to butt the tile directly against it. The space permits the grout to seep in between the tile and the wall, which helps to create a watertight seal.

As you cover large areas of the floor, place boards over the completed tiles. Walk on these boards rather than directly on the tiles, to prevent the tiles from shifting. Walking on the boards also helps press the tiles more firmly and evenly into the mastic. Be sure to wear clean shoes to prevent dirt from falling into the spaces between the tiles.

At the doorway, position your tiles so that their edges are even with the entrance from the inside edge of one door jamb to the other. You can lay a marble saddle in, now or later, as we have done in our demonstration.

Applying Grout to Floor Tiles

Check the can of adhesive to determine the manufacturer's required drying time. Once the mastic is dry you can apply the grout, using the same procedure described in working with wall tile. Mix the grout according to the manufacturer's instructions, until you obtain an almost pasty consistency. Spread the grout over the floor tile with

8. Continue to place the tiles along and out, rather than in one direction only. Notice that the chalk line serves as the guide against which all other tiles are laid.

9. As you cover large areas of the floor, lower boards onto the surface. Walk on these boards, rather than directly on the floor tiles.

10. The toilet has not yet been installed in the bathroom, and the tiling runs directly up to the waste pipe. It is preferable to remove the toilet and sink before tiling the floor so that the floor tile runs beneath the fixtures, rather than up to them.

11. Notice that the tiles along the base of the tub are placed as planned: only half of the tiles required cutting.

12. Grout is applied to the floor in the way described earlier. Press the pasty mixture into the crevices between the tiles with a hard rubber trowel.

13. Excess grout is wiped away with a damp sponge. Rinse the sponge frequently.

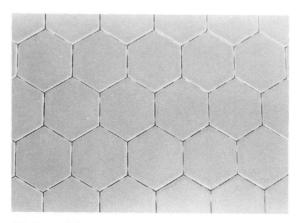

16. Spacer lugs between the tiles provide uniform spacing throughout.

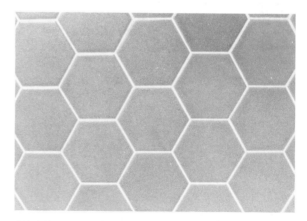

17. The grouted joints are neat and uniform. This has been achieved by carefully wiping away excess grout and by tooling the joints.

14. The crevices between the tiles can be tooled with an instrument—a toothbrush handle or a whittled piece of wood serves well—in order to obtain neat and concave joints.

15. The floor is completely tiled and grouted. Notice that grout fills the crevices surrounding the waste pipe.

18. The toilet has been installed over the tiled floor.

19. Baseboards are attached to the walls, concealing the ragged edges of the cut tiles.

the rubber trowel, forcing the substance into all the spaces. With a damp sponge, immediately wipe away the excess grout. Rinse the sponge often. Using the handle of a toothbrush, a clothespin, or similar instrument, you can tool the crevices if you want an even and concave joint between the tiles, but don't press in too hard. If the grout is recessed too deeply, the seams will be annoying dirt catchers later on.

Allow the grout to dry according to the manufacturer's specifications before replacing baseboards and fixtures.

Laying the Saddle

We were not ready to install the saddle across the threshold at the same time that we tiled the bathroom floor. But you may be, if your door is already installed. A marble saddle is placed from door jamb to door jamb, along the edge of the tiles. It is higher than the floor level, a deterrent to water flooding beneath the door.

Position the saddle at the door opening to be certain the size is correct. You may have to saw off the bottom of the door stops attached to the jambs so that the saddle can slip under them. (You can cut these small pieces of wood with a coping saw without removing them from the door jambs.)

Apply adhesive to the floor and to the underside of the saddle, just to be certain you have mastic covering all possible surfaces. Set the saddle into the mastic and position it so that there is equal space on either side between it and the door jambs. (This space allows for the expansion and contraction of the wooden door frame.) There should also be a small space between the saddle and the tiles, uniform with the spaces elsewhere on the floor between tiles. Apply grout to the inside seam, between tiles and saddle, and at the sides. The job is complete.

Because the saddle is higher than the floor, you will probably have to cut down the door. Follow our instructions in Chapter 15 for a good method of doing this.

1. Position the saddle at the threshold. The stop at each door jamb may have to be cut away in order for the saddle to slip under it.

2. Apply mastic to both the floor and the underside of the saddle.

3. Settle the marble saddle into the mastic. Position it so that there is an equal amount of space at each end between the saddle and the door jamb. This space will allow for the expansion and contraction of the wooden jambs.

4. Apply grout to the crevices surrounding the marble saddle.

CHAPTER 14

Rebuilding Old Steps

Few carpentry jobs are more complicated than constructing a brand-new stairway. Steps are so ornery to build, in fact, that there are specialists who do nothing else. The difficulty here arises because of the various features that must adapt to every situation: the angle of the staircase, the height and depth of the steps, their supports, and finally their decoration. Any miscalculation along the way creates a faulty job. If you have an old staircase in your home, therefore, we recommend that you consider rebuilding the steps rather than start from scratch. The hardest job has already been done for you and you can simply use the former structure as the framing for your new stairs.

form. The tread normally contains *nosing,* a rounded lip that extends over the riser.

Given these three features—the stringer, tread, and riser—you can rebuild any set of steps by following our demonstration, whether open- or closed-stringer. We rebuilt only three steps, but you can adapt the procedures to whatever set of stairs you have in your home. Reconstructing the steps is standard. The differences will occur in styling and decorating the stairway. Here we enter into the territory of cabinetmaking. Each stairway is different and each requires special care. Our steps are very simple and may give you an idea about how to handle the design of your own stairway. Our intention here is simply to provide you with the most basic elements in rebuilding stairs.

CONSTRUCTION OF A STAIRCASE

The variety of types of stairs is virtually endless, ranging from a short basement stair to complex main staircases. But in their simplest form all stairways have basic features in common: two pieces of wood (*stringers*) sloping from one floor to another with steps fixed between them. There are two basic types of staircase construction: (1) the *open-stringer* type in which the top edges of the stringers are cut out in a sawtooth fashion, and the steps fitted to them; (2) the *closed-stringer* type in which the edges of the stringers are straight and the steps fit in between them.

Many staircases are made by combining both open- and closed-stringer methods. For example, the steps may be fixed to a closed stringer on one side against a wall; on the other side they may rest on the edges of an open stringer.

Each step in a staircase is constructed with two boards: (1) a *tread,* which is the horizontal part of the step; (2) a *riser,* which is the vertical part of the step. The measurement of each riser is uniform, and the measurement of each tread is uni-

MATERIALS YOU WILL NEED

At the lumberyard you will order materials specially designed for stair construction.

Treads: Treads receive more wear and tear than any other part of the stairway, so if the steps will be exposed, you'll need a particularly hard wood. (Oak is common for this purpose.) If you intend to carpet the stairway, you can use a softer, and less expensive, wood for the treads, fir being the most common. The wood is milled specifically for treads, boards of uniform size, squared off at three sides and containing a nosing rounded off on one side. Treads are available in standard dimensions, between 8½″ and 11½″. (Remember, 9″ lumber is actually 8½″.) Measure the depth of the tread and order the largest size that comes close to this dimension. You may have to rip it to fit.

Risers: Some lumberyards still make risers available in fir or in harder woods. Because of the

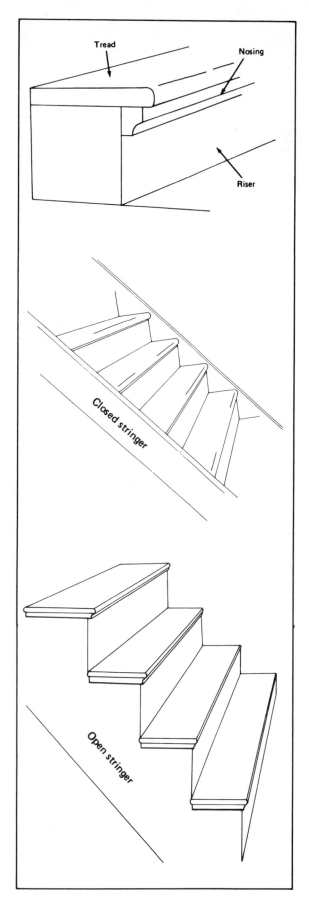

1. Anatomy of a staircase: a closed-stringer staircase; an open-stringer staircase. Each step contains a tread, riser, nosing, and stringer.

prohibitive cost of hardwood, however, most lumberyards now sell 1″ pine for this purpose instead. These measure traditionally between 6½″ and 8½″. (A riser tends to be 2″ shorter than the tread.) Count the number of risers you need in the dimension closest to the one on your stairway.

Decorative Wood: Just how you will finish your stairway is a matter of personal taste. The stringers should be encased in an attractive wood. You can use common pine or paneling and figure the amount on the basis of how much surface you intend to cover. We used barnboard.

Handrail or Balustrade: Depending on the way in which the stairway is designed, a handrail may be in order. If you have an inner staircase placed along a wall, for example, a handrail the length of the stairway is simply attached to the wall with brackets designed for this purpose. Balustrades—the stair rail with the spindles, or banisters—are more complex. If your stairway now contains balusters (spindles), we recommend that you refinish these rather than purchase new ones, because they are costly and tricky to install. If your balustrade is shaky, consult a home repair book on how to strengthen it. But try to avoid building a balustrade from scratch on your own. They are difficult and *very* costly!

Miscellaneous Tools: Circular saw, coping saw, ruler, hammer, pencil, scraps of pine.

STEP CONSTRUCTION

First you will reconstruct the steps, then the stringers. Check the old steps for surface irregularities. Hammer in protruding nails, and scrape off particles of plaster, cement, or spackle that may have become encrusted into the surface of the treads. Sweep the steps so that they are smooth and even.

Saw off the nosing from the old treads so that the end of each tread is flush with the riser below it. The old treads will serve as nailers for the new treads, and old risers will serve as nailers for the new ones. But if your staircase is open, having no risers (as many basement stairs are constructed), you must first install nailers. Nail a block of wood on each stringer immediately behind the tread, running vertically to the next tread above it.

First build the riser. Cut down the end of the pine board to exactly the width of the stairway, flush to the edges of both stringers. Now rip the wood so that its width (the height of the riser) is flush with the end of the tread above it. Do this

2. *Our steps are traditional for a basement stairway. The treads do not contain nosing or risers. If there is nosing on the treads, however, it must be cut off before you can attach new risers.*

3. *If the construction of the steps does not include risers, you must attach nailers to the stringers behind the treads. Notice that the outer edge of the nailer is flush with the outer edge of the old tread above it. Place these nailers on both stringers.*

4. *The sides of the first riser extend to the outer edges of the stringers. The riser has been ripped so that its top edge is flush with the top edge of the old tread. The riser is attached at the sides to the stringers and at the top to the tread. (The piece of wood you see beneath the first riser has been inserted temporarily to remind us to allow sufficient space for the finished flooring or carpeting to be installed later.)*

5. *Mark off the point at which the first oak tread should be cut. When cut, it should slip between the stringers.*

6. *The new tread has been sawed down so that it fits between the stringers, and it was ripped so that its nosing extends over the riser by no more than 1".*

7. *Attach the tread to the riser by using two 6-penny tempered steel nails. Later these nails will be countersunk and concealed with wood putty. Also drive in two nails at the back end of the tread. These will be concealed by the next riser.*

8. *The next riser is installed, cut so that it fits between the stringers with its top edge flush with the tread above it. It is attached to the nailers with finishing nails at the sides and to the tread along the top edge. Notice that the bottom edge of the riser conceals the steel nails driven into the back edge of the oak tread beneath it.*

9. *The next tread is installed in the same way as the first. Do not assume that all treads are the same measurement in an old staircase. They can vary from one step to the next.*

10. *The final riser and tread are installed. We have followed the work of three steps only. You can extend this to an entire flight of stairs in precisely the same manner.*

by leaning the uncut pine against the first step and scribing a line behind it, following the contour of the old tread with a pencil. Cutting along this pencil line should give you a riser whose top edge is flush with the top surface of the old tread above it. (You'll notice, in the photographs, that the first riser is sitting on a piece of wood. This is not meant to confuse you. We placed the wood on the floor so that we would remember to start the first riser slightly above the floor, giving us sufficient space to insert flooring or carpeting beneath the steps. This is unnecessary if you are working from a finished floor.)

Nail the riser at each edge with 6-penny finishing nails—three nails into each stringer, three nails along the riser.

Now lean the first tread up against the riser and mark off where it should be cut in order to fit between the stringers. Saw it down with the circular saw. The new tread will rest on top of the old one, the nosing extending over the edge by about 1″. You may have to rip the new board for an accurate fit. Hammer tempered nails into the tread to attach it—four nails will be sufficient: one at each end of the front edge, driven into the riser, and two at the back, driven into the old tread. Remember this surface may be exposed, so avoid marring the surface any more than necessary with the blows of the hammer. (If you're carpeting, you don't have to be fussy.) These nails will be countersunk later, filled with wood putty, and refinished with a sander.

The next riser will fit between the stringers, cut down to size using the same method as earlier. Three nails on each end attach the new riser to the old one or to the nailers. The next tread is placed over the riser, in the same way as the first. Continue in this manner until all the steps are rebuilt. Don't assume, incidentally, that each tread and riser will have the same dimensions in every case. In any older home, irregularities occur over the years, so measure each step—riser and tread—independently, and rip the new one to fit.

STRINGERS

Before running straight into the next phase of the job, study the old stairway and decide what has to be done and how you will do it. If the outside of the stringers is exposed, as ours is, you must decide how they will be finished. Do you want the steps to be a decorative element in the room or strictly functional? We decided upon barnboard trimming for the stringers to tie the stairway in with the barnboard used elsewhere in the room and to retain the rustic appearance of the home in general. But you can also make an attractive design from common pine or veneer paneling.

11. In the previous photograph you can see that the corners of the new risers and the nosing of the new treads extend considerably beyond the edge of the stringer. The top edge of the stringer is built up to conceal this. A piece of wood has been cut to the length, width, and depth necessary to conceal the corners and to remain flush with the sides of the stringer. Notice how the top and bottom ends have been angled.

12. Here is another view of the piece just attached to the stringer. Notice that it is flush at the side and that it has been cut at an angle at the top to bring it flush with the top tread. It has been anchored with several finishing nails.

13. The stringer on the opposite side of the stairway has been built up in the same way.

14. At the base of the steps a block of wood is nailed to each stringer to square off this part of the stairway.

15. Now a facing is placed over the sides of the stringers. Here we have used barnboard, cut to the size and angle necessary to bring it flush with all the outer edges of the stringer.

16. The interior sides of the stringer must be faced as well. Triangular shapes of wood—the same used for the outside facing—are cut to fit. With a coping saw, cut out an arch where the nosing will fit.

19. With facing nailed to both sides of the stringer, only one exposed edge remains to be concealed.

20. The exposed edge along the top of the stringer is "capped" with the same wood, cut slightly wider than the stringer itself to form a deliberate design element in the stairway.

17. *The facing for the inside of the stringer is attached with three finishing nails.*

18. *Continue to insert these triangular pieces at every step, on both sides.*

21. *Beneath the cap running down the length of the stringer, another piece of the same wood is inserted so that the base of the stairway is squared off.*

22. *A top view of the stringer reveals that no sign of the former stairway remains exposed.*

23. *The opposite stringer is treated in the same way: a piece of wood is inserted below the end of the cap.*

24. *The single remaining exposed area is now concealed.*

25. *The cut edges of the wood were stained to the same color as the barnboard. The steps were sanded, the nails countersunk. The heads of the nails were then concealed with wood putty mixed with the sawdust from the sanding. Then the steps were treated with polyurethane for protection.*

Attaching the new steps to the old caused the corner edges of the risers and nosing of the treads to jut out well beyond the stringers. These corners are unattractive and can be concealed by building up the top edge of each stringer. Rip a piece of wood the entire length and width of the stringer in a size sufficient to conceal these exposed corners. Angle the top and bottom cuts of this piece of wood as shown in the photograph. Attach it to the stringer with several 6-penny finishing nails. Do the same with the other stringer.

Pack out whatever edges of the pieces of wood are extending beyond the ends of the stringers so that everything is squared off at the base. Now that the tops of the stringers are built up to the desired height, you can conceal the old stringers and the sides as well. Simply face the sides with whatever attractive pieces of wood you've decided on as a finish for the stairs. Cut the wood to the size and angles necessary to finish off the sides of the stringers.

On the inner side of the stringers, immediately adjacent to the treads and risers, you can also make an attractive covering for the old surface. Cut out triangular shapes in the decorative wood to fit into the corners of each step. With the coping saw, notch out arches to permit the new facing to slip over the nosing of the tread. Attach this with three 6-penny finishing nails. It's unlikely that you'll be able to use a pattern or template to make a uniform triangular shape for each step. Variations—small as they may be from one step to the next—will always occur in older homes.

Now the stringers are faced on both sides, both inside and outside. An unattractive surface running down the top edge of each stringer will have to be concealed before the job is complete. Using the decorative wood here, you can attach a strip along the top edge of the stringer. We made ours slightly wider than the width of the stringer itself so that two lips extended over the sides of the stringer, an attractive capping of the edge all along the stairs. The edge of this cap was cut so that it was flush with another piece of wood attached at the base of the stairway. All remaining gaps were concealed with the decorative wood so that no signs of the former structure are exposed any longer.

FINISHING THE STEPS

Oak steps are finished like oak flooring: the nails are first countersunk. Then the surface is sanded (an electric vibrating sander is helpful here), first with coarse paper, then with finer paper. Save the sawdust from the sanding, mix it in with wood putty, and fill in the holes made from countersinking the nails. The sawdust will create a close match in color. If stains have somehow occurred on the treads since their installation, remove them with lacquer thinner. Thoroughly soak a white rag (do not use colored rags; lacquer thinner removes all dye) and wipe the steps. The stains will come right out. Treat the steps with a dark stain, if you want, and with a natural polyurethane finish for protection. Or, if you prefer, the steps may be carpeted.

HANDRAIL

Any flight of stairs must have a handrail or banisters on at least one side. We do not recommend that you construct your own balusters, but refinish these if you already have them on your stairway.

A handrail is easily installed along a wall. Place the rail about 39" above the stairs at the same angle as the stairway. Take a measurement off one nosing up the wall and a second measurement off another nosing. These points indicate the angle. Attach the hardware to the wall at these points and install the handrail onto these brackets.

PART THREE

Doors
and Windows

CHAPTER 15

How to Install Doors

No major renovation job can be accomplished in any home without encountering—somewhere along the line—a doorway. If you are doing any work that will alter the way you enter or exit from the building or room, you'll be installing a door, either exterior or interior. Even the construction of a simple closet will involve the installation of a door. Yet common as doors may be, their installation can present many headaches, and the amateur is easily discouraged from tackling the job. An error of only a fraction of an inch can produce a door that sticks or binds, or can create a variety of other nuisance problems.

Read this chapter closely before you dive headlong into the hanging of a door. We have arrived at what we think is the simplest, most sensible method of installing doors, and we might save you a good deal of frustration.

Installing a door is essentially a three-stage operation: the opening or doorway framing is constructed; the door is inserted into the opening; the hardware is installed into the jambs and door. We will explain all three operations, hoping to cover every kind of situation you will encounter.

TYPES OF DOORS

It's only when you shop for a door that you realize how many varieties are available. They fall into three groups, and within each style there are several variations. Exterior doors can also be purchased as combination doors, which are designed to hold a screen in the summer and a storm door in the winter. All doors arrive unfinished.

Flush Doors: These doors are smooth on both sides, squared off and even, their construction completely concealed by a skin of plywood or hardboard glued to a wooden frame. Flush exterior and interior doors can be solid or hollow, the former being more expensive. Over the skin of plywood or hardboard a veneer is glued. Lauan veneer is the least expensive, birch somewhat more expensive, and ash or oak even more expensive, and less readily available. The hollow, veneer flush doors are the least costly and vary greatly in quality. The least expensive versions do not have a particularly fine grain because it is assumed that these units will be painted. For staining, a higher-quality veneer is normally required. A contemporary solid flush door is constructed of a lumber core plywood-faced on both sides with a veneer of another wood.

The glue differs between the interior and exterior units, the exterior being weatherproof. Exterior doors are usually somewhat thicker than the interior variations, 1¾" rather than 1⅜". (Obviously, the thicker the door, the greater its resistance to warping.) Exterior flush doors can also be ordered with a panel of glass inserted.

Sash Doors: Unlike the flush door with its flat surface, sash doors are composed of several parts that can be combined in a variety of ways. A sash door can have panels or windows, for example, arranged in different combinations. A sash door can also be separated into two swinging units to form a *dutch door.* A *french door,* or *casement door,* contains panels of glass, like a colonial window. (Our sash door shown in the demonstration is a solid wood, six-paneled door.) The greater the amount of design work on the door, the higher the price. Sash doors are selected for exterior use because of their design possibilities. Study the catalogues at your lumberyard and select from the possible variations. Again, for exterior doors, the thickness is likely to be 1¾", and for interior doors, 1⅜".

Louver Doors: Doors that are louvered have slats running horizontally across them. Aside from their decorative potential, these louvers permit

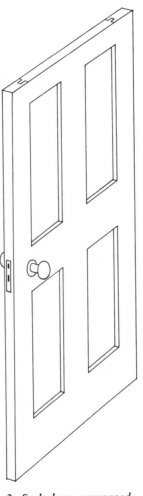

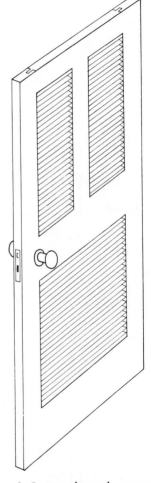

1. *Flush door: smooth on both sides.*

2. *Sash door: composed of several parts. This is a four-paneled door.*

3. *Louver door: slats permit air to circulate.*

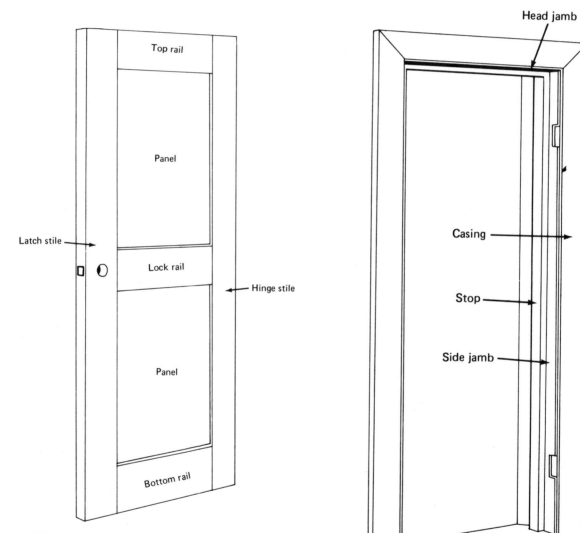

4. The components of a door: (1) *top rail;* (2) *bottom rail;* (3) *lock rail;* (4) *hinge stile;* (5) *latch stile;* (6) *panels.*

5. The framing of the door contains: (1) *side jambs;* (2) *head jamb;* (3) *saddle or threshold;* (4) *stop;* (5) *casing.*

the circulation of air and so are traditionally used for closets and pantries for ventilation.

COMPONENTS OF A DOOR

A door (like a window) is constructed with a frame that consists of *rails* and *stiles*. There are three rails on a door: one at the top, one at the bottom, and one at the middle, called a *lock rail*. There are two stiles, constructed vertically at the sides of the door: a *hinge stile* on one side, a *latch stile* on the other. Inserted within these stiles and rails are the panels of the door.

The frame into which the door is inserted consists of the following: two *side jambs* (one on each side); a *head jamb* overhead; and possibly a *saddle* or *threshold* at the door sill. A *door stop* is inserted along the middle of all three jambs to prevent the door from swinging through the opening. Casing or trim surrounds the edges of the door frame on both sides.

The door is connected to the jamb with hinges. Hollow interior doors swing on two or three hinges each $3\frac{1}{2}'' \times 3\frac{1}{2}''$; solid doors and doors that are thicker than $1\frac{3}{8}''$ swing on three hinges each $4'' \times 4''$. For heavier doors, special hinges are required.

Into the door itself is inserted the lockset used for opening and closing the unit: a handle or doorknob, which houses a latch or locking mechanism, and a *striker*. Into the jamb a *strike plate* is inserted to hold the striker in place.

The door must swing easily inside the jambs. Because the procedure for installing a door into its frame is time-consuming, precision work, it is now possible to order doors that are *pre-hung*, which means that the door arrives in an already assembled frame attached to the jamb with hinges. A pre-hung door is simply inserted into the opening—jambs and all—and adjusted so that it swings correctly; then the casing and lockset are installed into openings already prepared for them.

Doors are called right-hand and left-hand doors —depending on which direction they swing—but this terminology tends to vary from one lumberyard to the next and from one door manufacturer to the next. Not all doors swing. Some glide along tracks; some are *bi-folds,* which means that they push to either side, collapsing into an accordionlike arrangement as they are pushed to the left or right. Like swinging doors, gliding units and bi-folds can also be pre-hung.

DIMENSIONS OF THE DOOR

In Chapter 4, on partitioning, we gave some general information regarding the measurement of a

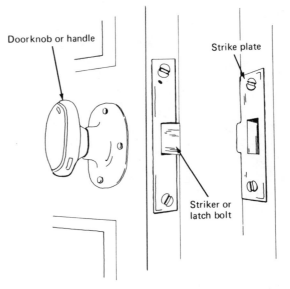

6. *The locks for a door contain:* (1) *doorknob or handle* (*which includes the latch mechanism*); (2) *striker or latch bolt;* (3) *strike plate.*

doorway, because the opening in the framework must be calculated on the basis of a door's dimensions. Standard doors—and we advise using these standard sizes whenever possible—are 6'8" high. The standard widths are available in increments of 2", starting from 2', up to 3'.

When you order a door, use the traditional methods of describing its dimensions. For example, a 2/0 door (called a "two-oh" door) is 2' wide, or 24"; a 2/6 door is 2'6" wide, or 30". (These dimensions refer to the door only, not to the framework or to the size of the opening into which it is installed.)

The most commonly used interior door is 2'6"×6'8", written 2/6×6/8. (*Note:* Width dimension always comes first.) For a small bathroom, a 2/0 door is frequently used; for an exterior back door, 2/8; for a front door, 3/0. Doors any more narrow than 2/0 are used in pairs as bi-folds. Into doorways wider than 3/0 are frequently installed double doors, a pair of doors that swing or slide.

ROUGH OPENING

You'll find that the terms used to describe doors and their openings are used for windows as well. The *rough opening* is the framing for the door, constructed from lumber in the exterior wall or in the partitioning of an interior wall. All rough openings—whether they are for windows or doors—have the same structural features in common.

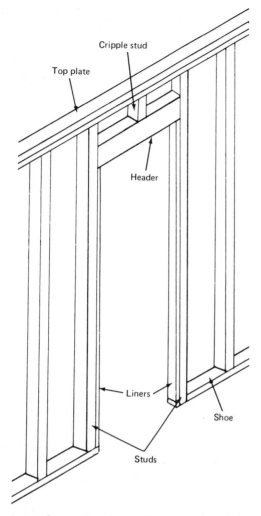

7. *A rough opening for a door contains:* (1) *two studs, one each side, anchored to the shoe and top plate;* (2) *two liners, one each side;* (3) *a header;* (4) *cripple studs.*

To the left and to the right of the door opening, *studs* are anchored to the shoe and then to the top plate (ceiling plate). In between these studs a *header* is nailed above the door opening. Supporting the header on each side are the *liners* (or *trimmer studs*), which are spiked into the studs alongside them. These liner studs are anchored at their base to the shoe, and at their top to the header. If room permits, *cripple studs* are anchored above the header and to the ceiling plate.

If you are installing a rough opening into a partition you've just erected, the chances are this partition is not a supporting wall. In this case, a header may be constructed with a pair of 2×4's. However, if the wall opening is being made into the exterior of the building, or is constructed in a bearing wall within the interior of the house, a heavier header (usually paired 2×8's) must be used over the door opening. Your local building code will specify the size of the header to be used in most cases. The construction of this framing allows for the support needed at the ceiling and prevents vibration from the operation of the door as it opens and closes.

CONSTRUCTING THE ROUGH OPENING

Regardless of whether you are cutting through a wall to create an opening from scratch or erecting a rough opening into a partition, the procedure is the same. Hanging an exterior door is the same as hanging an interior door. The only difference between the two is that the exterior door will require weather stripping and a saddle across the threshold.

First calculate the measurements you will need for the rough opening. Measure the width of the door first; write it down. Add to this the measurement for the jamb (¾″ on each side), and enough space for adjusting the door to a plumb line (½″ on each side). If the door is 2/6, your rough opening will be 30″, plus 1½″ (door jamb on each side), plus 1″ (for plumbing on each side), for a total of 32½″. Write this down.

Now calculate the height. Measure the door, add ¾″ for the jamb at the top, ¼″ for the door clearance at the bottom, and ½″ space for leveling the door. Figured this way, with a 6/8 door, you add 80″ plus ¾″ plus ¼″ plus ½″, for a total height of 81½″ from the floor.

In Chapter 4, on partitioning, we described how to calculate the width of a door opening because the measurement determined the placement of the shoe at the floor of the partitioned wall. We were not concerned with the height at that

1. First anchor the stud to the shoe. Allow 1½" alongside it for the liner.

2. Anchor the stud to the top plate. Be sure it is plumb. Mark off the placement of the cripple stud overhead.

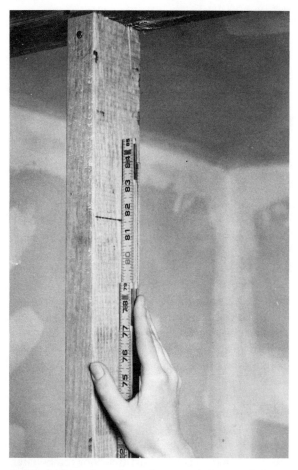

3. Mark the point where the top of the rough opening will fall. Allow ½" for plumb, ¼" for clearance beneath the door, ¾" for jamb. For a 6/8 door we marked the height at 81½" from the floor.

4. Saw two 2×4's to this height for the liners. With 10-penny common nails, anchor one to the stud at each side of the opening and toenail to the shoe. Be sure both liners are equal so that the header attached to them will be level.

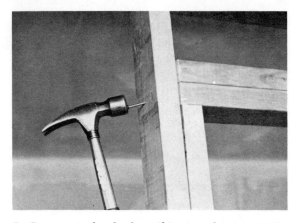

5. *Construct a header by spiking together two 2×4's. Rest its ends on the liner studs at both sides of the opening. Anchor the header to the studs with 10-penny nails. Make the header level.*

6. *Nail the cripple studs above the header.*

7. *Three cripple studs are inserted over the header: one at each end and one in the middle. They are toenailed into the header and into the top plate.*

point because the finished flooring had not yet been determined. (The flooring, obviously, affects the height of the opening, so be certain to take this into consideration. If you don't, you can cut down the door later, following our suggestions below.)

If you are cutting into a wall that has not been framed for a door, saw through the wallboard, remove the insulation (if it is an exterior wall), and inspect the wall for wires or pipes that may have to be rerouted. After this is done, cut through the sheathing and the siding, or through the other side of the partition; remove the studs; cut through the shoe exactly to the width of the rough opening you just calculated.

Both the stud and the liner are anchored to the shoe on either side of the opening. First toenail the stud into the shoe, allowing 1½″ alongside it for the liner. Lay the level on the stud and, when it is plumb, toenail the stud to the top plate. Do the same to a stud at the other side of the opening.

Now cut two liner studs to the height of the rough opening and anchor them to the studs at each side, toenailing them to the shoe as well. Be sure that they are equal. When the header is attached to them, it should be level.

Construct a header of suitable size (2×4's are sufficient for interior doors hung in nonbearing partitions; for exterior doors and bearing walls, consult your local building codes). The header should be the same length as the measurement between the two studs. Rest the ends of the header on top of the two liners, and anchor them at their sides to the studs with 10-penny common nails. In between the header and the top plate insert three cripple studs, one at each end and one in the middle, toenailing with 8-penny common nails. The rough opening is now complete. Now hang wallboard, or patch around the doorway.

As a final note, we cannot stress sufficiently how important it is to work toward an opening that is plumb on two sides and level at the header. The hinge side, in particular, should be plumb. It's far simpler to straighten the studs at this point than it is to adjust the door jambs later when hanging the door.

HANGING A PRE-HUNG DOOR

Hanging interior doors is just about the final job in home renovation. The walls have been painted, papered, or paneled, the floor finished, and all fixtures installed. Pre-hung doors reduce the frustration of this task.

A pre-hung door is exactly what the name suggests: the door arrives within an already as-

8. The framing for the door is now complete. (Here rough wiring was also installed.)

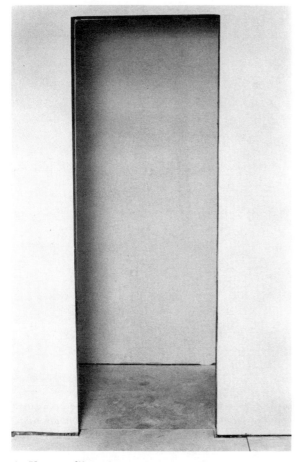

9. Hang wallboard or patch around the doorway.

sembled set of door jambs, attached to one side with hinges. The openings for the lockset have already been made in the door and into the jamb, and the stops and casing are generally included as well, already cut to size.

The manufacturer will tell you that pre-hung doors require only twenty minutes for installation, but we have yet to see one installed so rapidly. Still, when the time spent on hanging a pre-hung is compared to that devoted to the older method, you'll happily spend the extra money required. In fact, if you add the cost of jambs, stops, and so on, to the price of a door, you'll find that the pre-hung is not much more expensive than buying these items separately.

When the door is delivered, inspect it for damage. Some doors are guaranteed against warping and delaminating, so you might as well be certain you are starting off with a product that is in good shape. Take the door from its wrapping and remove the brace below the door, but don't take off the supports anchoring the door to the jambs. A swinging door will only interfere with the early stages of fitting. Measure the rough opening and compare this dimension with the measurement from one jamb of the door to the other. Will the pre-hung unit fit into the opening? Saw off the spacers (or horns, as they are also called) if you can't afford the space in the opening. And reduce the width of the opening if it is too large, as we have done in our demonstration.

Assemble the tools you need so that they are within easy reach: a hammer, 6-penny finishing nails, a level, and an assortment of shingles for shimming.

Check the rough opening with the level to see which sides are plumb. It's most important that the hinge side is plumb, and it will help greatly if the header is also level. If you can install the jambs directly onto these two sides of the rough opening, the third side is easily adjusted. Anticipate which sides will need adjusting and lift the door into the opening, being sure that it is placed so that it will swing in the desired direction from the desired side. The edges of the jambs should be flush with the wall surface on both sides of the doorway. Hold the door jamb against the liner on the hinge side and against the head jamb. If these two sides are plumb and level, tack them immediately. If the hinge side is not plumb, tack the hinge jamb at the narrow part of the opening, leaving the other end of the jamb swinging freely. Then shim out this end with shingles until it is plumb with the narrow part. Do the same with the head jamb. Tack it through the two jambs and through the shingles, leaving the nailheads protruding in case you may want to remove them later for further adjustment.

1. First establish which side of the opening is the hinge side. This should be plumb. It happened that our opening was too wide, so we reduced it by nailing a 1" board along the liner on the hinge side. The hinge side was already plumb, so we could use lumber of equal width. If the hinge side had not been plumb, this would have been a good time to correct it by using lumber of different thicknesses or by shimming the 1" board we did use.

2. If the opening is slightly short, you can reduce the size of the pre-hung by removing the so-called spacers, or horns, from the top of the jambs on each side.

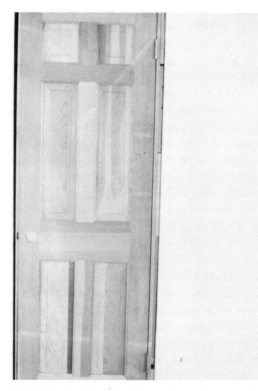

5. If the liner is plumb, the door is correctly positioned as soon as it is attached to the hinge side. Now it's simply a matter of adjusting the other two jambs to fit the door.

6. The door will swing freely if the space between it and the jamb is equal—$\frac{1}{8}$" or $\frac{1}{16}$"—on all sides. The slightest discrepancy in this space will affect the way the door will operate.

3. *Check the header. Is it level? If it is, lift the door into the opening so that the head jamb is up against the header. If the head jamb is not level, determine which side is the higher side, which the lower. With luck, the low side is on the hinge side and you can still lift the door so that it is up to the header. Otherwise, you'd better shim the top to make it level before you install the door. With the door in place, nail it to the hinge side with 6-penny finishing nails through the jamb into the liner.*

4. *Level the head jamb with shims, if necessary, and tack it to the header. You may have to remove these nails later for additional shimming, so don't drive them in all the way.*

7. *Start from the top of the jamb along the side jamb. Close the door. If the space is larger than it should be, insert a shingle between the liner stud and the jamb. Close the door again. Has the space been reduced? If not, slide the shingle still farther into the space, its wider end forcing the jamb still closer to the door until the space has been sufficiently reduced. Tack a 6-penny finishing nail through the jamb to hold the shingle in place.*

8. *Move down the door to the latch. Repeat the same procedures. If the space is considerable, use two pieces of shingle to force the jamb still closer to the door. Continue to close the door to check the space. Tack the shingles into place when the space is equal to that above it.*

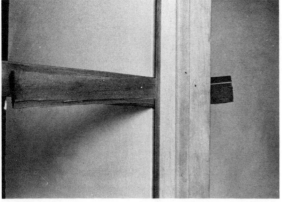

9. *Wherever the door jamb bows away from the door, shim it out with additional shingles.*

10. *Move all the way down to the bottom of the jamb. If the space is equal down the entire length of the door, drive the 6-penny finishing nails all the way in.*

11. *Now cut away the protruding shingles so that they are flush with the wall surface and with the jambs. The nails should hold them firmly in place as you cut them.*

12. *Close the door one final time to check that you did not affect anything when you drove in the finishing nails and cut shingles. If you did alter the space, shim out the jamb some more.*

The object is to plumb and level the door on all sides so that it swings freely, without dragging or binding. Once you have the hinge side plumb, you never again have to put the level against the door. The rest is accomplished by eye. The door is squared-off and rigid, and as long as it is plumb at the hinges, it should swing correctly from this position. From here it is simply a question of adjusting the jambs to fit the door.

The door will swing freely when the jambs are level and plumb and when you can see a ribbon of daylight between the edges of the door on all three sides, an unbroken and equal space about $\frac{1}{8}''$ or $\frac{1}{16}''$ on all sides. By shimming the jambs to the door you establish this equal space all around. Wedge shingles in between the jamb and the liner to force the jambs into closer proximity to the door, then tack finishing nails through the jambs, shingles, and stud to hold them in place. If greater thickness is required to push the jambs closer to the door, insert two shingles from opposite sides, their combined thicknesses increased to the point needed to force the jamb closer to the door. (Tack these shingles in—through the jamb—with 6-penny finishing nails also.) Insert these shingles wherever there is a bowing in the jamb. Open and close the door continually to check the space until you have arrived at a perfectly equal space around the entire door, as shown in the photographs. Once this is done, the door should swing freely.

Finally, anchor the jamb to the studs by nailing through the shingles sandwiched in between the jamb and the stud. Once the door is installed, you can saw off the ends of the shingles so that their edges are flush with the edges of the door jamb.

13. *The door is installed. Notice the uneven space between the stud and the jamb on the left where it was shimmed out with shingles to equalize the space between the jamb and the door.*

INSTALLING THE LOCK

Depending on the door and its use, various kinds of locks may be used. In residential use, the most common locks are the rim lock, the mortise lock, the tubular lock, and the cylindrical lock.

Rim Lock: This is mounted on the inside face of the door. One kind has a spring-loaded latch that can lock the door automatically; another kind has dead bolts.

Mortise Lock: This is installed into a single recess along the edge of the door. The mortise lock holds, in a single unit, both a spring-loaded latch and a dead bolt, which can be extracted and extended from the inside of the house by turning a knob without using the key.

Tubular Lock: This is most commonly used on interior doors and is the one we show in our demonstrations. Its installation requires two holes: a large one cut into the face of the door to hold the spindle and stems of the doorknob; a smaller one in the door edge for the latch bolt or striker. Some models of tubular locks have a push button in the knob or a small level button on the interior side. Some contain no locking mechanism at all—those used for closet doors, for example.

Cylindrical Lock: These are longer, larger, and stronger than tubular locks and provide more substantial security for exterior doors, but their design and installation are similar to those of the tubular lock. Two holes are also required for their insertion into the door.

1. *To install the lock, first insert the striker into the opening at the edge of the door. The striker also includes the latch mechanism.*

2. *Insert the stem of the doorknob on one side of the door into the holes of the latch mechanism. Do the same on the other side of the door, and secure the doorknob to the door with Phillips screws.*

3. *Attach the strike plate to the jamb, into the mortise designed to receive the plate.*

On a pre-hung door the openings have already been cut into the door and jamb to accept the doorknob, striker, and strike plate. It's simply a matter of following the manufacturer's instructions for their installation.

For a tubular lock, first install the latch—connected to the striker—into the opening along the edge of the door. Next install the knob at one side, inserting the stem (or spindle, as it is also called) into the holes in the latch case. Install the knob at the other side of the door in the same way and tighten the screws. You may find it easier to install these knobs if you press the striker as you insert the spindles into the latch holes.

Finally, insert the strike plate into the jambs. The construction of the strike plate should conform to the size and shape already made on the jamb.

STOPS

Our pre-hungs arrived with the stops already nailed into the jambs, but you may have to put in your own. This is simple enough. Close the door toward you so that you are facing the outside. With a pencil, trace a line 1/16" away from the edge of the door, down the side jambs and along the head jamb. This is the guide on which you lay the stops. Cut the stops to the size of the door opening. Open the door and nail them—with 4-penny finishing nails—along the edge of the line so that the door will close against them. Start with the hinge side first and test the door to see if it swings freely. Cut the stops down to fit if necessary. Try the door after each piece is nailed in place so you'll know immediately if it is in the correct position. If you've nailed the jambs to the studs along the center line, your stops should conceal these nails. Countersink all finishing nails.

HOW TO CUT DOWN A DOOR

It always seems to happen that after a door is installed something new is added to the floor, which means you can no longer swing the door freely. A saddle is inserted, carpeting is laid, or a new finished floor is installed and the door is too tall for the opening. Cutting down a door is so common that we decided to devote a section to it. Here are some tips on how to do it easily and properly.

Remove the door from the opening by extracting the pins from the hinges and lifting the door

1. To locate the placement of the stops along the jamb, close the door toward you and trace a line ¹⁄₁₆″ away from the edge of the door.

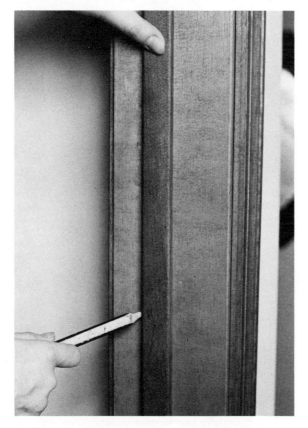

2. Open the door and attach the stops along the pencil line with 4-penny finishing nails. The stops will prevent the door from opening beyond its reach.

away from the jamb. Measure the distance between the floor (not the threshold) and the bottom edge of the lower hinge on the jamb. Then measure the distance between the bottom of the door and the bottom of its lower hinge. It should be ¼″ smaller (for clearance) than the measurement you just made from the jamb. From this difference you can determine how much should be cut off the door. Lay the door down on a pair of sawhorses and draw a line along the bottom of the door to indicate how much should be removed. (Using a carpenter's square will help you arrive at a line that is square.)

If you're working with a lauan door—or any door that is veneered—a special method is required. As the teeth of the saw rip through the veneer, the surface tends to splinter along the face side. This makes a very unattractive edge along the bottom of the door. To prevent this splitting, score the line with a utility knife. Press firmly into the veneer so that you cut through it. Pass over the line a few times with the knife until you're certain you've penetrated the surface. Now bring your saw up to the door and cut very slightly to the outside of the line. The blade of the saw will splinter the wood badly, but only along the edge that is being thrown away. (If you do splinter the door elsewhere, fill the cracks with wood putty.)

If you are cutting a large section from a hollow door, you may be cutting above the solid edge at the base. The groove along the base will have to be sealed. Scrape away the old glue and insert a new base with a piece of wood that fits into the frame. Then glue it into place.

Stain or paint the bottom edge and replace the door in its opening.

HANGING A STANDARD DOOR (FROM SCRATCH)

Frankly, we prefer to hang pre-hung doors. But we can't assume that you'll take the short way out, so we'll describe the more traditional method of hanging a door as well. Actually, our method is not so traditional. We have a shortcut, but we'll go into that later.

For installing a door from scratch you'll need to purchase the following items from your lumberyard:

Door Jambs: These can be ordered ready for installation. Interior jambs are made of 1″ pine and should be the same width as the wall. The two long pieces are notched to receive the shorter head jamb. The shorter jamb should conform to the width of your door opening.

Door: Order any door you please, according to

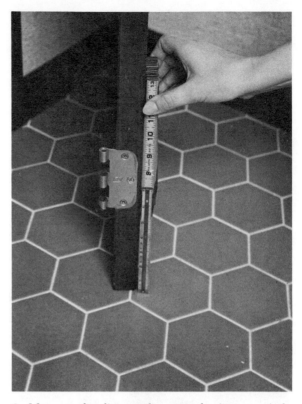

1. When a saddle was installed over this threshold, the door had to be cut down in order to clear it. To cut down a door, first measure the distance between the floor and the bottom edge of the lower hinge attached to the jamb.

2. Measure the distance between the bottom of the door and the bottom edge of its lower hinge. It should be ¼″ smaller than your first measurement for the door to clear the new floor.

4. Saw slightly to the outside of the scored line. As the saw rips through the veneer, it will splinter along the unwanted edge, not into the door.

5. Cut a straight line along the edge, then paint or stain the bottom of the door before replacing it in the opening. If the wood has splintered, fill the cracks with wood putty before painting or staining.

3. *Mark the bottom of the door with a line indicating where it should be cut. If you are cutting down a veneered door—such as lauan—first score this line with a utility knife, cutting through the surface of the veneer.*

the dimensions of your rough opening. It will arrive unfinished, with no indication for hinges or latches.

Hinges: You'll need two or three pairs of hinges, depending on the size of the door. A standard interior door requires one pair of 3½″×3½″ butt hinges. An exterior door requires 4″×4″ butts. You want hinges that can be taken apart and used for either right- or left-handed doors, so don't order simple butt hinges (these can't be taken apart). You want a loose-pin hinge. The two leaves for the hinge are held together with a pin that can be removed from the loops.

Stops: These are the strips of wood nailed along the jambs and across the head jamb to prevent the door from swinging beyond its frame.

Casing: This is the molding. Order door casing: four 7′ pieces of casing and two smaller pieces, in either colonial or clamshell style. (See Chapter 19, "How to Trim Standard Doors and Windows," for their selection and installation.)

The tools you'll need are standard: ruler, 1″ chisel, level, saw, pencil, and shingles for shimming. Only one tool is special here, and it is crucial: a *butt gauge*. This inexpensive tool is available at any hardware store and is designed for placing and cutting out the wood for the hinges. Order a butt gauge that corresponds to the dimensions of your butt hinges—3½″ or 4″. With these tools, then, you're set.

We mentioned earlier that we don't use a traditional method for hanging a door from scratch. We can't understand why anyone would! According to the older method, you fit the door into an opening already prepared with jambs. This tedious process requires that you lift the door onto wedges and lean it up against the opening. From this awkward position you are supposed to fit the door into the opening—cutting and planing it down if necessary—and install hinges that are perfectly matched to the jambs. Then you hope the door will swing once you're through. In fact, it almost never does, and you must make a number of small adjustments before it operates properly.

We avoid all this by hanging the door to the jambs right at the outset, and then treating it like a pre-hung. Since we know the door is square, why fit the door to the jambs when you can fit the jambs to the door?

First see if the jambs are the correct size for the opening. Assemble them by inserting the short head jamb into the notches at the top of the longer jambs. Don't nail them together. Lift the

1. Jambs are assembled by inserting the shorter jamb into the notch on the longer jamb. Do this first, then lift the assembled jambs into the opening to see if any adjustments in their size or in the size of the opening will be necessary (as we did when hanging the pre-hung unit earlier). If you cut down the jambs significantly, you may also have to cut down the door by as much, to avoid complications later. Also determine on which side the hinges will be installed. Mark the jamb for hinges now.

2. Notice the edges of the jambs—they are angled. When installed into the opening, these edges will taper into the surrounding wall, making it easier to trim the door later. The casing will lie flat.

5. To be certain your marks are correct, match up door to jamb. As they are placed side by side, you can see if the marks for the upper and lower hinges are accurate for both door and jamb.

6. Lay the butt gauge (3½" for interior doors, 4" for exterior) on the jamb, its top edge touching your mark. Tap the hammer firmly on the top of the gauge so that it sinks into the wood about 1/16".

9. Chip away the cuts you've just made. Use your hand here, not the hammer, for better control.

10. Stop when the mortise feels fairly even.

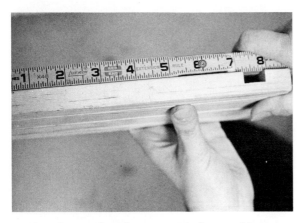

3. Now locate the placement of the top hinges on the jamb. Measure down from the notch and mark the jamb. (We marked off the jamb 7⅛" from the top.) Be certain your hinge marking is on the correct side of the jamb. Also mark off the bottom hinge on the jamb.

4. Now mark off the edge of the door for the top hinge. The measurement should be ⅛" smaller than that made on the jamb, to allow the door to clear. (We marked off 7".) Do the same for the bottom hinge, allowing ¼" for clearance here.

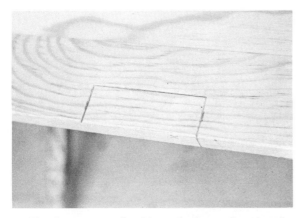

7. The butt gauge should mark the outline for the hinge leaf with an etched line, like this.

8. To create the mortise, make a series of closely spaced cuts crosswise from one end of the etched outline to the other with the chisel. It's better to take many small shots with the chisel than one big one.

11. Place a hinge leaf into the mortise and feel with your finger if it is flush on all edges. The hinge should lie flat. If it doesn't, chisel away the high spot.

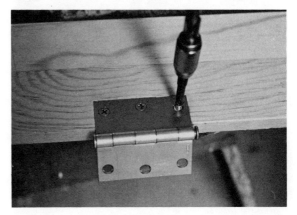

12. Place the hinge in the mortise, the pin at the top, then screw the hinge into the wood.

13. Chisel out the mortise along the door edge in the same way—with the butt gauge used as a guide here as well. Don't be alarmed if the veneer splits away from the edge as you work with the chisel. It springs back as soon as you withdraw the chisel.

14. Place the hinges side by side, matching butt to butt. A slight discrepancy in the position of the hinge loops may prevent the hinges from joining properly.

15. With the hammer, rap the hinge loops to shift their position enough (only slightly) to admit the matching loops.

16. As soon as the hinge leaves are joined, drop the pin through the loops—from the top—and repeat the same procedure with the other pair of hinge butts. Reassemble the jambs and proceed to hang the door as if it were a pre-hung unit (see our earlier demonstration).

jambs into the opening and see if they're the right size. You may have to reduce the size of the opening—as we did with the pre-hung earlier—or you may have to cut down the jambs to fit. Make a note of how much needs to be cut down. While you have the jambs in place, also establish on which side the door will swing—in or out—because that will affect which edge on the jamb will hold the hinges. (The door will swing *out* along the edge on which the hinge is attached.) As the jambs are standing in position, mark which one will hold the hinges along which edge.

Incidentally, while you have your jambs out, take a look at the way the long, narrow edges are angled. There's a good reason for this. When the jambs are installed into the opening, these edges are angled so that they will taper into the wall. This makes it easier for you to install trim later. You can lay the molding flat, free from interference with the jamb edges.

If you have to cut down the jambs, you may have to cut down the door at this time, too, to avoid any chance of error later. You'll want ⅛″ clearance at the top of the door and ¼″ clearance at the bottom, so the jambs should be ⅜″ longer than the door. Cut down the door to this dimension.

Now we'll attach the door to the hinge jamb. How high or low on the door you place the hinges should be determined by other doors in the room. You should conform to their dimensions. Traditionally, the top of the top hinge is 7″ down from the top of the door, and the bottom of the bottom hinge is 12″ up from the floor. (The middle hinge—if there is one—is equidistant from the other two.)

Take the jambs apart. Pick up the hinge jamb and lay your ruler along its edge, measuring off for the top hinge first. From the bottom of the notch on the jamb mark off the distance to the top of the hinge and add ⅛″ for the door to clear. (We marked off 7⅛″.) Then mark off the door to the same distance, less ⅛″. (We marked off 7″.) Then do the same with the bottom hinge. Mark it off from the bottom of the jamb to, say, 12″. Then mark off the door from its bottom edge the same dimension, less ¼″ for clearance —11¾″. Hold the jamb against the edge of the door, matching up your marks as they lie side by side, just to be certain you've calculated correctly.

Hinges for interior doors are composed of butts attached by loose pins. They must sit in a *mortise*—a recess made into the door wood—on the door and jamb, flush with the surface of the wood. The best way to mark the mortise is with a butt gauge. This is a metal pattern of a hinge that outlines the shape of the hinge leaf on the door and jamb by being driven into place with a ham-

mer. Its sharp edges mark the location of the butts. Lacking a butt gauge, you can mark with a pencil and square. If you do this, remember that the open edge of each hinge leaf is set in ¼″ from the back of the door and is set in from the edge of the jamb the same distance. This allows room for the loops holding the pins.

Place the butt gauge on the mark and up against the edge of the jamb. With the hammer, rap the butt gauge sharply so that it sinks into the wood. This is the outline for the mortise, etched at the correct depth.

With the chisel, make a series of closely spaced crosswise cuts from one etched line to the other. Remove the chips by hand, scraping and cutting away as you go. Try the hinge in the mortise. It should lie flat and not wobble. If it does, a high spot must be chiseled away. The hinge leaves should be flush with the surrounding wood.

Now chisel out the mortise for the lower hinge on the jamb and do the same for both hinges on the door. As you chisel the door—if it's veneer—the surface may split, the veneer pulling away from the door edge. Don't be concerned if it does this, because it springs back into position as soon as the chisel is withdrawn.

Remove the pin from one hinge, separating the butts so that you can place one butt on the door, the other on the jamb. Settle each butt into its mortise and screw it into place. Screw in the other hinge in the same way. Be certain you have allowed for the pins to be on top, not on the bottom, so that they will swing in the correct direction.

Now lift the hinge jamb alongside the hinge side of the door and join the matching hinge butts. No matter how careful you've been until now, you'll probably find that they won't fit precisely. Rap the loops with the hammer, forcing the hinge into the precise position needed to accept its mate. As soon as the butts are interlocked, drop the pin (from the top) through the loops. Do the same with the other hinge.

After the door is hinged to the jamb, simply reassemble the jambs by joining them at their notched ends. If you calculated correctly, there should be ⅛″ space between the top of the door and the head jamb, and ¼″ space between the bottom of the door and the base of the side jambs. Nail the jambs together with 6-penny finishing nails. Lift the door, jambs and all, into the opening and proceed from here just as you would a pre-hung, following the instructions we gave earlier.

Now, after all, doesn't this seem simpler than the traditional method? With practice, you'll hang doors more and more efficiently, encountering few of the original difficulties.

OPENINGS FOR THE LOCK

The door you have just hung will not have any openings for the lock. Making the appropriate openings in the door and jamb to hold the lock is not difficult, but it does demand close attention to detail and following the manufacturer's instructions carefully.

For a cylindrical or tubular lock you'll have to drill two holes into the door: a large one through the face of the door, and a smaller hole in the edge of the door. Two mortises are required: one along the edge of the door for the plate surrounding the striker, and another for the strike plate on the jamb.

The new lock will be packaged with a paper template that fits around the edge of the door and enables you to mark the door correctly for the openings. First determine how high you want the knob to be on the door. Normally it is placed about 36″ above the floor, but it's more important that the position of the knob match the other doors in the room.

Fold and position the paper template in place and, with an awl, puncture a hole in the door through the face of the template, marking the center of the hole for the lock on the face of the door. Do the same for the hole on the edge of the door that will hold the striker or latch bolt. Make sure your template is placed correctly for a 1⅜″ door or a 1¾″ door.

Into the face of the door drill a hole 2⅛″ in diameter. We used a heavy-duty ¾″ drill, the largest power drill manufactured. This costly tool is not necessary, providing you have a hand drill and an expansion bit that can create a hole of this dimension. Place the tip of the bit onto the hole you've just made with the awl and drill straight through into the surface of the wood.

Continue to drill through the face of the door until you see the point of the drill breaking through the surface of the other side. Stop and go around to the other side of the door and finish the hole from there. This prevents the door from splitting.

Now place a 1″ bit into the drill and hold its point at the edge of the door where your second mark was made with the awl. Drill until you reach the large hole, being sure that your bit is straight, at a right angle to the door edge.

Insert the latch bolt into this hole; trace the outline of the latch bolt plate and, with a 1″ chisel, mortise out the wood until the plate fits into it, flush with the wood. (Remember to score the outline of the mortise first by tapping in the chisel around the perimeter to prevent the tool from slipping beyond the boundary of the mortise.) After the mortise is completed, insert the latch bolt and knob spindles into the two open-

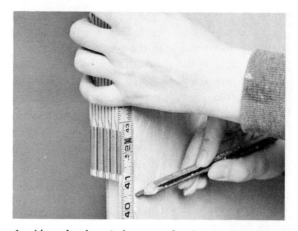

1. After the door is hung, make the openings for the lock and strike plate. Measure up from the floor to where you want the doorknob to be placed (36″ is standard, but match the other doors in the room).

4. Using a large drill or an expansion bit for a hand drill, make a hole in the door 2⅛″ in diameter. Place the tip of the drill on the point made earlier with the awl. Continue until you see the point come through the other side of the door, then withdraw the drill.

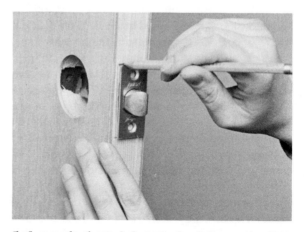

7. Insert the latch bolt into the hole on the door edge and trace the outline of the plate.

2. Placing the paper template in position, puncture a hole through the center of the circle—using an awl—into the surface of the door. This locates the hole for the doorknob.

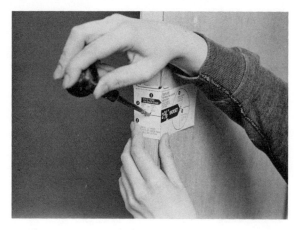

3. Now puncture a hole through the template at the end of the door to locate the position of the striker.

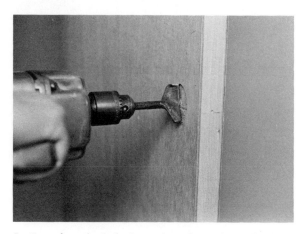

5. Complete the hole from the other side of the door to avoid splitting the wood.

6. With a 1″ bit, drill through the edge of the door, into the point made earlier with the awl. Continue to drill until you enter the larger hole.

8. Using this outline as a boundary, chisel out a mortise about 1/16″ deep.

9. After inserting the knobs into the latch bolt, swing the door nearly closed and mark the top and bottom edge of the striker where it hits the jamb.

10. *Measure the distance between the edge of the door and the edge of the striker.*

11. *Transfer this last measurement to the jamb and mark it between the two points made earlier.*

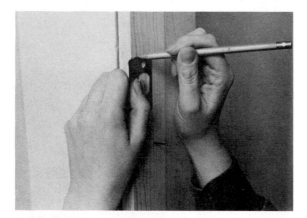

12. *Centering the opening of the strike plate over the mark on the jamb, trace its outline.*

13. *Drill a 1" hole about ½" deep into the door jamb at the point you marked for the entry of the striker.*

14. *Chisel out a mortise about ¹⁄₁₆" deep, following the outline drawn on the jamb. Insert the strike plate.*

ings on the door (as described in the manufacturer's instructions and shown earlier in this chapter).

Your instructions may also include a template for locating the position of the strike plate on the jamb, but it's just as simple to locate it yourself. Swing the door to a near-closing position, and make marks at the top and bottom of the striker where it touches the jamb. Now measure the precise distance between the striker and the edge of the door. Transfer this measurement to the jamb, between the two points marked earlier for the striker. Position the strike plate over this point and trace its outline onto the jamb.

Now drill a 1" hole ½" deep into the door jamb at the point where it will take the striker. Be careful not to drill through the jamb. Mortise out the jamb, following the shape of the strike plate you traced earlier. The plate should fit flush (about ¹⁄₁₆" into the wood) with the jamb. Anchor it to the jamb with screws and install it.

Other kinds of locks are no more difficult to install. Follow the manufacturer's instructions.

CHAPTER 16

Installing Windows

Even if you've never before tackled a major renovation job, you have probably been able to handle nearly every procedure already described in this book with self-assurance. When it comes to installing windows, however, you are bound to come to a screeching halt. In our own renovation work, we've noticed that our windows seemed to draw the greatest attention. It seemed magical that we could create an opening where none existed before and install a new window during the course of a single day, dramatically altering the appearance of the building. (We timed it once, in fact. It took us exactly 2½ hours to create an opening and to install a new window!)

Installing windows seems overwhelming, perhaps, because the work is visible from both indoors and out—a public display of your skill (or lack of it). Truthfully, we found it far simpler to install a window where none existed before than to replace an old window with a new one the same size. All you do is make an opening in a wall, prepare the rough stud framing to receive the window, slip the window in—frame and all—level and plumb it, and then fasten it.

One word of caution before you begin. Windows do affect the exterior of the house. It is not within the realm of this book to describe exterior work in any great detail (there are enough variables in this subject alone to create another volume!). Before you tear up the exterior of your house, therefore, be certain to anticipate just how much alteration will be necessary outside. In particular, sheathing and siding may have to be patched. If you are not prepared to handle this work yourself (although we hope to give you enough information so that you *can* do it yourself), consult with a builder first, preferably one who specializes in siding.

COMPONENTS OF A WINDOW

All windows have certain details of construction in common. As we discuss windows, we'll be referring to these terms, so look them over first before reading on.

The frame of a window contains three general parts. (1) *Head:* The top of the frame, consisting of a horizontal member called the *yoke* or *head jamb,* and an outside *head casing.* (2) *Jambs:* The two vertical members, at the sides of the window frame. (3) *Sill:* The lower, horizontal part of the window frame. An outside *casing* is constructed around the four sides of the window—generally as a single unit with the window. The casing is a frame used as a guide for siding. Casing is also placed on the inside of a window after installation (discussed in Chapter 19, "How to Trim Standard Doors and Windows").

The *sash* is the frame that holds the window pane. It is constructed with *rails* at the top and bottom and *stiles* at the sides. If there is more than one pane of glass in the sash, the dividing members into which the panes are fitted are known as *muntins* or *muntin bars.*

TYPES OF WINDOW

When you begin to plan for new windows in your home, you'll find a greater variety than you had ever imagined. Your decision, of course, may be determined largely by other windows in the home that you are attempting to match, but even within each category you'll find quite a number of styles. All windows either slide, swing, or are stationary.

Double-hung Windows: This is the most traditional of windows, called double-hung because it has an upper—or outside—sash that slides down, and a lower—or inside—sash that slides up. These movements may be controlled by pulleys equipped with cords and weights or by springs concealed in the side jamb sections of the unit. Some double-hung sashes are aluminum; most are wood. This type of window is adaptable to many architectural styles and has been used in houses for hundreds of years.

Casement Windows: A casement window is attached to its frame by means of hinges and is operated by turning a crank. It is a vertical, long, **narrow window**, and the hinges are attached at the side.

Awning Windows: Awning windows are like casement windows placed on their side. They are hinged at the top and swing out at the bottom, and they are usually operated with a crank or with a scissors-type linkage that permits rapid adjustment. They are generally installed for maximum ventilation and provide protection against rain damage while the window is open.

Jalousie Windows: These are made of horizontal glass slats set in metal clips at each end. The metal frames are connected by levers, which close and open the glass slats. The jalousies operate like awning windows, but they do not protrude as far and so can be used in more limited space. They are better suited to warm than to cold climates because they cannot be made completely weather-tight. They are also used in rooms that are not kept heated in the winter or air-conditioned in the summer.

Hopper Windows: These are the reverse of awning windows. They are opened from the top, their hinges attached at the sill.

Gliding Windows: Though some horizontal gliding windows are made of wood, most are aluminum. They move along a closely fitted track at the top and bottom. To facilitate ease and smoothness of window operation, the bottom track contains nylon glides.

Picture Windows: This term usually describes large windows whose glass is fixed; they are most often combined with other types of windows. A fixed picture window can, for example, be flanked on either side by two casement windows or by two double-hung windows.

Bay and Bow Windows: These are multiple windows that extend out beyond the framing of the house and so require their own roofing. A bay window consists of a fixed glass unit in the center flanked by operating casement or double-hung windows attached at a 45-degree angle to the center and to the walls of the building. A bow window consists of four or more operational units (generally casement), which are attached to each

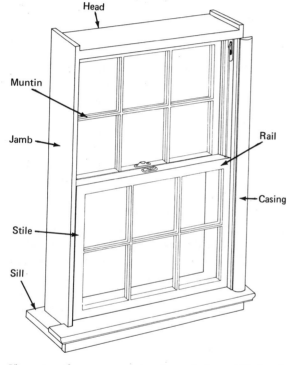

Here are the components of a window: (1) head; (2) jambs; (3) sill; (4) casing; (5) rails; (6) stiles; (7) muntins.

Double-hung window.

Casement window.

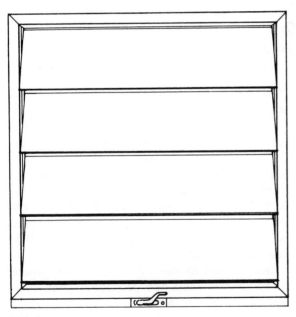

Jalousie window.

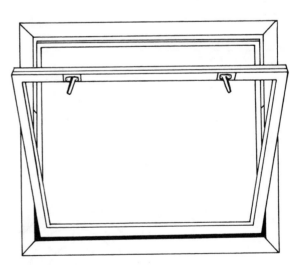

Hopper window.

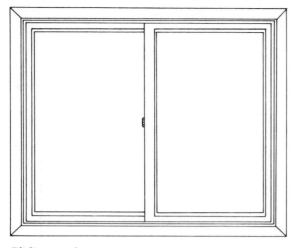

Gliding window.

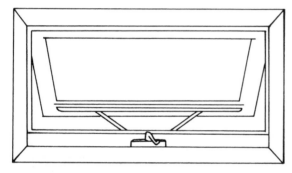

Awning window.

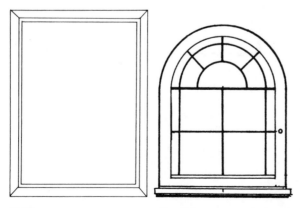

*Stationary or
fixed window.*   *Special-purpose window.*

other at smaller angles so that the unit appears almost curved. These windows require special and unusual consideration for installation and trimming, so we have included them in our Chapter 18, "How to Install Special Doors and Windows," and Chapter 21, "How to Trim Special Doors and Windows."

Special-purpose Windows: Small windows designed for use in stairways and hallways and over entries, beside garage doors, and in gable ends are available in a number of designs, including half-circle, quarter-circle, full circle, and octagonal frames. (We describe the installation and trimming of an octagonal unit in Chapter 18 and Chapter 21.) A basement window is generally a fixed, small unit installed permanently in a masonry wall.

Major window manufacturers have nearly all these styles available, with the possible exception, perhaps, of the small special-purpose windows just discussed (which are made by small custom houses, most likely). Catalogues from manufacturers will indicate which windows can be combined. For example, a fixed unit can be combined with an awning unit or a double-hung unit. When windows are joined in this way, they are *mullioned* by a thin strip that holds them together and gives the impression of a single unit.

SELECTING A WINDOW: LIGHTING

The placement, size and shape, and number of windows in a room have a dramatic effect on the way in which natural light illuminates a room. The ideal is uniformity of daylight across an entire room through all seasons—no hot spots, no dark corners. There are a variety of factors that affect the distribution of light: the direction the room faces; the shape and position of the window; the type of window and glass; the reflections of light within the room; and the type of sunlight controls within and outside the house.

Bearing this in mind, here are some general principles that could help determine the selection and placement of windows.*

•The glass area in the walls of a room should be more than 20 per cent of the floor area.

•A short, wide window produces a broad, shallow distribution of light. A tall, narrow window gives a thin, deep distribution.

•The higher the window, the deeper the light will penetrate.

* Our discussion of selecting a window is based on detailed studies made by the University of Illinois Small Homes Council.

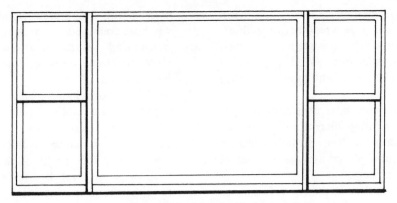

Picture window, flanked by double-hung windows.

Bay window.

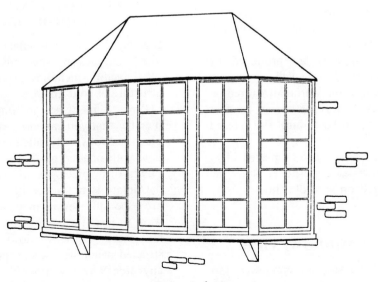

Bow window.

•Glare is generally caused by contrast between the windows and the dark areas between them. Less glare is produced with a single large opening than with several smaller ones. Windows grouped together give a more even light than when they are separated.

•Corner windows, and those near corners, produce less effective lighting than those well away from the exterior corners. Bay and bow windows also do not substantially increase the amount of light admitted into a room.

•Place the main window in the room facing toward the south for best light and warmth, toward the north if you prefer to limit the sun's heat and to provide a constant, unchanging light.

•Translucent glass increases privacy; tinted glass reduces heat and glare.

•Screens absorb a good deal of light, as much as 50 per cent.

SELECTING A WINDOW: VENTILATION

The size and the placement of windows greatly affect the movement of air in the room. Air currents through the house are vital (and should not be confused with drafts). Air moves because of differences in temperature and pressure, from high pressure to low. The side of the house facing the breeze has the high pressure; low pressure occurs on the downwind side. Air currents move from the sunny to the shady side of the house. With this in mind, read these principles of windows and ventilation:

•Windows that can be opened should account for more than 10 per cent of the floor area in a room.

•Try to locate the windows to take best advantage of prevailing breezes.

•Corner windows and those near corners produce less effective ventilation than those well away from exterior corners.

•Good comfort conditions are produced by pairs of openings low on opposite walls.

•High openings carry off warm air stored at ceiling level, but they do less for human comfort than window openings of the same size placed lower.

•The effectiveness of one opening placed high, the other placed low—at opposite ends of the room—depends largely on wind direction.

SELECTING A WINDOW: VIEW

What will you see from your window after it is installed? The window is no problem if you're blessed with a fine view. Some of us are not, so we must create our own. A fenced yard or a few well-placed shrubs may resolve this problem. Here are some considerations you should also bear in mind:

•Scale your windows to the view. A long horizontal window is logical if you look out on a range of mountains. But a narrow garden may call for a glass wall that is tall and not so wide.

•Consider the height of the window. Place a window at eye level. Eye level can vary from one room to the next. The ideal for an open view is between 42″ and 80″ from the floor in the kitchen and 48″ and 80″ in the bedroom. In a living room, the ideal is to have a clear view from 10″ above the floor to 80″.

•Minimize obstructions to the line of sight: avoid unnecessarily wide window divisions any greater than 4″, especially horizontal ones.

•Windows that open will require screens. Will these impede your vision?

SELECTING A WINDOW: DESIGN

Design considerations affect both the interior and the exterior of your home, so it is important to keep these in mind as well when you decide upon the window.

•Be consistent with the period. If your home or windows are colonial, for example, a modern window unit will seem out of place.

•Study the arrangement of windows as they appear from the outside. A scattering of different-sized windows can be unattractive. Group the windows, or arrange them in an interesting pattern.

SELECTING A WINDOW: OTHER CONSIDERATIONS

Beyond the decisions affecting light, ventilation, view, and design, you must also bear in mind other factors, including privacy, climate, and the structure of your home.

Privacy may be an important factor. Remember that you can also protect your privacy by placing shrubs and walls outside, selecting a window with opaque glass, by installing drapes and blinds, or by placing windows high in the walls.

Climate is not so easily controlled. If winters are especially severe in your area, you may not want to install a large expanse of glass. You will also need storm windows or multi-pane-constructed windows. Avoid jalousied windows in any area where you require insulation. On the other hand, too much sun may be the problem in your area. Glass comes in many colors for this purpose alone, gray and blue being the most desirable for reducing the sun's heat and shutting out glare from the desert or seashore.

The structure of your home may also determine your choice of windows. How is the house covered? If it is covered with brick veneer, solid masonry, cement, or stucco, you'll probably be able to put in only the exact kind and size of window you are taking out. You can't remove these materials easily to accommodate a larger window. You could install a smaller one by building framework up inside, but we suspect it is unlikely you will want to do this. On the other hand, if you have any kind of wooden shingle or siding, clapboard, or asbestos siding, you won't have too much trouble because you can remove pieces of siding fairly easily to make a new window fit in.

ORDERING THE WINDOW

When you've decided on the style and shape of the window, you'll select a manufacturer next. Windows vary enormously in price from one brand to another, and there is generally good reason for this. The quality of materials and workmanship varies with the price. Generally speaking, we would recommend paying the extra for higher-quality windows. Inferior windows are a constant source of problems. They do not open or close easily, or they are flimsy.

In general, wood windows are better than metal windows because they seal better and don't twist as much as metal. Aluminum windows tend to be flimsy and insubstantial. Steel casement windows can be a hazard during a fire, because they cannot be broken apart easily in an emergency. Moreover, putting storm windows on steel casement windows is difficult at best.

The best combination is a window made of wood with a metal weather stripping. This reduces drafts. The highest-quality windows (which we used for our demonstrations, incidentally) are framed in wood and encased in vinyl so that they never require painting.

When you calculate the cost of the window, don't forget to include the price of storm windows. Better window manufacturers now make a window with a double-pane (and even triple-pane) construction, which is about 20 per cent more efficient in shutting out the cold air than the traditional storm window arrangement. We discovered that it was just about as expensive to purchase medium-quality windows with storms as it was to purchase the highest-quality windows with multiple-pane construction. (For our demonstration we used double-pane windows.)

When you order the windows, have them delivered. They are heavy and bulky and you may damage them if you try to handle them on your own. Always lay the windows with the glass side up.

WINDOW DIMENSIONS

Assuming that you have decided upon the style, basic shape, and manufacturer of the window, let's get more specific: exactly what size window will you order? Calculating the correct dimensions is critical to your window installation. First, keep your terms straight. For example, an "opening" can refer to the window opening itself or to the opening in the wall into which you are installing the window. Here are the three terms most frequently used, listed by the largest size to the smallest. Don't confuse them.

Rough Opening: This is the opening in the wall into which you are placing the window. The rough opening is the framework of lumber holding the window.

Actual Size: Also called the *over-all size,* this dimension refers to the window unit itself, from the sill to the head, from jamb to jamb.

Nominal Size: Also called the *sash size,* this dimension refers to the size—height and width—of the sash only, independent of the framing around it.

You'll be using all three dimensions at one time or another, so keep them straight. When you order a window, you give the size of the sash only (nominal size), independent of the framing or the opening into which it will be placed. Always give the nominal dimensions with the width first, the height second. Tradition has created a standard terminology for double-hung windows, similar to the one used for doors. The nominal size of a double-hung window can be, for example, 2/4×3/2. In other words, 2'4"×3'2", or 28"× 38". The terminology for all other styles of window varies from one manufacturer to another, but double-hung units normally follow this system. Remember again that this measurement applies only to the size of the *sash,* not to the actual window or the rough opening.

ROUGH OPENING

The rough opening, as we explained earlier, is the opening into which the window is installed, framed with lumber on all four sides. (Framing a doorway and framing a rough opening are very similar.) The rough opening consists of the following components:

Studs: At the extreme left and right of the rough opening are studs, one on each side, attached at the shoe and to the ceiling plate.

Header: This is needed in a bearing wall. Overhead, a horizontal header is anchored to the two studs, constructed of two pieces of lumber spiked together at their sides. Depending on the size of the opening, this lumber may be as large as 2×12 or as small as 2×4. If the opening is large enough, the header is anchored to the ceiling plate; if not, *cripple studs* are inserted between the header and the ceiling plate. (A header is needed only in a bearing wall. In general, walls that run parallel to the ridge of the roof are bearing—or supporting—walls. Those that run across the gable ends are not. If the window opening is more than average length, however, a header should be used even in a wall that is nonbearing, to prevent cracks in the wallboard or plaster.)

Liner Studs: These are also called *trimmer studs* or *jack studs*. The header is supported below by two liners, at the left and right. These studs are spiked into the studs alongside them, anchored to the shoes and to the header.

Sill: Running parallel to the header at the bottom side of the rough opening is a sill, which can be constructed of a single or double layer of 2×4's.

Legs: These are also called *cripple studs*. These short 2×4's support the sill. They are anchored to the shoe and to the sill.

The rough opening should be 1" wider and 1" longer than the actual window. This extra space of ½" on each side of the window allows for room to level and plumb the unit before it is anchored to the building.

The most difficult and time-consuming part of installing a new window is creating the rough opening. If this is done properly, the window is inserted in only a matter of minutes. So we will focus, in this chapter, on creating rough openings in a variety of different circumstances. The window itself is installed in the same way in each situation. We anticipate that you'll be installing a window under any one of three conditions: you'll be replacing an old window with a new one of the same dimensions; you'll be enlarging or reducing the size of an already existing opening; or you'll be starting from scratch by constructing an entirely new rough opening. We'll describe all three.

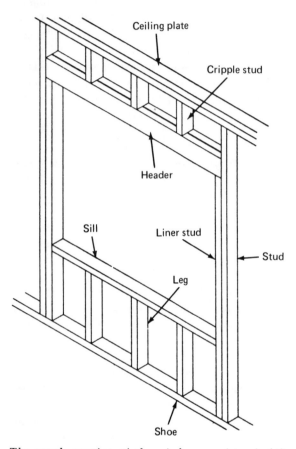

The rough opening of the window consists of: (1) studs; (2) liner studs; (3) header; (4) sill; (5) legs; (6) cripple studs.

1. *An old barn window is the simplest to replace. Because the window was not inserted on a bearing wall, no header was used. A window the precise size of the opening was ordered. Since it was old-fashioned—tall and narrow—it was a custom order.*

2. *The old window was removed from its opening.*

3. *The old opening was modified for greater support. A pair of studs and liners were inserted, the opening 1″ larger than the actual window.*

4. *The new window was inserted. All other jobs described in this chapter were somewhat more complex.*

1. Because there are no wallboards concealing the structure of this window, it is relatively easy to see how an opening can be modified to accommodate a window of a different size. (This is not a bearing wall, so there are no headers involved.)

2. The old unit was removed from the opening.

3. After the window was removed, the frame was rebuilt. The old studs were used for legs under the sill and for additional support on the sides. The sheathing was patched outdoors. The window was installed at the center of the opening between two new liner studs.

4. After new insulation is placed around the window, gypsum wallboard nailed to the framing completely conceals the former opening.

REPLACING A WINDOW

The most straightforward task of all is replacing an old window with a new one of the same dimensions. The rough opening has already been created for you and you can install a new window without rebuilding the exterior or the interior of your home, except perhaps installing casing indoors around the new window.

First establish the size of the rough opening. There are methods of calculating this dimension by measuring the window currently in the opening, adding a few inches, and so on, but we'd prefer to take the easy way out by measuring the rough opening directly. Remove all the casings (trim) around the old window so that the rough opening is exposed on all four sides. Measure the opening from liner stud to liner stud, from sill to header. Remember that this opening is 1″ larger than the window itself. With the dimensions of the rough opening in hand, go down to the dealer and select a window whose over-all dimensions are smaller than the rough opening by 1″ or more.

It's simplest to replace the old window with a new one precisely the same size, but this may not be practical. You can easily enlarge the opening at the base of the window without encountering any great structural changes in the rough opening. (Be sure that the window is at least 6″ above any radiator or convector below.) If you increase the height of the window, however, you must install a new header, and if you alter the width, you will also have to reconstruct the header. If you want a window that is substantially more narrow than the old one, you can alter the rough opening simply by reframing it with new liners, but remember you will have to patch the exterior siding.

After you have the new window delivered, remove the old window. Indoors, remove all trim around the window with a claw hammer or with a flat bar. Don't worry about creating a mess. You've only just begun.

Since you are replacing the window with a new one of the same size, try to avoid damaging the siding any more than necessary. With luck, you can simply replace the window without having to patch any new siding.

The next step depends on the siding of your house. Shingles—either asbestos or cedar—are attached to the sheathing by nails. Study them carefully to see how you can extract these nails without damaging the shingles. It would be ideal if you could re-use the shingles you remove. From the shingles surrounding the window remove the nailheads or pry them loose, and cut through the calking around the window with a utility knife. Some shingles should lift off, some can be folded back, others must be destroyed. Every house presents its own individual circumstances.

Clapboard can also be pried loose. To remove clapboard around a window, pry the boards up slightly and pull out the nails if you can. Pry the nails loose, cut off their heads, or drive them through the board with a nail set. Try to remove the boards without splitting or breaking them, if possible. Obviously you can always replace them with new boards, but matching paint is never ideal.

Masonry and aluminum siding are much too difficult for the amateur to tackle. Call on a specialist for this aspect of the job. It's well worth it.

Don't try to salvage the drip cap as you remove the siding over the top side of the window. Many new windows have their own drip caps attached and replacing one isn't expensive anyway. After you've moved the siding out of the way, cut through the tar paper and study the construction of the old window. Some windows are attached to the sheathing and must be pried loose from the outside; others are nailed directly to the lining studs and can be removed from indoors. It's relatively easy to locate the nails that have anchored the old window to the house, so pry them away. (It's wise to have someone working with you, incidentally. Removing windows can be tricky, and another set of hands may be valuable.)

Once the window is removed, all exposed nails extracted, and debris cleared away, you install the new window just as you would in any rough opening. This procedure is described below, under "Installing the Window."

CONSTRUCTING A HEADER

The next sections will describe the situations in which you will build or rebuild a rough opening. Before going on, we should take time out to explain more about headers.

Headers are the support needed above any opening in a bearing wall. A bearing wall supports a portion of the house above it and is normally supported with studs. If you create an opening—for a door or a window—you will be removing some of these important studs from the framing, and you must substitute some other means of support. This is the function of the header. A header is a double thickness of dimension lumber that runs horizontally at the top of an opening, its ends resting on shorter studs, called liners, or trimming studs, or jack studs.

In new construction all headers are the same width regardless of the opening they span. A

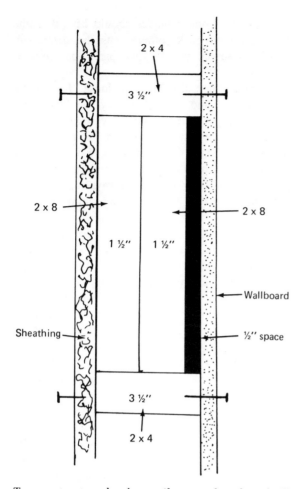

2 x 4

3 ½"

2 x 8

2 x 8

1 ½"   1 ½"

Wallboard

Sheathing

½" space

3 ½"

2 x 4

To construct a header, spike two lengths of 2"
dimension lumber together. For our headers we
nailed together two pieces of 2×8. On the top and
bottom sides of the header we also nailed 2×4's.
These two pieces, laid flat, gave us the thickness we
needed for the walls so that we had a nailing surface
for the sheathing on one side and the wallboard on
the other.

header for a 2′ window is the same as that used for a 10′ window. Consequently, the top sides of all windows are in line. Bear this in mind when you install your header: it should line up with the others in the room. If the distance between the top sides of two windows and the ceiling varies to any degree in a room, this difference will be immediately apparent. The differences are even further exaggerated with drapery or blinds. On the other hand, window sills may vary considerably in height without attracting any notice whatsoever.

The wisest thing you can do is to consult the building inspector in your area regarding the building codes that govern the size of headers. This way you are certain to install an acceptably sturdy support over the window.

Remember, the header is supported by a liner stud on each side; your measurement for the header should take this 3″ into consideration. So when you calculate the length of the header, always add 3″ beyond the size of the rough opening. If the rough opening is 36″, the header should be 39″.

Above most of our windows we constructed our headers from two pieces of 2×8 spiked together and sandwiched between two 2×4's. Here's why. The thickness of our walls was 3½″. Two pieces of 2″ lumber spiked together gave us a thickness of only 3″. By nailing a 2×4 to the top and bottom edges of the header, we obtained the desired 3½″ at the top and at the bottom. This gave us a nailing surface for the sheathing outside and for the wallboard attached over the top of the window inside. (See our diagram.)

One further word of advice: if, at any time in the course of your work, you will be working with an opening that is not supported by a header, you'd be wise to install some form of temporary support until the work is completed. For example, if you remove an old header, or if you cut a wide opening into a wall where none existed before, you should construct temporary supports for the ceiling, a kind of wall running parallel to the wall section being removed. Locate this wall about 30″ from the window wall, to give you enough space for working. When we installed the window shown in this demonstration—8′ wide—we installed an 8′ temporary support for the ceiling while we worked. Place a 2×4 on the floor, nail another to the ceiling directly over it, and wedge studs in between, forcing them tightly between the 2×4's below and above (or you can also use a plank against the ceiling). We used four studs in this way, tacking them above and below with 10-penny nails. After our work was complete, the new header in place, we removed the temporary wall. (Protect a finished ceiling with towels or blanket and a good floor finish with a plank or piece of plywood.)

A final word on headers: always install them crown side up.

HOW TO ENLARGE AN OPENING

Installing a window in an opening that already exists is simple enough if the new window is the same size as the old one. Enlarging the size of an opening is another question. Here you have to rip out not only the old window, but a good part of the framing for the old rough opening as well. Then you'll have to patch sheathing and siding on the outside of the building. Now you see why we said earlier that it is easier to start from scratch in building an entirely new opening than it is to alter one that already exists.

Wait until your new window is delivered before you dismantle the old unit. It's always best to build a rough opening only after you have the new window in hand so that you can measure and remeasure continually to be certain you're on the right track. There are too many things that can become confused in calculating the measurements, and we'd rather be safe than sorry.

It's also wise to make a careful diagrammatic drawing of the rough opening in advance (such as ours), calculating the dimensions of the window opening in relation to the header and studs surrounding it. Refer to this drawing whenever you find yourself a little confused—which is bound to happen the first time!

We are assuming here, as in the demonstration, that you are replacing a tall, narrow window with one that is shorter and wider. This is most common nowadays because newer designs call for this shape, no doubt because ceilings in homes are lower than they were in former times.

Remove the casing from the old window and study the rough opening. The old window was installed between two liner studs, and it would be preferable to retain one stud for the new opening. (Although the liner will have to be removed from the rough opening in order to rebuild the header, you can at least take your early measurements from it.)

Let's assume you've decided to retain the stud to the left of the window (as we did). First measure the width of the new window and add 1″ to this. Working off the left-hand stud of the old rough opening, measure off the width on the right-hand side of the wall. (Since you're working off an existing stud, you allow only 1½″ for the liner on the left, but 3″ for the stud and liner on the right.) Place the 4′ level against this mark on the wall and continue a straight and plumb pencil line down the length of the wall. The width has been established.

If, for any period of time, you work with a fairly large opening from which the header has been removed or in which it is not yet installed, build a temporary support for the ceiling 30″ away from the work area.

223

1. This is a conventional old-fashioned window, to be replaced by a modern double-hung unit that is wider and shorter. The opening will be altered without removing any more wallboard than necessary.

2. First remove the casing of the old window to study the rough opening beneath it.

3. Measure the width of the new unit, from jamb to jamb.

4. Measure the height of the new window, from header to sill.

Now mark off the height of the new window, adding 1″ here as well for the new rough opening. Allow for the new header, and remember to take the sill into account. In our demonstration there was no header for the old window, so we allowed 10¼″ from the ceiling plate for the installation of this header. (We constructed our header from 2×8's sandwiched in between two 2×4's, a total of 10¼″.) Stand back from the wall and look at the marks. Is this where you'll want the new window? Check your measurements again, just to be on the safe side. Consult the diagrammatic drawing you made earlier. Check to be certain that the horizontal line marked on the wall is level and the vertical line is plumb. Now remove the old window. Pry it loose from the siding, remove the panes and framing, and clear away the debris.

Following the lines marked on the wall, saw through the wallboard or plaster. You can use a keyhole saw and the hammer for this purpose, but we found that a reciprocating saw made our work on windows almost effortless. Remove the wallboard and insulation beneath it. You may find wires or plumbing beneath the surface of the wall. If they traverse the new opening, they will have to be rerouted before the window is installed. (It is unlikely, however, that this will happen.) You can build around wires running beneath the window by notching the studs and legs.

Now cut into the sheathing, following the line of the wallboard you've just cut. Cut right through the siding and let it fall away. Cut away any studs that traverse the new opening. Remove the old header and the liners supporting it. Saw the studs below the window to the height of the legs needed to support the new sill. If you are using one 2×4 for a sill, for example, cut the studs 1½″ below the rough opening. The new sill, anchored to these legs, will be at the correct height for the rough opening.

By now you have a hole in the wall. All that's left is to construct a new framing for this opening. First install the studs—to the left and to the right, or on only one side if you are retaining one of the old studs. Measure the space between the two studs. This is the size you will make the header (it should be 3″ wider than the rough opening; remember, two liner studs—each 1½″—are supporting the header.)

Cut the two liners to the height they must be in order to support the header. If the header is going to be tight against the ceiling plate (as ours is), follow this procedure: lean the top ends of the liner studs against the studs on each side of the opening. Rest the header on top of these liners and push one liner flush against the stud

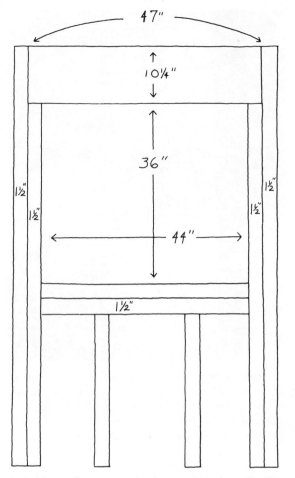

5. *Make a diagrammatic drawing of the measurements for the rough opening, based on the measurements for the window you have just measured. This is important. It's easy to miscalculate these dimensions, and referring to a diagram such as this will help keep you on the track. Make note of the existing studs in your drawing.*

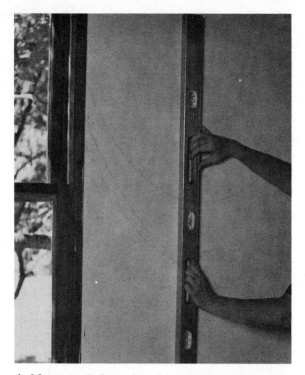

6. *Measure off the width of the rough opening, starting from the stud that you are retaining (on the left of the window here) and continuing to the point where the next stud will be inserted. Draw a plumb line down the wall, using the level as a guide.*

7. *Measure the lengths of the rough opening in the same way. Be certain to allow for the header at the top (ours was 10¼").*

alongside it, lifting the header in position against the ceiling plate. Tack both header and liner into place. Then lift the other side of the header into place by driving in the second liner stud. Nail every member in solid.

If the header is narrow and is not resting up against the ceiling plate, simply install the liner studs first, nail the header to the studs, and install cripple studs overhead, 16″ on center, as you would for a door opening. Use 10-penny common nails for attaching studs to each other and header to studs. Toenail with 8-penny common nails.

Now nail the sill into position. Anchor it to the legs below the window and toenail it to the two liners. Most instructions for installing windows advise you to make the sill level. Although this is certainly desirable, we were far more concerned with the header than with the sill. Since we wanted all the windows in the room to be equidistant to the ceiling, we fastened the windows to the headers, not to the sills. So it didn't really matter if the sills were out of level. Most windows, in fact, are designed to be fastened at both sides and at the top only.

Now go outside and fill in the sheathing. You need sheathing outside because you'll be nailing the window to it. Check first to be certain that you have a nailing surface on which to attach the edges of all new sheathing and siding. If not, you'll have to install cats or nailers on the inside for this purpose. After you've patched the sheathing, staple tar paper around all exposed edges of the wood outside. You are now ready to install the window. Follow the instructions under "Installing the Window," below.

HOW TO REDUCE AN OPENING

Reducing the size of an opening is far simpler than enlarging it. Here you only have the nuisance of patching new sheathing and siding to match the old. The supports for the old window should certainly be suitable for a smaller unit, so you should not be required to do more than to construct a simple frame for the new window with 2×4's.

After you remove the old window and make your calculations for the size of the new unit, simply rebuild the framing. Attach all new 2×4's to the old ones. First construct a new sill off the former one. If you are using the same header for this window that you did for the old unit, you can attach the liner studs to the header and toenail them into the sill. If your new window is to be installed lower than the former unit, simply construct a smaller version of the header, using 2×4's anchored into the new liner studs.

8. *Pry loose the old window, and remove the sash.*

9. *Remove the remaining frame from the opening. Wear gloves to avoid damage to your hands.*

10. *Now cut along the lines you have marked on the wall.*

11. *Remove the wallboard only.*

12. *Now cut the wallboard down the length of the wall where you marked the line in pencil.*

13. *Remove the wallboard.*

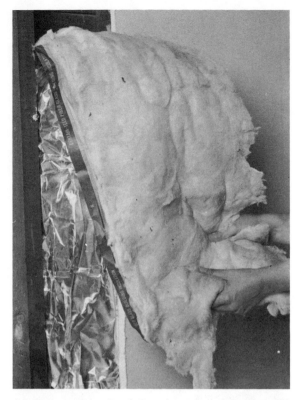

14. Remove the insulation from beneath the wallboard. Once the wall is exposed, you can examine for wires and pipes that may interfere with your work.

15. Cut through the sheathing and siding, following the same lines, and then remove the sections of the old framing that will not be used.

18. There are many ways to install a header, but here is one method that works. Install one liner first, then rest the header on this and insert the other liner on the other side of the header, forcing the header against the ceiling plate.

19. The header is placed in position.

16. Construct a header. The measurement for the length of the header is the distance between the two studs. It will be supported by two liner studs. We made a header from two pieces of 2×8.

17. The two 2×8's were sandwiched between two 2×4's. The members were all attached with 10-penny common nails.

20. Although the walls conceal the two studs on either side of the header, you can see from this angle that the liner is supporting the header.

21. Install the sill by attaching the legs below and toenailing it to the two liner studs.

22. *Patch the sheathing on the outside of the window.*

23. *Outside, tack tar paper around the edges of the rough opening.*

24. *The rough opening is complete. The most difficult task of installing the window is now over.*

Patch the new sheathing outside to match the old. Tack tar paper over the new sheathing, and install the window as described below (see "Installing the Window").

MAKING A NEW OPENING

If you've managed to follow the procedures described for enlarging an opening, you'll have no trouble starting from scratch. In fact, if you install this window correctly, you can probably avoid doing any major work on the exterior whatsoever.

First locate the position on the wall where you intend to install the new window. Your work will be somewhat easier if you can work off at least one existing stud. If it's only a question of shifting the window 2″ or 3″ either way, try to locate it alongside an existing stud. Tap the wall, or look for seams that will tell you where the stud is below. If you think you've found it, simply tap a nail through the wallboard, inching your way to the right or left, until you've located the side of the stud. This will determine one side of the rough opening.

Hold a 4′ level vertically against the wall, its edge touching the nail hole you've just made. Draw a plumb line above and below the nail hole, following the edge of the level as the guide.

Now measure the rest of the opening. Remember, this stud will have a liner stud attached alongside it, so allow for an extra 1½″ in your measurement. Press the lip of a retractable ruler into the wallboard at the pencil line and pull out the ruler the full width of the window, marking on the wall where the other stud will be located. Remember to allow an extra 1½″ on the other side for the liner stud as well.

Now mark on the wall the location of the top side of the rough opening. Remember to allow for the header. Use a right angle to be sure your horizontal line is perpendicular to the vertical. Continue the line across the wall with the level as your guide. Now mark off the lower part of the rough opening. Consult your diagrammatic drawing every step of the way to be certain you have kept all the correct dimensions in order. It's easy to miscalculate.

After you have constructed a temporary support for the ceiling (see earlier description), cut through the wallboard along the pencil lines and remove the portion you have cut away. Our window was so large—8′ by 4′—that we decided to cut away all the wallboard, from floor to ceiling, to make our work easier. Although you can always work around wallboard, you may prefer to patch wallboard later, as we did. (It also made our work more visible for photography.)

1. If you are starting a rough opening from scratch, decide first where you will place the window. Work off an existing stud if you can possibly arrange it. Here we located the stud by tapping a nail into the wallboard, inching slightly to the right until we were certain we had found the side of the stud.

2. Using the nail hole as the fixed point, lay the level vertically against it.

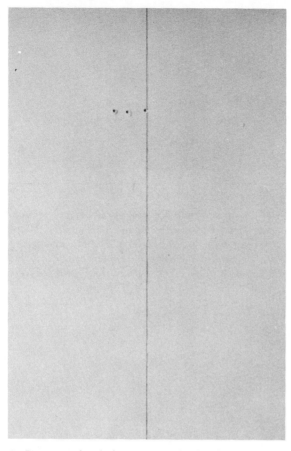

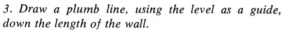

3. *Draw a plumb line, using the level as a guide, down the length of the wall.*

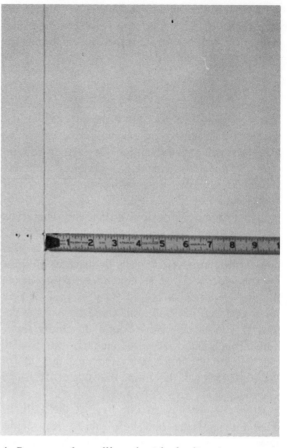

4. *Puncture the wallboard with the lip of a retractable ruler. Press it into the pencil line and extend the ruler out to the full width of the rough opening.*

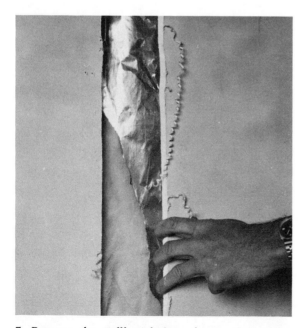

7. *Remove the wallboard. In order to give greater visibility to our work, we removed the wall above and below the window. We wanted you to see the structure of the rough opening for this large window.*

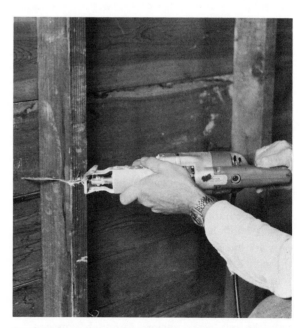

8. *Cut the studs to the height necessary to support the sill.*

5. *Allowing for the space to be taken by the header, mark off the horizontal line of the rough opening. A carpenter's square will help you establish a line that is perpendicular to the vertical line. Continue this line with the level until you reach the other side of the rough opening.*

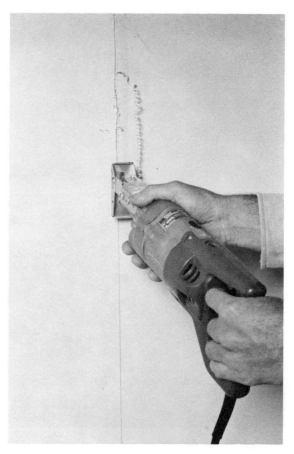

6. *Now cut into the wallboard.*

9. *Rip off the studs from the sheathing by pounding them loose with the hammer.*

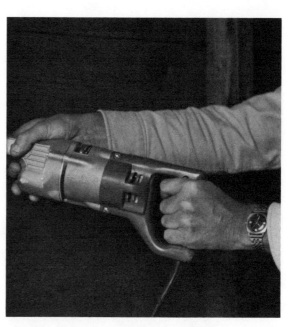

10. *Now cut into the sheathing and siding.*

11. *The opening has been cut into the wall. These legs will hold the sill, bringing it flush with the rough opening cut into the siding of the house.*

12. *Toenail the header into the stud.*

14. *A short leg is attached to the liner stud, as additional support for the sill.*

15. *The sill is anchored to the legs with 10-penny common nails.*

13. The liner stud is inserted below the header for support. It is spiked into the stud alongside it.

16. The rough opening is complete. The unit to be installed here is a bow window, described later in the chapter on special doors and windows.

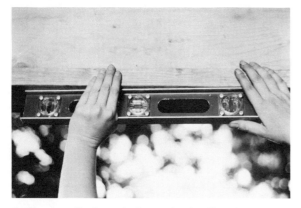

1. To install the window, check all sides of the rough opening first to determine which side is plumb or level. With luck, the header is level.

2. Slip the window into the opening. Hold it in position against the header (which happens to be level here).

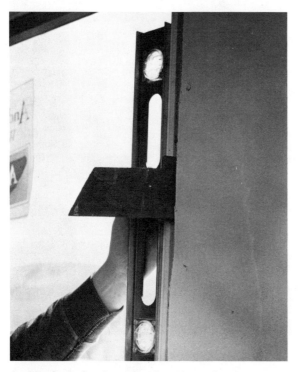

3. Check the level on all sides. Shim where necessary for plumb.

Saw through the framing studs. If the header is not going to sit up against the ceiling plate, saw off the studs at the point where the header will be attached, using these for cripple studs over the header. If the header is going to sit against the ceiling plate, rip the studs away and remove the old nails from the framing so that the surface is even enough to permit tight contact with the header.

Once the opening has been cut—according to the dimensions shown on your diagrammatic drawing—nail in a new stud, and construct the header. Install the new header overhead, the liner studs supporting it at each end. (Installing the header has been described earlier, under "Constructing a Header.") After the studs, header, and liners are all anchored with 8- and 10-penny nails, attach the sill over the legs.

Go outside and remove just enough siding around the edges of the rough opening for the casing of the new window. If you do this carefully, you can remove only enough for attaching the new window to the sheathing, no more, so that you will not have to do any additional work on the siding. You may even be able to remove the siding without damaging the old tar paper beneath it. If this is not possible, pull away the old tar paper and staple in new strips along the four edges of the rough opening. When the window is installed, the calking should conceal the rough edges of siding around the window, unless you've gone too far.

Now you're ready to install the window.

INSTALLING THE WINDOW

Installing the window is the same procedure regardless of how you arrived at the rough opening. Whether you are placing a new window in an old opening of the correct size, or have enlarged or reduced an old opening, or have created the opening from scratch, the installation of the window is the same in every case.

Just before you lift the window into the rough opening, measure it one last time as a final check. Measure the rough opening again also. Is the opening 1″ wider and 1″ longer than the actual size of the window? If it is smaller, the window will not fit; if it is too much larger, you will not have any surface to which the window can be attached.

Before you struggle with the window unit, establish in advance which sides of the rough opening are level or plumb, and which sides are not. At least one end of the window should be brought into contact with the header, so that the height of the window is the same as that of every

236

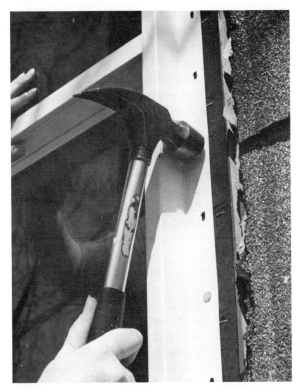

4. *When the window seems level, it is nailed into position.*

5. *Sometimes it can happen that the sheer weight of the unit causes it to sag slightly, even though it has been anchored securely. Here the window dropped slightly at the right.*

6. *A soft block of wood is tapped beneath the jamb, forcing the window back into its correct position.*

7. *The window is installed. What remains to be done now is patching the wallboard, spackling, and painting. The casing will be added later, a procedure described in Chapter 19, "How to Trim Standard Doors and Windows." The exterior is also patched.*

other window in the room, as you had planned. Obviously, it would be ideal if the header were level, but you may not be so lucky. At least you should anticipate in advance which side of the window will have to be lowered from the header.

The window is meant to be installed from the outside, but this may mean carrying the unit up a ladder, an acrobatic feat not always welcomed by those of us who feel uncertain about heights even in the best of circumstances! Although it is awkward, we preferred to install the window from indoors, lifting the unit sideways to pass through the rough opening and then pulling it toward us. It's not as risky as it sounds. The window is suspended in mid-air for only a few seconds. Once it is in the opening, resting on the sill, no muscle power is required. It will balance easily with one hand, until you are ready to lift it to the header. From inside you may be able to lean out the open window and hammer the nails into the side of the house. After the window is tacked into position, you can climb the ladder outside to complete the nailing job.

In any event, it is advisable to have an assistant work with you, someone to guide the window into the opening, and to hold it in position while you reach for the level and hammer. Good teamwork will go a long way here.

When the window is placed in the opening, center it between the liner studs and bring it into close contact with the sheathing. Lift it to the header and, while your assistant is holding it in place, hold the level along the top edge. One side will most likely be higher than the other. On the high side, drive in one galvanized nail through the casing at the upper corner, through the sheathing, and into the stud. Don't drive it in all the way. You may want to pull it out later.

With one corner attached, you can swing the window slightly to where it will be plumb and level. You may have to insert shims—slivers of wood shingles—along the side of the window to get it plumb, just as you would in hanging a door. If you can't get it right, remove one of the nails and start over. Once the window is correctly placed—and it should open and close properly—complete all the nailing around the casing, one galvanized nail every 4″ or 5″.

Even after you have attached the window thoroughly, the unit may sag slightly from its own weight. (This happened with our window in the demonstration.) Tap a block of soft wood under the sill at the sagging side of the window. This wedge will force the window back to where it belongs.

Don't be alarmed if the jamb of the window is not flush with the interior wall surface. This edge can be built up easily, a procedure we discuss in our chapter on trimming windows.

Once the window is in place, the patching work begins all over again. Stuff loose insulation into the spaces around the window. Repairs in the wall may have to be made, including spackling and painting; the casing around the window must be installed indoors (see Chapter 19, "How to Trim Standard Doors and Windows"); and the exterior work must be completed. For outdoor work, you may have to call in a specialist to patch up the signs of your latest efforts, depending on the kind of siding on your house. If the new window does not include a drip cap, a new one must be installed over the top of the window; the siding will have to be repaired and calking placed all around the perimeter of the new unit.

CHAPTER 17

Installing a Sliding Glass Door

The increasing popularity of sliding glass doors in the home is due, in all probability, to their convenience and versatility. A sliding glass door expands the living space by making a deck, patio, or pool area a part of the interior life of your home. A glass door admits light and air, and its operation does not consume any floor space.

If you know how to hang a door and how to install a window, the sliding glass door will seem easy to install. The entire door and frame may be ordered from most manufacturers as one complete unit. Assembly, when required, presents no difficulty whatsoever.

ORDERING A SLIDING-DOOR UNIT

Unlike windows, sliding doors are fairly uniform in design. They do vary considerably, however, in quality. These words of advice may come in handy when the cost differential puts you in a state of shock.

If the climate in your area varies considerably from one season to the next, you would be wise to order a unit with insulated glass. A large expanse of uninsulated glass drains the efficiency of heating the room in colder weather, a fact that should seem obvious. But it creates other problems as well, somewhat less expected: uninsulated glass will fog up during the winter, condensation forming on its surface as soon as the warm interior comes into contact with the cold exterior.

One further note of caution: you may encounter similar difficulties in cold climates with an aluminum-framed unit. Because of the way aluminum conducts heat and cold, condensation tends to form on the tracks during the winter and ice over as soon as the temperature plummets below freezing. So, before you dismiss the more expensive units because their favorable qualities are not immediately apparent, bear these points in mind. You'll also find that the most expensive units glide more easily, feel sturdier, and are easier to install.

Sliding-door units include glass panels and screens. Standard units have two or three panels of glass, with one panel operating, the others stationary. Standard sizes, for example, come in 6′ or 8′ widths, with either a right- or a left-hand door opening, and 9′ and 12′ widths with the center panel opening. Like windows and doors, these measurements describe only the size of the glass, not the framing or the rough opening into which the door will be installed. Standard heights for sliding units are 6′8″ (like other doors) and 6′10″. (Remember that you will need clearance for the header above the door. Are your ceilings high enough to accommodate both door and header?)

Sliding-door units are constructed like windows: jambs on two sides, a head on top, and a sill at the floor. Both head and sill contain tracks along which the unit slides. The units also contain hardware attachments, including a handle, indoor latch, and lock.

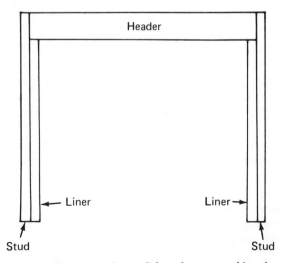

1. A rough opening for a sliding door resembles that for any window or door because it contains the same components: studs, liner studs, and header.

PREPARATIONS

If the wall into which you are installing the unit is a bearing wall—as most exterior walls are—be sure to install a temporary supporting device under the ceiling beams parallel to the wall section being removed. A support made of 2×4's will be sufficient. A finished ceiling may be protected with blankets or towels for cushioning, the floor with a plank or piece of plywood placed beneath the supporting 2×4's.

First remove anything from the wall that will interfere with the work: pictures, baseboard, and so on. If you are removing a window from the wall, dismantle it now, removing casing, panes, and frames.

Before you cut into the wall, be certain you know the actual size of the frame that will hold the sliding door. This may mean assembling the frame before you do anything else: a wise precaution. Follow the manufacturer's instructions for assembling—each brand has its own variations. The frame is joined at four corners, creating two side jambs, a head jamb, and a sill. Brackets are placed into the head jamb and sill—directly into holes that have been predrilled for this purpose. These brackets are designed to hold the stationary unit in place. Calking is applied to the ends of the side jambs.

Once it is assembled, stand the frame up on end, the sill at the floor, and lean it against a wall. Measure the frame carefully. Your rough opening will be 1″ wider and 1″ higher than this. Make a diagrammatic drawing, noting down all the dimensions.

ROUGH OPENING

Like windows, sliding-door units will be installed into an opening in the wall that is framed out with two studs, two liner studs, and a header. The opening is made precisely the same way as that for a window, except that there is no sill to be constructed. The floor is the sill of the gliding-door unit.

Try to work off an existing stud, if you can, as we recommended in the previous chapter where we described how to make a rough opening for a window. Using the level as a guide, mark the vertical lines of the rough opening directly on the wallboard. Then, allowing for the size of the header, mark off the horizontal line to indicate the top of the rough opening. You can pop a line with a chalk marker for this purpose.

Now cut through all these lines made on the wall. Cut through the wallboard first, remove the insulation, examine for wires or pipes that may have to be rerouted, then cut through the sheath-

2. After a deck was installed outside this house, the windows were no longer serviceable. These are to be removed and replaced by the sliding glass door. The existing stud to the right of the right-hand window remained in place. The rough opening was constructed from this stud.

5. Remove the framing of any windows or doors in the wall.

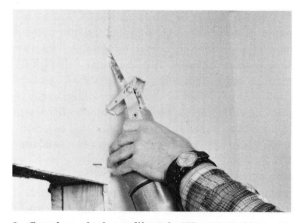

8. Cut through the wallboard. (Here it is being cut along the edge of the existing stud.) Remove insulation and check for wires or pipes that may have to be rerouted. Then cut through the sheathing and siding.

240

3. *Install a temporary supporting device under the ceiling beams, parallel to the wall section being removed.*

4. *Remove all trim that may interfere with the work on the wall you are about to work on. Remove baseboards carefully. They can be cut down in size after installation of the sliding door unit, and replaced along the same wall.*

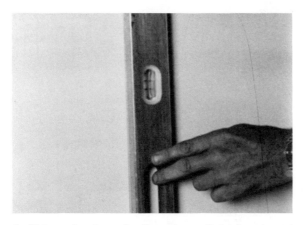

6. *Using a level, mark off on the wall the location of the liner stud in the rough opening.*

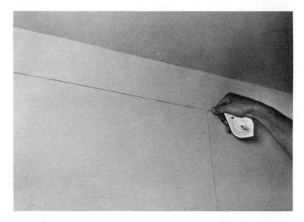

7. *Allow room for the header when you mark off the horizontal side of the rough opening. A chalk marker was used here.*

9. *We were particularly careful in cutting through this opening, in order to avoid any more patching than necessary. The studs in the framing were removed from the wall from the point at which they were anchored in the ceiling plate. This left space for us to insert the header.*

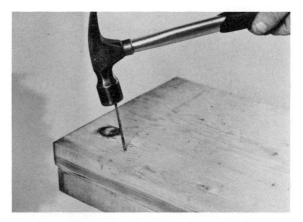

10. *Assemble the header. For a wide expanse, your building codes may well call for two 2×12's spiked together.*

11. Lift the header, crown side up, into the space between the interior and exterior walls, up against the ceiling plate or cripple studs above. Toenail it into the studs alongside it.

12. The header is supported on the left with a liner stud. It was driven snugly beneath the header, forcing the header tightly against the ceiling plate.

13. The rough opening is framed out: a stud and a liner on the left and right, and the header above. The open area on the left must be patched before going any further.

14. The open area to the left of the rough opening was patched. Pieces of 1×6 were used for sheathing, nailed from the outside to close up the space. (Exterior plywood could also have been used for patching.)

15. Chances are that the finished flooring indoors will not be on the same level as the subflooring running across the threshold of the door opening.

16. The threshold is built up with particle board, bringing it flush with the finished flooring inside. The sill must be level and firm, since much of the weight in the sliding door will rest upon it.

ing and the siding. Cut through the studs, and pull them loose from the frame. Cut through the shoe, if there is one, at the floor. Continue to refer to your diagrammatic drawing to be certain you are cutting away exactly what you need to construct a new opening.

Insert studs on both sides of the opening, each anchored to the shoe and to the ceiling plate. (Use 8- and 10-penny common nails for framing out the rough opening.) Now construct the header, much as you would for a window. With a wide expanse such as this, you will probably need a sturdy header (consult the building codes in your area), perhaps as much as two 2×12's spiked together. (Be certain to calculate this before purchasing the door unit so that you know you will have sufficient clearance overhead to accommodate both the door and the header in the room.) Ideally, you can remove the studs in the framing and bring the header into direct contact with the ceiling plate overhead. This should give you just enough room.

Push the header into position, crown side up, and toenail it to the studs on each side. Insert a pair of liner studs below, one on each side, forcing the header into tight contact with the ceiling plate or cripple studs above it. (This is the same procedure as used in making a rough opening for a window.) The framing for the rough opening is now complete.

Make whatever repairs on the sheathing may be necessary. The threshold of the opening should be checked. The subfloor must be firm at this point because it supports a portion of the sliding door's weight. It should have a firm bearing and should be level. Chances are that the finished flooring indoors is higher than the threshold across the entrance. Build up the floor with patches of wood or particle board to bring it to the same level as the finished floor indoors.

Unless you live in a concrete-slab-floor house with outside paving level with the inside floor, you'll have to install flashing along the base of the opening. Flashing is made of a strip of metal sheeting that prevents water seeping through. Butt the vertical flange of the flashing to the edge of the subfloor; then nail or screw it into place. Then apply a bead of mastic along the length of the flashing, as recommended by the manufacturer, and across the two ends to form a dam. On a concrete slab that sits above the ground, this is an especially important job.

HANGING THE DOOR

Now that the rough opening is complete—studs, liner studs, and header in place—check the open-

17. Check the rough opening to determine which sides are plumb or level.

18. Lift the frame of the sliding-door unit into the opening, rest it in the sill, and press the side jamb against the stud you know to be plumb. It should be level. If not, adjustments must be made.

19. After leveling the sill, secure it to the floor by nailing along the inside edge with 8-penny coated box nails spaced approximately 12″ apart.

20. *Jambs must be plumb and straight. Check all sides.*

21. *Shim the jambs and the header wherever necessary to remove any bow and to achieve a level or plumb line on all sides.*

24. *Lay the stationary panel in the outer run of the frame, making sure the bottom rail is straight with the sill and the predrilled holes all line up. Anchor the panel at the sill and at the head by driving screws through the brackets.*

25. *The stationary panel is anchored along the top edges with screws driven through the parting stop into the top rail.*

28. *Tar paper has been tacked to the sheathing in preparation for the new siding to be placed over it. With already existing siding, simply calk around the edges.*

29. *Indoors, the wallboard is in need of repair.*

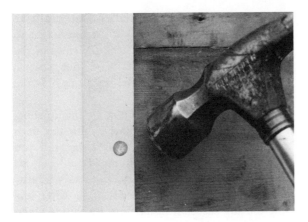

22. Once the frame is installed so that all sides are plumb and level, attach it to the sheathing of the house with galvanized nails driven into the casing every 8″ or 10″ along the sides and top.

23. Now anchor the side jambs to the liner studs by driving screws through predrilled holes in the frame. Secure the head in the same way.

26. Now slip the sliding-door panel into the opening. Position the rollers of the door on the rib of the metal sill. Tip the door at the top and lean it into the opening. Once it is in place, drive in screws at the head stop, so that the door will slide easily. If it doesn't move easily, consult the manufacturer's instructions for methods of adjustment. (Notice that the head was shimmed with shingles to obtain a level.)

27. Following the manufacturer's instructions, install the hardware, the handle latch, and the lock.

30. Insulation is stuffed into all crevices and between the studs.

31. The wallboard is patched to fill in damaged areas, and the seams are taped and spackled.

32. After painting, baseboard and casing were added and the job was complete.

ing against the frame to be certain that you have an extra 1″ at the width and 1″ at the height to plumb and level the frame. Check the sides of the rough opening to see if you have one that is plumb (ours was plumb on the right side). Is the header level?

Lift the frame and position it in the opening from the outside, pressing the sill into the door opening. Press the jamb up against the stud you know to be plumb. The sill must be level, so check it carefully and make the necessary adjustments. (Shimming may be necessary.) After leveling the sill, secure it to the floor by nailing along the inside edge with 8-penny coated box nails spaced approximately every 12″.

Check for plumb and level on all other sides of the frame. Shim the head and the jambs where necessary to achieve the level or plumb line. Anchor the side jambs to the liner studs by driving screws through the predrilled holes in the frame, but don't fasten it so tightly that the jamb bows. You may have to use shims under the jamb where the screws are inserted. Secure the head in the same way. Anchor the frame to the sheathing outside, driving galvanized nails every 8″ or 10″ down the side of the casing. Once the frame is secured and is level and plumb on all four sides, you are ready to insert the glass panels.

First position the stationary door panel in the outer run of the frame, being sure the bottom rail is straight with the sill. If the panel is in position, the predrilled holes will line up. Into these holes screws are driven to anchor the panel to the frame. Anchor the panel at the sill and at the head with the brackets installed at the time you assembled the frame. Screws are then driven through the *parting stop* at the head into the top rail of the stationary panel.

Once the stationary panel is secured, you can install the sliding panel. Place the operating door in the opening. Position the rollers of the door on the rib of the metal sill. Tip the door at the top and lean it into the opening. Position the head stop and drive in screws to hold it in place. Now the door should slide easily along the track. If the door does not slide easily, or is not parallel with the side jamb, adjustments can be made. Follow the manufacturer's instructions. No doubt there are screws that can be loosened at the bottom rail to enable you to raise or lower the door.

Finally, following the manufacturer's instructions, install the screen. Insert the top rail into the appropriate channel in the head jamb, and force the screen into position. It will ride on the rib of the sill track on its own rollers.

Follow the manufacturer's instructions for installing the hardware in the door as well. All that remains is the work to be done inside and out.

CHAPTER 18

How to Install Special Doors and Windows

It's virtually impossible to anticipate all the situations you're going to encounter when you renovate a home. Each job has its own peculiarities. We'd like you to feel, however, that there is a solution for every situation and that a little ingenuity is a skill you'll develop naturally with experience. The purpose of this chapter, briefly, is not necessarily to give you specific projects but to help you develop an attitude toward a special situation. You'll learn how to look at what you're about to do and to ask yourself: what is unusual about this particular project? This kind of interrogation will lead to the solution for any kind of special situation.

HANGING AN UNUSUAL DOOR

Perhaps you've just finished an attic and there was only one place you could put a closet door: below the rafters. This situation is not altogether uncommon and the lazy method of resolving it—with a curtain or drape—is also fairly common. But here's a way of handling the situation that is far less common, altogether more satisfactory, and not very difficult to do: hanging an angled door.

Installing the Jambs

The first thing you'll want to do is to establish the height of the longer jamb—the hinge side. See if it will fit in the opening. If not, cut the jamb down to size. You may also have to cut down the door at this time.

Now hang the door on the hinge jamb, just as you would a traditional door. Read the section in Chapter 15, "Hanging a Standard Door (from Scratch)," if you don't know how to do this. Follow the same procedure exactly: line up the hinges on the door and jamb, cut out mortises for the hinge butts, and test out the fit by connecting the two hinge leaves, so that you know the door will swing in a normal opening, providing the hinge jamb is plumb.

Check the liner on the hinge side of the door opening, to see if it is plumb. In our doorway the liner was very much out of plumb and the opening was much too wide. We corrected both by installing a 2×4 next to the liner. The width of the opening was reduced and the hinge side was made plumb by shimming with blocks of wood and shingles. After plumbing the liner, tack in the hinge jamb.

Now measure the distance from the notch on the hinge jamb to the ceiling. Draw a line on the opposite liner stud at exactly the same distance from the ceiling. The head jamb—when it is attached at those points—will be parallel to the angle of the ceiling.

Cut the other side jamb down to size so that its notch will be the correct distance from the ceiling. Tack it into position and check its size. Are the notches on both the side jambs equidistant from the ceiling?

Obviously the jambs are notched to accept a head jamb that is *perpendicular* to the sides. To accommodate an *angled* head jamb, the notch must be adjusted so that the head jamb can be inserted in it at an angle. Do this with a chisel on both jambs. Also angle the ends of the head jamb so that it will fit into the notches. Insert the head jamb into the two side jambs. It should run parallel with the ceiling.

Cutting the Door to Fit

Now comes the tricky part: cutting the door to fit the angle. It's not as difficult as it sounds. Here's a simple way to accomplish the feat.

Take a 4′ level and hold one end at the inside top corner of the short side jamb. Hold it there steadily, and raise and lower the opposite side

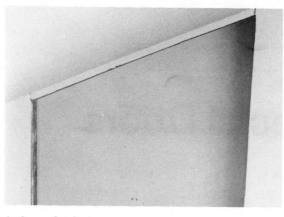

1. In a finished attic it's quite common to find a door opening that is angled to fit beneath the rafters.

2. First correct the opening if necessary. The hinge side is the longer of the two sides. Our opening was too wide and out of plumb. We corrected both defects by installing a 2×4 against the liner on the hinge side and shimming with blocks of wood. After hanging the door on the jamb, tack the hinge jamb to the longer side of the opening.

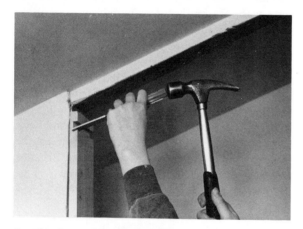

5. Chisel out the notches in both jambs so that they are angled in the direction of the ceiling.

6. Mark the head jamb on the sides where it should be angled as well. Saw off this edge with a handsaw.

9. Hold a level from the top inside corner of the short side jamb across the opening to the other side. Without letting the level slip from the corner on the short side jamb, raise or lower the instrument on the other side until it is exactly level. Mark on the hinge jamb where this point is.

10. Measure the distance from the top inside corner of the hinge jamb to the point you've just marked on the jamb with the level. Our mark was 12" below the corner.

3. On the hinge side, measure the distance from the notch to the ceiling. Mark off this measurement on the other side of the door opening. When the head jamb is attached to this mark, it should run parallel with the ceiling.

4. Cut the other side jamb down to size so that its notch is exactly where you made the pencil line. Tack the jamb to the liner.

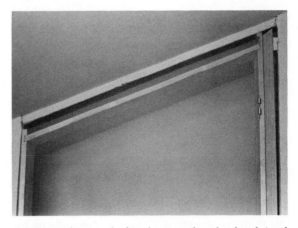

7. After the notches in the side jambs and the ends of the head jamb have been chiseled, the jambs can be joined at an angle.

8. If you have calculated correctly, the head jamb should be parallel to the ceiling.

11. Transfer this mark to the door. Mark off one edge of the door—opposite the hinge side—the distance you've just measured on the jamb. (Ours was 12".)

12. With a straightedge, connect the corner of the door with the mark you've just made on the door, to establish the angle of the cut. Cut the door along the pencil line.

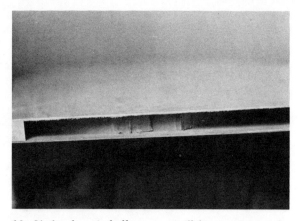

13. *If the door is hollow, you will have cut into the hollow core when you sawed the angle. Scrape away the glue and push aside the cardboard stiffeners.*

14. *Insert a strip of wood between the two veneered sides of the door, and glue it into place to conceal the hollow edge.*

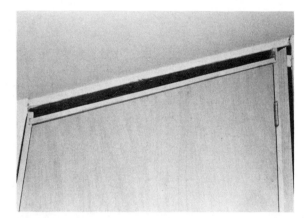

15. *If you've calculated correctly, the angle of the door should be exact when it is hung. Open and close it very gently.*

16. *The higher inside corner will probably rub against the head jamb. Draw a pencil line to indicate how much is to be removed to prevent the rubbing.*

17. *Cut along the pencil line at an angle so that the cut is not apparent from the front of the door.*

18. *Return the door to its hinges. It should swing easily without rubbing the head jamb.*

until the bubble indicates that it is level. Mark the opposite side jamb at exactly this point.

Now take a ruler and measure the distance from the top inside corner of the tall side jamb to the point you just marked off against the level. Ours measured 12″. Now carry these marks over to the door. You know the door is at its full height at the hinge side and must be shortened at the other side. Measure down along the door edge—opposite the hinge side—to the distance you just measured on the jamb. (Our measurement was 12″.) Connect this point with the corner at the hinge side. This is your angle. Cut the door in the way we showed you in Chapter 15, in the section "How to Cut Down a Door." If the door is hollow, you'll cut into the core. Scrape out the glue and push away the cardboard from between the two veneered sides and seal the edge by gluing a new piece of wood in between.

If you've measured and cut correctly, the door should fit neatly into the angled opening. Swing it open gently. You'll probably find that the top edge of the door on the hinge side rubs against the head jamb. This is easily corrected. Draw a pencil line along the inside of the door and cut along this line. Angle the cut so that what you remove is not visible from the other side of the door, but just enough to prevent it from rubbing the head jamb.

Now patch the wallboard and trim the door. Because the angles involved in trimming this door are unusual, we have described this procedure in Chapter 21, "How to Trim Special Doors and Windows."

19. Finally, the hardware has been installed.

INSTALLING AN OCTAGONAL WINDOW

It's much more difficult to *trim* an octagonal window than it is to *install* it. The calculations are easily arrived at and the window is so small that it generally requires no additional support.

Here we have demonstrated the installation of this unit in an exposed wall so that you can more easily see how to construct the rough opening.

An octagonal is based on the square. As long as you have the dimension of one side, you can establish all the others. All the sides are equal in size, and each pair of opposite sides is the same distance apart as all the other pairs. If you extend their lines, they will touch to form a square.

Draw the octagonal shape on the wall and cut it out with a reciprocating saw or by hand with a keyhole saw. Frame it on four sides with 2×4's to form a square, as shown in the photograph. Then measure one side of the octagonal unit and center it on each of the four sides of the square. Cut

20. The door swings open easily. Patch the wallboard, if needed, and paint the walls.

1. *An octagonal is based on the square. Cut out the octagonal shape into the wall. Then frame out the opening with 2×4's of equal length to form a square. Place the octagonal window inside the square and mark off where the angles of the window fall on the sides of the square.*

2. *Complete the rough opening by inserting 2×4's —each cut at 45-degree angles to the size of the sides on the octagonal unit—and nail them to the sill, header, and studs.*

3. *Insert the octagonal unit in the opening.*

4. *Patch wallboard all around the sides of the octagonal unit.*

2×4's to this dimension and saw each of their ends at 45-degree angles. Center these pieces across the corners of the square and nail them to the studs. Once this is done, the rough opening is complete.

Since the window is small, it is easily inserted into the opening and nailed to the siding. Patch wallboard around the perimeter of the window, tape and spackle, and you're ready for trim. Here's the clincher: trimming this window is not easy. We'll describe the procedure in detail in Chapter 21, "How to Trim Special Doors and Windows."

INSTALLING A BOW WINDOW

The most difficult thing about inserting a large window into a large opening is that it takes power! Because of the strength needed to lift headers and windows, and so on, we turned this demonstration over to stronger workers. The principle is still the same as that used on any other window, however, so if you have help there's no reason that you can't do it just as easily.

What we want to show here, above all, is how to handle the unit of this size once it's inserted into the opening. Bay and bow windows extend out beyond the structure of the building, which means they need their own roof and their own exterior support. Don't try to undertake this job if you haven't had some experience working with the exterior of your house, or unless you plan to re-side the house entirely. It's a big job that has a major influence on the exterior of your home. We were going to re-side the house anyway, so we didn't mind tearing off the siding that was necessary to build the roof and supports. Think this over before you begin.

You should erect scaffolding for working outdoors. This is not like installing a simple double hung window where a few moments on the ladder will be sufficient time spent outdoors and high up. For a bow window you will have to construct a roof and supports beneath it, so you should be able to work in comfort during the time spent on the work. We constructed a temporary scaffolding with 2×4's, which supported boards placed across them.

It's also important to construct a ceiling brace while you're cutting into the side of the house. Until the header is in place, the area around the opening is weak and you run the risk of a sagging ceiling if you don't brace it first. Use the kind of bracing arrangement shown in Chapter 16, "Installing Windows."

Making an opening for a bow window is ex-

1. The rough opening is made for the window in the same manner as for any other window. Construct scaffolding so that you have a sturdy and sufficiently large area for working on the unit outdoors.

2. Outside, along the sides of the rough opening we nailed 2×4's. The window unit will be nailed to these, then to the sheathing. By extending the unit this much farther out, we could obtain a greater sweep of the roof overhead and a deeper window seat indoors. This is optional, however. You can also attach the window directly to the side of the house.

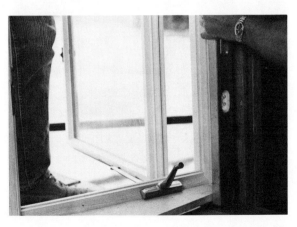

3. After the window is inserted in the opening, it's wise to have one person balance the unit—from the scaffolding outdoors—while another person plumbs the unit from indoors, shimming where necessary.

4. When the unit has been leveled properly, it is nailed to the exterior of the house. We have nailed our unit to the 2×4's alongside the rough opening.

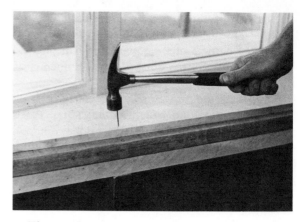

5. The window sits on the sill for support and is anchored to it with 6-penny finishing nails.

8. Outside, from the scaffolding, begin to work on the construction of the roof. The top of the window unit is exposed, like this, and must be built up to support the framing for the roof.

9. Angle a 2×4 so that it fits against the side of the building and up to the first window division. Anchor it to the window with 10-penny common nails.

6. Shim the top of the window unit with blocks of wood to provide a firm nailing support.

7. The bow window is now nailed to the rough opening, firmly supported by the sill and level and plumb on all sides.

10. Continue to place 2×4's along the top of the window unit, four pieces nailed to the window for a four-window unit.

11. Nail the flanges of the window to the 2×4's, inserting the protective drip caps at the joints where provided.

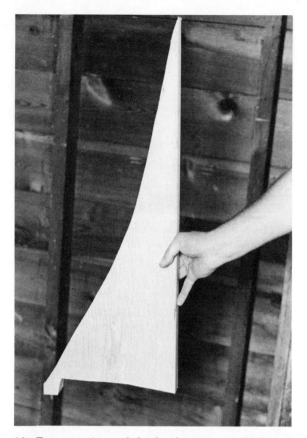

12. *From a piece of 2" lumber (we used the remainder of the lumber from the header), cut a frame like this for the roof. The frame should be wide enough at its base to span the top of the window, tapering off at the top in a gentle curve.*

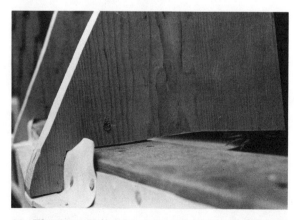

13. *The foot of the frame extends over the edge of the window. The frame is toenailed to the 2×4's just inserted.*

actly the same as making one for any other kind of window. (In fact, in our chapter on installing windows, we showed this opening when we described how to create a rough opening from scratch.) We modified the rule in one way only. We wanted a deeper window seat indoors and a bigger sweep in the roof line, so we extended the window out even farther beyond the house. Before inserting the window in the opening, we nailed a 2×4 to each side of the window outdoors, alongside the rough opening. When the window was installed, therefore, we anchored it to the 2×4's rather than to the sheathing of the house, extending the window that much farther beyond the siding.

Inserting the Window

After the rough opening is complete, lift the unit into the opening. This will require more than one person, since the unit is bulky and awkward to handle. While one person is standing on the scaffolding outdoors, balancing the window in the opening, the other person should be holding a level to the window, shimming the unit where necessary. Finally, the window is anchored to the sheathing or siding of the house (or onto the 2×4's nailed alongside the rough opening, as in our case).

After the window is anchored to the building, adjust the head and sill of the bow window with shims. Since the window is so large, shims must be inserted in several places to prevent it warping or shifting. Face-nail the window to the sill. The unit should be firmly in place.

Building the Roof

A bow window requires its own roof. This can be handled in a variety of ways, but here's one method we found attractive and easy to install.

First build up the foundation for the roof framing directly onto the window unit. Pieces of 2×4 cut to fit the angles of the window should be nailed above the unit with 10-penny common nails. The flanges along the top of the window are nailed to this.

Now build the underpinnings for the roof, a frame onto which sheathing is nailed. Three supports (or frames) will be sufficient for a bow window the size of ours, a frame shaped with a gentle arch that will form an attractive line for the roof. Cut these supports from a piece of 2" lumber—we used the leftover portion from the header—in a pleasing shape that has a small foot extending at its base. Use a saber saw to cut this. Nail the three frames to the top of the window, the feet overlapping the window edge, and shim

14. *The frames are nailed to the side of the house, shimmed out with blocks of wood so that they are firmly anchored. Three frames are needed for this window.*

15. *The sheathing for the roof is ⅜" exterior plywood. For a four-unit bow window, cut four pieces of sheathing, each to be matched to form a pleasing arrangement over the window. The sheathing is made flexible by sawing with a circular saw, the blade lowered just enough to make grooves in the wood without penetrating to the other side. These grooves are made with the grain every 1" or 1½" on the underside of the plywood.*

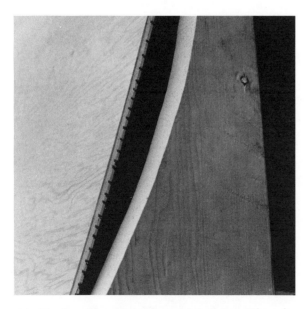

16. *Fit the plywood to the roof framing. The edge of the plywood should fall midway along the edge of the frame, so that each sheet can butt alongside the next.*

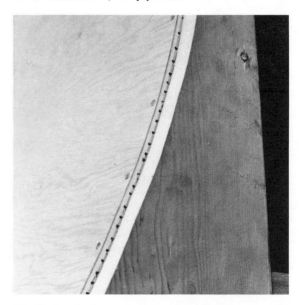

17. *If the fit is good, press the plywood into the curve of the frame. The grooves along the underside will enable you to bend the wood without cracking it. Attach the plywood to the frame with ¾" galvanized nails placed every 2" or 3".*

18. *The next sheet of plywood is attached to the frame, butting up against its neighbor and following the same curve of the brace beneath it.*

19. *The two end sheets of plywood are triangular in shape, and also grooved on their undersides.*

20. *The four sheets of plywood have been attached to the framing of the roof. Notice that they combine to form an attractive shape over the window.*

to the side of the house so that they are firm.

Now build the sheathing for the roof from ⅜″ exterior plywood. You will need as many pieces as you have window units. Each piece will butt its neighbor, nailed along the edges of the frames you just anchored above the window. Cut the pieces in pleasing shapes that will match and form an interesting pattern for the roof. The grain of the plywood should run horizontally along the selected shape.

Here's a good trick: to create the curve in the roof, you will bend the plywood to fit along the edge of the supports you just constructed. Set the circular saw for a shallow cut and saw a groove —from one edge to the other—along the grain every 1″ or 1½″. Be certain that the blade is deep enough to make a groove, but not so deep that it penetrates to the other side of the wood. These grooves will make the plywood flexible and you can bend it to fit the contour of the frame you just installed.

Place the plywood on the frame so that its edge runs midway down the edge of the frame. Press the plywood into the contour of the frame and nail it with ¾″ galvanized nails. Attach the next sheet of plywood—the underside also grooved— along the edge of the frame and anchor it in the same way. The sheets in the center of the bow window will be cut according to one pattern; the two sheets at the ends will be cut in another, to form a graceful pattern over the entire window unit. Anchor them all to the frame you've made for the roof, using galvanized nails.

Once the sheathing has been installed, it's time to put shingles on the roof. These are applied in horizontal rows with galvanized roofing nails in the traditional manner, one row overlapping the next, from the lowest to the highest row. Cut the shingles at the edges to conform to the shape of the roof, and attach a final row of shingles along the joints above the sheets of plywood sheathing. This is added protection and emphasizes the division of units—and the curve—of the bow window. Finally, nail flashing (strips of aluminum) to the side of the house and to the roof of the bow window so that there is no chance of rain water seeping through the joint.

Constructing the Window Supports

Outside, the bow window must be supported from below. This provides an opportunity for you to construct an attractive finishing touch to the unit. Again, there are a variety of ways to treat this support. Ours is designed to conform to the rustic appearance of the barn.

First the window must be packed out from below, just as you reinforced the top of the unit

21. Begin to place shingles over the sheathing on the roof.

22. The shingles are cut at their edges to follow the contour of the roof line. The first row of shingles always contains two layers for added protection of the sheathing. On the right, both layers have been nailed to the sheathing; on the left, only the first layer has been installed.

23. The shingles have been installed in horizontal rows, and a final row of shingles is placed along the three joints for added protection and to emphasize the design of the window. Flashing has been nailed to the roof of the window and to the side of the house to prevent water seeping through.

24. *After the roof is complete, remove the scaffolding and begin to work on the lower portion of the unit. First the underside of the window must be packed out. Scribe the angle of the window on a piece of 1" pine.*

25. *The second piece of pine, inserted beneath the window, completes the job of packing out the unit.*

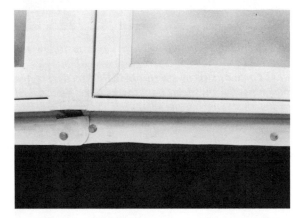

26. *Nail the flanges of the window to the pine you've just nailed to the underside of the window. Use galvanized nails.*

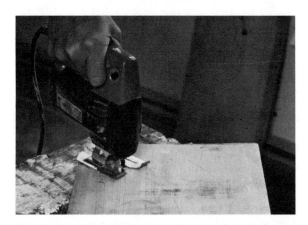

27. *Design a brace that is as deep as the window at the top and tapers off at the bottom in a graceful curve. Trace this line on a piece of 2" lumber and cut it out with a saber saw.*

28. *Place the brace beneath the window and check it for fit and design. If it's acceptable, use it as a pattern for the second brace.*

29. *Both braces are tacked into position now. They provide support for the window and add a decorative touch to the exterior of the house.*

before you constructed the roofing frame. Scribe the angle of the protruding bow window on a piece of 1″ pine and cut the pine to this shape. Insert the pine beneath the window. If the window is fairly deep—as ours is—you'll need two pieces of pine to fill out the entire base of the window. Nail the wood to the window with 6-penny finishing nails. Now attach the flanges of the window unit to this case with ¾″ galvanized nails.

On a piece of 2″ lumber draw the contour of a brace for the window—its widest part just wide enough to give maximum support to the window, its narrow part tapering off into a graceful curve against the building. With a saber saw, cut this shape out of the lumber. Fit it to the window, and if it is acceptable, use it as a pattern for a second brace. Attach both braces to the window and to the side of the house. These can be painted or stained to match the window or to match the siding. In our case, we chose to paint them white, to match the window, and to contrast with the dark

30. The seams are concealed with siding. The braces have been painted white to match the window and to contrast with the dark siding. The flanges at the base of the window have been concealed with a fascia made of the same material as the siding.

siding. With siding, any number of decorative treatments can finish off the job. The flanges can be concealed with a fascia tacked to the window (constructed of the same siding material). The 2×4's at the side of the window and the flashing around the roof are also concealed with siding.

Trimming this window is far less complicated than installing it. We have described this procedure in Chapter 21, "How to Trim Special Doors and Windows."

PART FOUR

Moldings

CHAPTER 19

How to Trim Standard Doors and Windows

Moldings are installed around the perimeters of the windows and doors, along the base of the wall, and possibly along the wall where it meets the ceiling, or as corner guards for exposed outside corners. Moldings serve two main functions: they're decorative, and they conceal irregular joints. Carpenters tend to use molding only where necessary to hide unattractive gaps, so that the absence of moldings tends to suggest good craftsmanship. In our chapter on spackling, for example, we recommended that you tape the seams between wall and ceiling rather than install molding around these seams to conceal them. Greater skill is required for taping, so the results display superior craftsmanship.

Molding, where used properly, is handsome and, like spackling, can distinguish the poor craftsman from the superior one. In fact, no matter how straight the walls are, or how well the floor has been installed, or what kind of lumber you have used, the one thing that shows off a good job or exposes a bad one is the trim.

Molding is the finishing touch. It should be installed after the walls and floors are finished, and after all painting and papering are completed. Moldings are stained or painted the same color as the walls or are in contrast to the walls. If they are of a different color, we advise you to paint or stain all molding in advance of installation. This way you can be certain to avoid contaminating the color of the trim or the walls with the other color.

Because molding follows the shape of a door or window, it is necessary to join moldings so that they turn the corners. Before we go any further, therefore, we'd better take time out to describe the method of making these joints.

MITERED JOINTS

Molding will surround the shapes you trim, their ends meeting at the desired angle to make the proper turns. The angles cut into the moldings are *mitered*. A saw designed for cutting wood at an angle is called a *mitering saw*. It is a backsaw placed into a *mitering box*—an instrument that can be adjusted to guide the saw at the appropriate angle. The molding is laid against the mitering box and held firmly in place, and the saw cuts at the angle for which it has been set.

Mitering saws are the traditional tool used by carpenters for trimming. The better saws are more expensive because they do a better job, making trimming easier in the long run. We preferred the *mitering knife,* however, a tool more commonly used by picture framers. A good mitering saw is no less expensive than a mitering knife, and so we were not influenced by any cost differential. The mitering knife is more precise, capable of cutting to $\frac{1}{32}''$ of the desired measurement, unlike the mitering saw, which is less accurate. But even more important to us was the kind of cut made by the mitering knife, totally clean and free of rough edges. (The teeth of the mitering saw tend to create small splinters at the edge of the cut.) We also preferred the knife because of the way the angles are set. With a mitering saw, each angle must be set for each cut. If you cut one piece of wood at a certain angle, you must reset the machine to cut the next piece at another angle. Two angles may be set on the mitering knife, so that you can change angles without stopping to reset.

One word of caution: a mitering knife can be exceedingly dangerous. We have been told that carpenters are uneasy about transporting the knife from job to job because of the temptation to grab it carelessly at the opening, lifting the knife with the edge of the blade pressing into the palm of the hand. The razor-sharp blade is perilous, so treat the instrument with great respect: move it as little as possible, and lift it only by the handle provided for this purpose. To avoid any more movement than necessary, we did all our

1. To join two pieces of molding at a 90-degree angle, cut two pieces each at opposing 45-degree angles. Insert the molding into a mitering knife (as used in these demonstrations) or mitering saw, and cut the first piece at a 45-degree angle, the shorter part of the angle at the thin part of the molding.

2. Place the second piece of molding into the mitering knife and cut it at the opposite 45-degree angle.

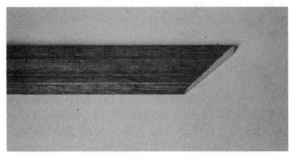

3. Notice that the shorter part of the 45-degree angle is always at the thinner side of the molding.

4. The opposite angle is cut at 45 degrees. Notice that the thinner edge is always the shorter one.

5. When the two pieces of molding are joined, their angles matched, the turn is 90 degrees.

1. A door is ready for trimming after it's been painted or stained. The casing will conceal the gaps between the jambs and the rough opening. This is the same door shown in Chapter 15, under "Hanging a Pre-hung Door."

mitering with the knife on the floor, placed in the center of the room.

A 45-degree angle is most frequently used for trimming. Two pieces of molding, each cut at opposing 45-degree angles and joined, will create a 90-degree turn, one piece being perpendicular to the other.

Set the mitering saw or knife at a 45-degree angle. The error most easily made is placing the wood so that it faces the wrong direction, the 45-degree angle cut to the wrong side. This error may mean wasting a perfectly good length of molding, so be careful in positioning the wood in the box or knife, facing it in the correct direction before cutting.

When you've cut one piece of molding to 45 degrees, cut the second piece with the angle facing the opposite direction at 45 degrees. (In a mitering saw you'll readjust the mitering box; in the mitering knife you simply place the molding at the other side of the instrument against the angle set previously.) Placed together, end to end, these two 45-degree angles should give you a mitered joint of 90 degrees.

Before you begin, practice some joints with your mitering knife or saw, using scraps of molding. Hold the cut pieces together tightly on a flat surface and line them up square to check the fit at the joints. Is there a space at the outside or inside end of the joint? If so, you should adjust the mitering knife or saw to the correct angle so that it makes a perfect joint. Also be certain that during the cutting of the molding you hold the wood firmly against the back of the box. A poor joint can result if the molding is held in place improperly.

Other kinds of moldings will have to turn around inside as well as outside corners. For an inside corner, these moldings must be cut at the correct 45-degree angle, first with the mitering saw or knife, then undercut to the proper curvature with a coping saw. The coped joint is described in greater detail in the next chapter, "Baseboards and Corner Moldings."

MOLDINGS FOR DOORS

The molding that surrounds the doorway, concealing the gaps between rough opening, jamb, and door, is called *casing*. Casing is available in two styles: (1) *Clamshell casing* is 2¼″ wide, ⅛″ along one edge, and ⅝″ along the other, a smooth surface curving from one edge to the other; (2) *Colonial casing* is 2¼″ or 2½″ wide and is also ⅛″ at one edge and ⅝″ at the other, but the surface is molded in a traditional design rather than the smooth, plain curve of the clam-

2. Make a mark on the side jamb, ¼" away from the inside edge, exactly where the corner makes the turn.

3. Mark the head jamb—¼" away from the inside edge—exactly where the corner makes the turn. These two pencil marks make an L on one side of the door. Do the same on the opposite side, making a reverse L at the points where the top and side turn the corner ¼" away from the inside edge of the jamb.

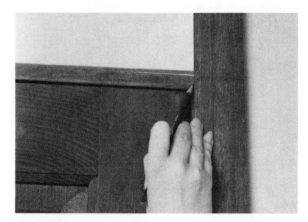

4. Holding the piece of molding against the jamb, its thin edge nearest the door, mark the point at which it touches the pencil mark. This is the shorter edge of a 45-degree angle. Mark it for the cut, and miter it to this mark. Do the same with the casing along the other side of the door.

5. Take the short piece of casing and miter one side to the correct 45-degree angle. Hold it in position over the door, ¼" above the inside edge of the head jamb, the mitered edge touching the pencil mark.

6. While the mitered edge is touching the pencil mark on one side, mark the casing at the point where it touches the pencil mark on the other side. Miter the angle to this mark.

7. Cut all three pieces of casing to the correct dimension. Tack the first piece of casing, with a 4-penny finishing nail placed 4" below the corner, into the jamb through its thinner side. Don't drive the nail in all the way.

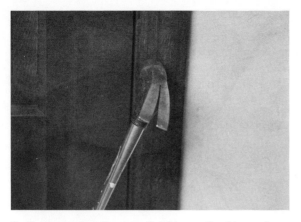

8. Tack another 4-penny finishing nail midway down the casing. Be sure that the casing is ¼" away from the inside edge of the jamb.

9. Attach the casing along the other side of the door with two 4-penny finishing nails, one placed about 4" below the corner, the other about midway down the casing.

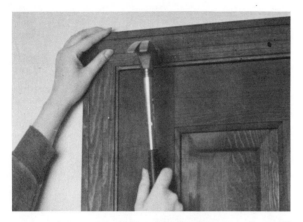

12. Tack the other side of the head casing about 4" from that corner.

13. Now set the corners. By placing the 4-penny nails 4" from the corners, you have a good deal of play at the corners. Here a nail is driven through the side of the casing so that the corners are attached correctly. You can do the same through the top.

16. Only two more nails are needed to anchor the casing at the head, each placed about midway, though not lined up exactly with each other. Drive a 4-penny finishing nail into the thinner part of the casing, a 6-penny finishing nail through the thicker part.

17. By anchoring the casing to the walls you probably upset the corners again, though we know they are correctly placed because they were matched earlier. The irregularities of the wall behind the casing have probably separated the moldings so that their surfaces are not flush with each other, even though their angles match. A wedge behind the seam may help by pulling them away from the wall just enough to bring them into flush contact.

10. Slide the head casing into position, matching the mitered angles.

11. Tack a 4-penny finishing nail—through the thinner side of the casing into the jamb—about 4" away from the corner.

14. After the corners are set, anchor the casing to the wall. First drive 4-penny finishing nails along the thinner side of the casing into the jambs: about four will be sufficient.

15. Then drive 6-penny finishing nails through the thicker side of the casing into the studs. About four will be sufficient, but stagger their position with the 4-penny nails you already placed. If you line up the nails opposite each other, you weaken the wood.

18. Cut away the excess shim with a utility knife and anchor the corner tightly with a 4-penny finishing nail on both pieces of casing. Countersink the nails.

19. *You may have to play with the corners a bit more to get them perfect, but ultimately they will fit into place because they are the correct length and they are at correct 45-degree angles. Finally the door has been trimmed. Only baseboards are required to complete the trimming operation.*

shell. Clamshell is generally used for more contemporary homes, colonial for more traditional homes. (We used colonial for all our demonstrations.)

MOLDINGS FOR STANDARD WINDOWS

Like doors, windows are trimmed with casing. Window casing, like that for doors, is available in clamshell and colonial styles. In addition to the casing surrounding the perimeter of the window, another kind of molding called a *stool* is placed horizontally across the sill of a double-hung window. Although the stool is commonly called a window sill, this is a misnomer. The sill is the window itself, and the stool is a molding that overlaps the sill, blocking the space underneath the window to prevent drafts from seeping through.

TRIMMING A DOOR

Doors are trimmed on both sides of their opening, so you'll need four long pieces of casing for the sides and two shorter pieces for the heads.

Trimming a door accurately is very easy. What's most important is that you cut each piece to the correct length and at the correct 45-degree angle. And there's a good way to do this simply.

Door casing is always placed about ¼" away from the inside edge of the door jambs, so that there is ample room for the hinges and an equal margin on all sides. The first thing to do is to mark the jambs where the casing will be placed. Mark the inside corner of the jamb where the casing will make the turn, ¼" away from the inside edge of the side jamb. Then mark the corner where the casing at the top will make the turn on the head jamb, again ¼" above the edge. Join these two points to form an *L* or a reverse *L*, depending on which side you've marked. Now do the same with the other side of the doorway, marking where the side and head casing will join, ¼" away from the inside corner.

Pick up one of the longer pieces of molding and place it along the hinge side of the doorway —the thin edge of the molding on the side of the door opening—and mark it at the point where it touches the pencil mark you've just made on the jamb. Remember: this mark is placed at the thin side of the casing and represents the shorter end of the miter. It helps to mark the molding with a little crow's foot to remind you in which direction the angle should be cut.

Now carry the molding to the mitering saw or knife and set the instrument for the 45-degree angle that will correspond to the angle of the crow's foot just marked on the molding. Place the molding into the box and think before you cut. Is the angle correct? Is the molding facing so that the shorter side is placed at the thin side of the casing?

Cut to the crow's foot mark, and return the casing for a fitting. Lean it up against the jamb, ¼" away from the edge, and check its size. Does the shorter side of the angle touch the pencil mark? If more needs to be cut, do it now. If it is slightly short, you can lift it from the floor when you attach it.

Now take the other long piece of casing and mark it at the point where it touches the pencil mark on the other side of the jamb. Cut it down, with a 45-degree angle opposite to the one you used for the other piece of casing. Fit the casing against the jamb and check to be certain it touches the pencil mark.

Take the short piece of casing and cut a 45-degree angle at the end, again being certain that the shorter side of the angle is at the thin side of the casing. Hold the casing in place on the head jamb, the mitered end placed exactly where the pencil mark has been drawn, and mark the opposite end of the casing where the pencil mark indicates. Cut the head casing—at the correct angle —to this mark. All three pieces should now be correctly mitered, each to the correct length. If the ends of each piece touch the appropriate pencil marks, you know all three should fit perfectly.

With a 4-penny finishing nail placed about 4″ from the corner, tack the first side piece of casing into place through the thin part of the casing into the jamb. Do the same with the long casing on the other side as well. Don't drive the nails in all the way; you may want to pull them out later if adjustments are necessary. Tack in a second 4-penny finishing nail midway down the casing. Be sure the casing has an equal margin of ¼″ away from the inside edge of the jamb.

After both pieces of casing have been tacked into place, drop in the head casing. Tack it into place in the same way, with two 4-penny finishing nails placed about 4″ from the corners, through the thin part of the casing into the jamb.

Now set the corners. By tacking the 4-penny finishing nails 4″ away from the corners, you have greater play at the corners for adjustments. Shift them to where they match, then drive a 4-penny finishing nail into the side of the casing —through the corners, from the side edge near the wall, joining the pieces at the corner. If the corner looks perfectly matched, leave it alone. Or you may drive another nail through the top side of the corner. Continue to play with the corners until they are matched.

Now anchor the casing to the wall. Drive 4-penny finishing nails through the thin side of the casing into the jambs. About four (including those already tacked in) will be sufficient for each of the side casings. Through the thick sides of the casing drive 6-penny finishing nails into the studs —about four will do for each long piece of casing here as well, but don't line them up exactly opposite the 4-penny nails you've just driven or you'll run the risk of splitting the wood.

Anchor the head casing with only two more nails: a 4-penny finishing nail into the jamb midway across the casing and a 6-penny finishing nail into the header about midway across the casing, but not directly above the other nail. Drive in the finishing nails you already placed at the corners.

By anchoring these pieces to the walls you've probably upset the corner joints. Their position has shifted slightly because they are making close contact with the irregular surface of the wall, but you know that their angles are correctly set because you matched them earlier. Only the surfaces are out of alignment, not the angles.

You can shim out a corner with a sliver of shingle (even cardboard will work!), pulling it forward sufficiently to bring the two wood surfaces flush with each other. After the shim is correctly placed behind the corner, anchor it with a finishing nail inserted through the casing. Cut away the exposed shingle with a utility knife so that no part of it extends beyond the edge of the casing. The corner will be flush and the minute space between the wall and the casing will never be seen. Do the same with both corners if necessary.

The door is now trimmed on one side. Follow precisely this procedure for trimming the door on the other side.

Door Stops

If the door is a pre-hung unit, the stops may already have been installed in the jamb. If not, you'll have to put them in yourself. Refer to Chapter 15, "How to Install Doors."

TRIMMING A WINDOW

If your new window has been installed in a newly constructed home, it's very possible that the window can be trimmed immediately with no preparation. Chances are, however, that the window has been installed in an older home, which means that certain adjustments must be made before the casing can be installed.

1. Here is the window to be trimmed. Notice that the jambs are exposed on all sides. If wallboard extends too far into the window, cut it away so that the jambs are exposed.

271

2. *This is typical of a new window installed into an older home: the jambs are not flush with the surface of the wall. Here they recede by about ⅝″.*

3. *Hold a length of 1×6 up against the jamb so that it is positioned correctly along the window.*

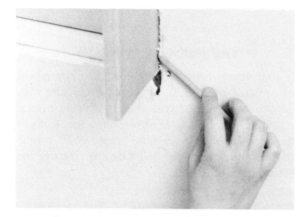

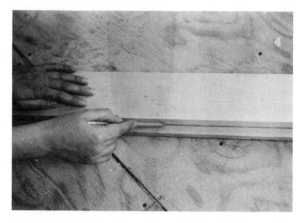

6. *Don't assume that one measurement is sufficient. There can be irregularities that cause a discrepancy between its dimensions. Mark the lower part also where it must be ripped in order to be flush with the finished wall surface.*

7. *Join the two marks with a single pencil line, using a straightedge as a guide.*

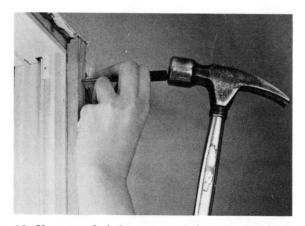

10. *You may find that a part of the extension jamb is slightly too thick, extending somewhat beyond the surface of the wall. Countersink the finishing nail along this edge.*

11. *Plane along the edge that is too thick until you've made it flush with the wall. By countersinking the nail you avoid chipping the blade of the plane.*

4. While you're holding the 1×6 in position, mark it for length. Cut the 1×6 to this length.

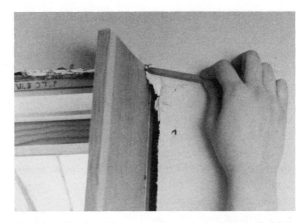

5. After the 1×6 is cut to the correct length, hold it in position against the jamb. Mark it near the top with a sharp pencil where it should be ripped in order to be flush with the finished wall surface alongside it.

8. Anchor the 1×6 to a sawhorse to prepare it for ripping. The pencil line should extend beyond the sawhorse so that you can rip along the line.

9. After you've ripped the 1×6 along the pencil line, attach it to the jamb. The edge of the wood should be flush with the exposed window jamb and flush along the cut edge with the finished wall.

12. Attach the other extension jambs to the window in the same way. If the corners are not exactly flush, countersink the nail on the thicker piece and plane it so that the corners are flush with each other.

13. Nail the corners together with finishing nails to close any gaps between the pieces. The window is now ready for trimming.

Preparing the Window: Extension Jambs

In order for the casing to be nailed around the perimeter of the window, the edges of the window jambs must be flush with the surface of the finished wall. In an older home the jambs may well recess slightly below the wall surface. Moreover, you'll probably find they are more recessed at one part of the window than at another. Irregularities in the framing or in the wallboard, or in the way the window was installed, may mean that one end of the window is more deeply recessed than the other.

So before you can nail in any casing, you must build up (or "pack out," as it is said in the trade) the window jambs so that they are flush with the wall surface. These are called *extension jambs*. For this purpose of constructing extension jambs, 1×6 lumber is ideal. You will probably need one or two lengths of lumber for each window, depending on how recessed the unit is from the wall. The window in our demonstration receded by only about ⅝"; we've seen other windows that have receded as much as 3½". (Awning units usually recede even more, and for this reason awning units have grooves into which extension jambs can be inserted, though the procedure for their installation is the same as that described here.) Order one or more pieces of 1×6 in a length that will extend from one corner of the window to another in a continuous strip. (For a 5' window, for example, order a 6' length of 1×6.)

First pack out the longer sides of the window. Cut down the 1×6 to the inside measurement of the actual window. Hold it in place along the jamb of the window and mark it, with a sharp pencil, at the top and at the bottom where it must be cut to be flush with the wall surface. Don't assume this dimension is the same down the entire length of the window. Take two measurements, one on each end of the jamb. There may be as much as ¾" difference between the top and bottom. Mark the two points on the 1×6 and connect the marks with a straight pencil line. With a circular saw, rip the 1×6 along the pencil line.

Place the edge of the 1×6 along the edge of the window jamb. If you have ripped the piece correctly, its cut edge should be flush with the wall surface. Nail the extension jamb into the window jamb, using whatever length finishing nail is necessary to penetrate the ripped wood and the window jamb. If the jamb is not quite right—too wide or too narrow—don't feel you have to dismantle it entirely and start over. You can make adjustments while it is in place. If it is slightly too deep—extending beyond the wall surface—countersink the nails and plane down the surface that extends too far. If the wood recedes slightly, you

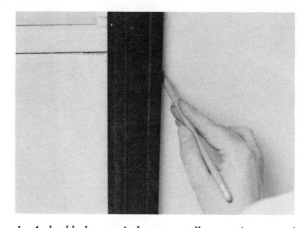

1. A double-hung window normally contains a stool attached to the window sill. This is the first part of the window to be trimmed. Mark the walls for the placement and size of stool and apron. Hold a piece of molding along the edge of the window and trace along its outside edge, using a sharp pencil, about 2" above the sill to about 4" below the sill.

4. Hold the stool up to the window again. Its ends should touch the outside lines you made on the wall. Now mark the inside dimensions for notching. Here the sill will be notched to fit around the window jamb.

7. Anchor the stool to the window sill with 6-penny finishing nails.

2. Turn the molding on its wider edge, directly alongside—and outside of—the mark you've just made on the wall. Trace this as well. The two parallel lines are about ¾″ apart. The outside line indicates the placement of the stool; the inner line indicates the placement of the apron beneath it. Make these marks on both sides of the window.

3. Hold the stool against the marks. Place one end against the outside pencil line and mark where it hits the other outside line. Cut the stool along this mark.

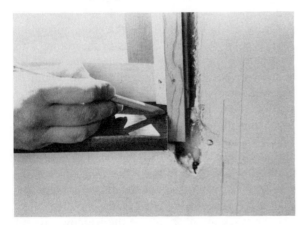

5. Mark the outer edge of the sill. Cut the stool along these two pencil marks with a handsaw. Do the same with the other side of the window and with any other projections that may prevent the stool from sliding into place.

6. Check the stool for position. Its square edge should be about ¹⁄₁₆″ away from the window sash, with ends fitting tightly against the wall.

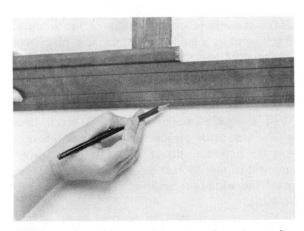

8. The apron is cut at the point where it touches the inner pencil lines you made earlier on the wall. Hold a piece of molding up against the stool, one end alongside the inner line, and mark it where it touches the other inner line. Cut it to size.

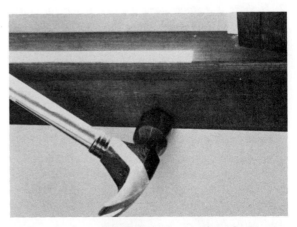

9. Attach the apron below the stool with 6-penny finishing nails driven into the wall. The stool is placed in a direction opposite to that of the casing: its wider edge is fixed under the stool, and the thinner edge is placed away from the window opening.

1. A window can be picture-framed on all four sides —with no stool or apron.

2. If there is a stool, stand a piece of molding on it and rest the thin edge along the edge of the side jamb.

3. Mark the casing at the inside corner of the jamb. Cut the 45-degree angle from this point.

can make the wall flush with it by pounding the wallboard with the hammer, tapping just enough and just in the needed area to make it flush with the extension jamb. Insert jambs on the other sides of the window and nail the jambs to each other at the corners to close whatever gaps may appear.

If you are trimming a double-hung window and intend to place a stool at the base, attach extension jambs on three sides only. If you are not putting a stool on the window, pack out all four sides of the window.

When the jambs have been extended so that they are flush with the surrounding wall, you're ready to attach the casing to them.

Installing a Stool and Apron

Not all windows require stools. Only a double-hung unit traditionally contains a stool: it is nailed to the window sill inside primarily to block the air that seeps through the bottom of the lower window.

Order a stool in the same thickness and width as that used on other windows in the room. This is usually quite standard. Calculate the length of a stool to be about 6" longer than the width of the window opening.

First mark the wall for the placement of the stool and the apron that will be nailed below it. There's an easy trick for this: hold a piece of casing alongside one edge of the window and continuing below the window—the thin edge of the casing flush with the side jamb—and mark the wall along the outside edge of the molding, placing the mark about 2" above the window sill and continuing the line about 4" below the window sill. Now turn the casing on its wider edge and hold it along and to the outside of the line you've just made. Trace a second line along the casing, parallel to the first and the same length. (The two parallel lines, therefore, are about ¾" apart.) Make these lines on both sides of the window. They serve as a guide for the size and placement of the stool and the apron beneath it. The lines are long enough to be seen from above and below the stool after it is in place.

Now cut the stool to length. Hold the uncut stool alongside one of the outside pencil lines you've just made on the wall and mark where it hits the opposite outside line. This is the measurement of the stool. It will extend about ¾" beyond the window casing. (Cut the stool to this length.)

Now the stool must be notched to fit around the projections in the window. Hold the stool in so that both ends are touching the pencil marks on the window and mark it where any projections on the window may occur. Notch these out with a handsaw, and slide the stool into position so that

4. *Cut one 45-degree angle out of the head casing, and hold it in position flush with the edge of the head jamb. Mark where the other angle should be cut to turn to the corner.*

5. *After all three pieces of casing have been cut to the correct length and at the correct angle, tack each piece to the jambs with 4-penny finishing nails placed about 4" from the corners.*

6. *Tack each side piece of casing about 4" from the stool as well.*

7. *Play with the corners until they are matched perfectly. By placing the nails 4" from the corner, you have the flexibility to shift the angles sufficiently. Attach the corners at their sides when they are matched.*

8. *After the angles are matched, anchor the casing to the wall: 4-penny finishing nails along the thin part of the casing, 6-penny finishing nails into the thicker part of the casing.*

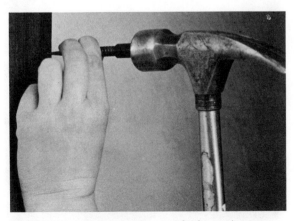

9. *After setting the corners—with shims if necessary—countersink the nails.*

its square edge is about ⅟₁₆″ from the window sash, with ends fitting tightly against the wall. Make whatever adjustments are needed in the stool for a proper fit, then attach it by nailing the stool to the sill, through the face, with 6-penny finishing nails.

The apron is attached just below the stool. It is constructed of the same molding as the casing on the other sides of the window. Hold a piece of uncut molding up under the stool, placing one edge alongside the inner pencil line you made earlier on the wall. Mark the molding where it touches the matching line on the other side of the window. Cut the molding to length. Attach it to the wall with 6-penny finishing nails, the wider edge under the stool.

Window Casing

Like casing around doors, casing around windows is mitered at the corners. It is possible to "picture-frame" a window, so that the casing surrounds the window on all four sides and no stool is nailed to the sill. This is simply a matter of mitering four corners and joining the pieces as you did with a doorway. If a stool has been installed, casing is nailed around the three sides of the window. Unlike casing for trimming doors, the casing is flush with the edge of the jamb, not ¼″ away from it. If you're not picture-framing the window, install the casing after the stool is in.

Take the first piece of casing and square it off at one end. Rest the squared-off end on the stool and hold the casing against the wall, its thin edge lined up with the inside edge of the side jamb on the window. At the first corner, mark with a pencil where the casing should be cut to turn the corner. Make a crow's foot to remind you in which direction the angle should be cut. Now cut a 45-degree angle and set it aside.

Take the molding for the head of the window, cut a 45-degree angle at one end, and hold the piece in position along the edge of the window head jamb, marking the corner where the piece should be cut. Finally, rest the last piece of casing on the stool, hold it against the jamb, and mark it for the cut. After all three pieces have been cut to the correct length, tack them to the jambs with 4-penny finishing nails placed about 4″ from the corners.

Now play with the corners as you would when trimming a door. Drive in nails from the sides, or make whatever adjustments are needed to match the angles. Then anchor the casing to the walls—with 4-penny nails driven into the jambs through the thin part of the casing, and 6-penny finishing nails driven into the studs and header at the wide part of the casing. Return to the corners to make whatever adjustments may be necessary and set them. Shim out the angles—as described earlier under "Trimming a Door"—if they are not flush, and finally countersink the nails. The window is now completely trimmed. Only stain or paint is needed to finish the job.

10. The window is trimmed.

11. Stain or paint the parts of the window that are still exposed and the job is complete.

CHAPTER 20

Baseboards and Corner Moldings

Like casing around windows and doors, baseboard is designed to conceal a whole host of sins. You may have a gap below the wallboard, for example, or the finished flooring in the room may not have been installed flush with the wall. (Baseboard can cover a space 3½″ high and ½″ wide.) In concealing these unattractive spaces, baseboard also places the final touch in the room, the decorative element that unifies all the work you've done so far. Baseboard is nailed to the walls after the walls have been painted or papered, the finished flooring laid, and the casing around the doors installed. Baseboard can be either part of the wall—painted in the same color—or in contrast—painted or stained in a different color. In either case, it's advisable to paint or stain the full lengths of baseboard before you cut them down. Even the splinters that may occur in cutting pieces can be touched up later, after the baseboard is installed, and the work will still be neater than if you try to paint or stain baseboard after it is nailed to the wall.

ORDERING BASEBOARD

Before you go to the lumberyard, look over the room and establish what you need. Like casing for windows and doors, baseboard is available as clamshell (a flat surface, slightly curved from ½″ at the base to ⅛″ at the top edge) or colonial (fluted and shaped along the sides). If your room is contemporary and you've used clamshell casing around the doors and windows, select clamshell baseboard. Likewise, if the room is more traditional and you've used colonial casing, select colonial baseboard.

Now measure the uninterrupted walls and make a note of how many lengths you'll need of 6′, 8′, 12′, 16′, or 20′. (Order these larger strips to avoid patching baseboard along an uninterrupted wall.) Shorter pieces can usually be made from extra pieces cut down from the longer ones.

If the gap between the wall and the floor is greater than ½″, baseboard alone will be insufficient to cover it. You'll need to order lengths of quarter round molding as well so that you can install a "shoe" at the base of the wall.

BASEBOARD AROUND AN OUTSIDE CORNER

At each end of a wall you'll encounter an outside or an inside corner. Each corner involves mitering the baseboard so that the two boards can make a 90-degree turn. On an outside corner, both pieces are mitered at 45 degrees. On an inside corner, one end is flat and squared off, the other baseboard is mitered and "coped."

An outside corner is the simpler of the two corners. Let's assume that you have a wall with an inside corner at one end, an outside corner at the other, a common occurrence. Square off one end of the baseboard so that it will fit into the inside corner at the opposite end of the wall. Now measure from one end of the wall to the other, and lay the ruler down on the underside of the baseboard, marking off the measurement from the squared-off end to precisely the point at which the outside corner occurs. Mark the underside at this point, where the corner turns. This will be the inside of a mitered angle.

In mitering casing, you cut the angle into the face of the molding. In baseboard, the mitering is cut along the inside flat edge of the molding, the angle being sliced into the underside of the wood. Place the baseboard into the mitering box or knife along the flat side so that the underside is severed at the pencil line, the face jutting out at a 45-degree angle to the underside. Place the baseboard against the wall for a fit, positioning the squared-off end into the corner and the mitered end at the outside corner. The underside should line up with the edge of the outside corner. If it is

1. *This wall is typical: there is an unattractive gap at the base and it contains both an inside and an outside corner.*

2. *Square off one piece of baseboard to fit into one end.*

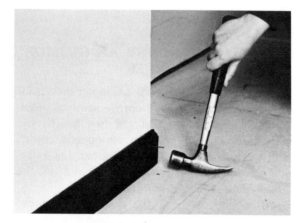

5. *Tack the baseboard with a 6-penny finishing nail placed about two thirds of the way up the baseboard from the floor, and about ¾" from the corner so that you're certain to nail into a stud.*

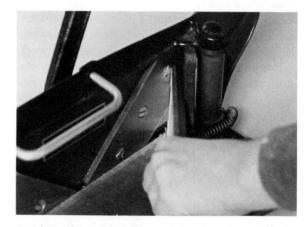

6. *Miter the second piece of baseboard at a 45-degree angle opposite to the other piece you've just prepared.*

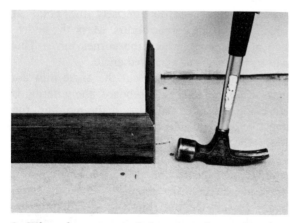

9. *When the corner is fitting precisely—with no adjustments necessary—drive the nails into the wood and countersink them.*

10. *Place a 6-penny finishing nail into the baseboard every 16" so that you are certain to attach it to the studs behind the wallboard.*

3. For the outside corner at the other end, miter a 45-degree angle along the surface of the baseboard.

4. Place the baseboard against the wall for a fitting. Here we are looking down on the outside corner. Notice that the corner of the wall lines up with the underside edge of the baseboard.

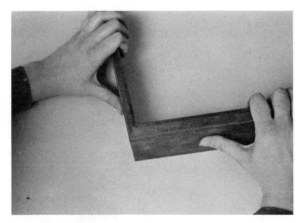

7. Notice that if you place two 45-degree angles together, you form a right-angle turn.

8. Tack the second piece of baseboard into position, making the 90-degree turn around the outside corner.

11. For an inside corner, make a straight cut with one piece, no mitering necessary.

12. Cut the second piece of baseboard at a 45-degree angle (opposite to that used for an outside corner).

13. *The two pieces of baseboard should look like this if they are being matched for an inside corner: one piece mitered at 45 degrees and one with a straight cut.*

14. *Cut away the exposed wood from the mitered piece of baseboard with a coping saw. If you can't see the edge clearly, draw a pencil line along the contour of the miter and cut to that line. Here the wood has been stained so it is easy to follow the line with the coping saw.*

15. *When you place the mitered baseboard over the other piece, you can form a 90-degree angle turning inward.*

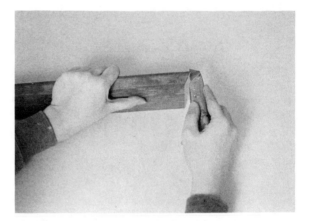

16. *Irregularities in your cut may mean that there are small gaps along the joint. Cut away the small protrusions creating this gap with a sharp utility knife. Continue to place the baseboard against its mate, working until you get a good match.*

17. *Slide the baseboard into position for a final check. If the joints are well matched, set the baseboard along the wall.*

18. *The baseboard completes the trim on the wall.*

too long, cut down the the board at the squared-off end. If it's a bit short, slide the board up to the outside corner into the correct position. (It's not important for the squared-off end to fit tightly at the opposite corner. The small space at the joint can be concealed later with the other baseboard.)

With a 6-penny finishing nail, tack the baseboard into position. Place the nail about two thirds of the way up the baseboard from the floor, and about ¾" from the corner so that you're certain to anchor it to a corner stud.

Now join the other baseboard in the same way. Measure the wall from one corner to the other, miter the end at a 45-degree angle, and slip it into place so that its mitered end joins the other miter to form a 90-degree angle at the corner. Tack it into the wall in the same way you nailed the first board. Drive one or two extra nails into the corner on both boards. Once you are certain that the corner is properly joined, anchor the remainder of both baseboards into the walls. Locate the studs every 16" or 24" along the wall and drive one 6-penny finishing nail through the baseboard and into each stud. Again, position the nail about two thirds of the way up the baseboard from the floor so that you are sure to drive it into the stud. (If you drive the nail lower, through the baseboard and into the shoe, you'll pull the top edge away from the wall because the board will be drawn into the gap below the wallboard.)

Press down on the baseboard, pushing it firmly against the floor, then nail it in place. As you work, avoid damaging the surface of the board with the head of the hammer. Drive in the nails carefully, and not too far, countersinking the heads later.

BASEBOARD AROUND AN INSIDE CORNER

Fitting the inside corner is slightly more difficult than mitering an outside corner. Before you risk a full length of board, therefore, practice with some short pieces of baseboard you intend to discard.

An inside corner is made with two baseboards, one squared off and placed into the corner, the other with a coped joint.

To cope a joint is to cut a 45-degree miter into one of the baseboards and cut away the excess wood along the mitered outline. Cut the excess at an angle, making an undercut. Cut closely to the mitered joint without damaging the contour of the baseboard. Once the cutting is completed, the contour of the baseboard will conform to the outline of the adjacent baseboard.

Here's a trick with coping: it's not always easy to see the precise contour of the edge you are cutting against. If you paint or stain the baseboard first, this edge will be clearly visible as you slice it away with the knife or mitering saw. If the wood is unpainted or unstained—so that it is the same color as the trimmed edge—you should use another method of seeing it clearly. Trace the contour with a pencil and cope up to this pencil line.

Another trick: don't use a coping saw with a sharp blade. A sharp saw rips the wood so rapidly that the edges have a tendency to splinter and destroy the contour. Use a dull blade instead; you'll have to work at it a bit harder, but you'll have more control. If you're using a new blade, dull it first by scraping along the teeth with the back of a knife blade.

After the baseboard joint has been coped, slide it into the corner so that it butts against the other baseboard already positioned there. If the joint is not altogether satisfactory, slice away any protruding pieces with a sharp utility knife until it fits perfectly. Every corner will be different; each is tailor-made to suit the peculiarities of the angle. So you'll be on your hands and knees for a while, slicing and sanding until the joints are exactly right.

The joint correct now, anchor the board to the studs as described earlier. Countersink the nails.

OTHER TRICKS WITH BASEBOARD

If you should run short of baseboard during the course of a wall, patch the two lengths. You'll get a better joint if you miter the two sections of baseboard rather than butt them at their squared-off ends. Slice one board at a 45-degree angle in one direction, the other board in a 45-degree angle in the other direction. Slip them together.

If the baseboard should end abruptly at an outside corner, with no piece coming to meet it at the turn, miter the edge of the baseboard so that it angles toward the corner. This is a neater edge.

If the length of wall to be covered is too small for you to anchor a baseboard adequately with nails, glue it instead.

After the baseboard is fully installed, return to it with a small brush and touch up sections with the stain or paint where splinters may have occurred.

CORNER MOLDINGS

You may have occasion to use moldings in corners—to conceal gaps between walls and ceiling, as corner guards along the outside corner of a

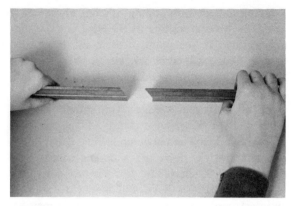

19. If you run short of baseboard, and two lengths must be joined, miter the pieces at opposite 45-degree angles like this. Joining lengths of baseboard by mitering makes a better join than by butting them.

20. If the baseboard ends abruptly at the edge of a wall, miter it so that the edge tapers into the wall.

21. Touch up with stain or paint.

wall, or between the baseboard and the floor. For these purposes, a three-dimensional molding is used, which has its own inside or outside corner running along its length so that you can insert it into a corner seam.

The moldings most likely to be used for corners are:

Quarter Round: Round on one side, squared off at two sides, quarter round is used most commonly at the angle between baseboard and finished flooring. Used for this purpose, quarter round is called *shoe molding.*

Crown: Flat at its underside, with two sides angling out from the back, crown molding bridges a corner between the wall and ceiling.

Cove: A right-angle corner along its underside, the front of this molding is curved outward into a convex shape. Cove molding is used as trim between the wall and ceiling.

Corner Guard: This molding is used to cover wallboard or paneling on outside corners.

Quarter round, crown, and cove moldings are handled like baseboard. For outside corners, they are mitered at 45-degree angles. To turn an inside corner, do the same as you would with baseboard. One molding is squared off and placed at the corner; the other molding is mitered and then coped. Cut a 45-degree angle in the correct direction, then cut away the excess with a coping saw so that it butts directly up against the other end.

When two corner guards are joined at an outside corner, both pieces are mitered at 45-degree angles. This is more easily said than done, however, because mitering three-dimensional molding can be very tricky. There are no real short cuts here, even though we may have a few suggestions to make the job easier. You'll have to arrive at the correct angle by trial and error. Take a few scraps and practice.

The difficulty in mitering these corner guards derives from the fact that there are four possible ways to miter, yet only one will be right for a particular corner. You can form a right angle up, down, toward you, or away from you the four ways the molding can be cut. One suggestion: with crosses, mark the molding on the edge that goes on top, but place the molding in the mitering box so that the marked edge is down. When you make the cut, the angle should be as planned.

Experiment by making all four miters. Hold the molding in four different positions in the mitering box to see how this affects the angle you get. Then do the same with 45-degree angles in the other direction. Use these pieces of wood for your patterns, so you have some guide to use later.

1. This is crown molding. It is traditionally used along the seam between wall and ceiling. An outside corner is made by mitering two pieces at 45-degree angles.

2. The inside corner of crown molding is made in the same way as in baseboard: one piece is a straight cut, the other is mitered, then coped.

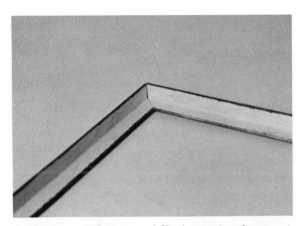

3. Corner guard is more difficult to miter because it is three-dimensional. Using scraps, make patterns for the angles you need before cutting up the good pieces. Here is the underside of a 90-degree turn made with corner guard.

4. This is the face side of corner guard. Look simple enough? Try it!

SHOE MOLDING

If the baseboard itself is insufficient to conceal the gap in the flooring around the edges of the room, install shoe molding at the base of the boards.

Shoe molding is constructed from quarter rounds, cut to the proper lengths of the walls. Miter or cope all the corners, and use 4-penny finishing nails, long enough to penetrate the subfloor as well as the finished flooring.

At the points where the shoe molding meets the door casing, make it a curve to the door jamb. The job will look much better if you round it off this way rather than leaving a straight end. Place the molding in the box or knife and shave it at an angle. Finish it by setting the finishing nail head below the surface of the molding with a nail set. Stain or paint exposed cuts.

1. *Shoe molding is nothing more than quarter round. An outside corner is made by mitering two pieces at 45-degree angles.*

2. *An inside corner is made by mitering one piece and coping it, as you did with baseboard.*

3. *Shoe molding is used to cover gaps that may appear at the base of the baseboard. It is nailed into the floor with 4-penny finishing nails placed at 45-degree angles.*

4. *Where shoe molding terminates at a doorway, miter its end so that it tapers into the door casing.*

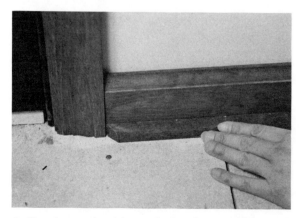

5. *Touch up the edges of the shoe molding with stain or paint after it is installed.*

CHAPTER 21

How to Trim Special Doors and Windows

In Chapter 18 we described how to install special doors and windows so that you could see some variations on a theme. Doors and windows that present problems in installation do not necessarily present difficulties in trimming, and vice versa, and the trimming of these unconventional units can apply to just about any other trimming jobs you may encounter.

What makes trimming seem difficult is not the complexity of the work but the patience that is required. There is no single solution to all trimming jobs. Each is different, demanding its own resolution. And there are no true short cuts to a good job. So we can't provide any easy answers to all the situations you encounter, but we can give you a few tips on how to resolve an unusual problem when it arises so that you can think it out on your own. After that, only experience can be your instructor.

TRIMMING AN ANGLED DOOR

In Chapter 18 we inserted a door beneath the rafters of an attic closet, meeting the angle in the ceiling with a door cut to fit. Trimming out the door is simply a matter of getting these angles correct.

Begin as if you were trimming a standard door. Mark the jambs at the inside corner of the joints. Make these marks on the inside corners of the head and side jambs, ¼" away from the inner edge of the jamb. (Remember, casing is placed ¼" away from the inside edge of the jambs on all sides.)

Now hold a piece of molding up to that mark on the side jamb, ¼" away from the edge of the jamb. With a sharp pencil, trace the outside edge of the casing just about where the outside corner of the mitered joint should fall, a line about 2" long. Then hold a piece of molding over the head jamb and do the same: trace its top edge so that

the horizontal line intersects with the vertical line made earlier with the side casing. Finally, do the same with the piece of molding on the other side of the doorway, marking the walls with two intersecting lines.

Cut one piece of side casing down to its approximate length and hold it against the jamb, maintaining an equal margin of ¼" down its length from the inside edge of the jamb. Holding it firmly, mark the molding on two sides—first,

1. This is the angled door we installed earlier, as described in Chapter 18. The wallboard has been patched, spackled, and painted, and the door has been stained.

2. Mark the side and head jamb at both inside corners—¼" away from the edge of the jamb—to indicate where the point at which the casings will be mitered to turn the corners.

3. Hold a piece of molding up against the pencil mark you've just made on the side jamb. With a sharp pencil, trace the side of the casing—a line about 2" long—at the approximate place where the outside corner of the mitered joint should fall.

6. Hold a piece of casing along the side jamb, maintaining a ¼" margin between its edge and the inner edge of the jamb down the length of the casing. This margin is important. If the casing is out of line, the angle will not be marked accurately.

7. With the pencil, mark the inside edge of the casing where it touches the first mark you made on the inside edge of the side jamb.

10. Now mark the head casing. It's important that it should not shift position while you are marking it, so tack it to the wall with a 4-penny finishing nail to hold it in place.

11. When the head casing is in place, mark the inside edge where it touches the pencil mark on the head jamb.

4. Hold the molding up against the mark made on the head jamb and trace its other edge at the point where the angle will make its turn. The two lines should intersect.

5. Do the same on the other side of the door opening: trace two lines, with the molding, along the side and head jambs. These lines will intersect.

8. Still holding the casing firmly in place, mark the outside edge where it touches the point at which the pencil lines intersect on the wall. Remove the casing and connect these two marks with a pencil line drawn across the surface of the casing. Cut the casing to this angle with a mitering knife or saw, or with a handsaw.

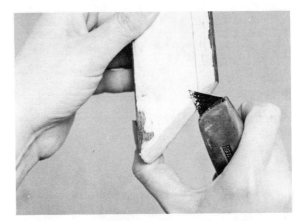

9. After mitering the angle from the casing, we carved out the wood about ⅛″—from the underside—along the inside edge of the cut. This undercutting will allow for the irregularities in the wall at the joint; it is helpful when you can't nail the corners of molding together from the sides of the joint because a wall or ceiling is too close for hammering.

12. Mark the other edge where it touches the point at which the two pencil lines intersect on the wall. Do the same with the other end of the head casing as well. Remove the casing and draw the angles at each side by connecting the pencil marks. Finally, mark the other side casing.

13. After you've cut all the angles in the casing along the pencil lines, tack the first piece in place and check to be sure that one end touches the pencil mark on the jamb and the other end touches the corner, where the two pencil lines intersect.

14. Nail the side casing into position under the head casing.

15. Nail in the other side casing. If the angles match properly, anchor the trim to the wall with 4-penny finishing nails driven into the thinner part of the casing into the jamb and 6-penny finishing nails driven into the wider part of the casing into the stud.

16. The trim around the door is complete. Baseboard has been added.

17. When the door is opened, the angles form an attractive line with the frame and with the ceiling.

where it touches the inside pencil mark on the jamb, and second, where it touches the intersecting pencil lines above. Remove the casing and connect these two points. This is your angle.

Trim this angle carefully along the pencil line. If you have a mitering knife or saw, set the instrument for this unusual angle. If not, saw along the pencil line with a handsaw. Hold the molding up against the door and see if it touches the pencil marks on both sides—the point where the lines intersect and the mark on the jamb. Continue to trim until you get a perfect fit.

Our molding was so close to the ceiling that we knew we would not be able to hammer nails into the corners from above the casing. To get a closer fit, we undercut the molding slightly with a utility knife. Undercutting prevents the irregularities in the wall from pushing the joint away from its surface. This way the molding is notched to fit any humps in the wall below it.

Now hold a piece of molding over the head jamb and mark its corners. It's very important that you do not shift the position of this molding as you go from one side to the other, so tack it into place with a 4-penny finishing nail and be certain its position stays fixed. Cut each piece of molding in the same way, matching the angles to the pencil marks on the wall and jambs. You should have a good fit if they all match. It's painstaking work, so don't rush it.

After the pieces are all trimmed, tack them to the jambs with 4-penny finishing nails placed 4″ from the corners, just as you would when trimming a standard door. Play with the corners until you get them right, removing them from the jambs if further adjustments are necessary. Once the corners are placed, anchor the casing to the jambs and to the studs. Reset the corners if necessary, and the job is done.

The procedure for trimming this door is the same as that used for any door where the angles are other than 90 degrees. As a footnote, two things are worth emphasizing. First, always use a sharp pencil so that you can trust the accuracy of your pencil lines. The work here is so precise that even the thickness of a graphite pencil can upset the joints. Second, always be certain that the moldings are correctly placed when you trace the outlines on the wall. The margin of ¼″ along the jambs must be equal. If it is not, your angle will be upset when you attach the casing to the jambs later.

TRIMMING AN OCTAGONAL WINDOW

As we said earlier, trimming presents a problem only when the angles are other than 45 or 90 de-

1. After the window was installed, we patched around it with wallboard, taping and spackling to conceal the joints.

2. We scraped away bumps and particles of spackle along the edge of the wallboard until it was exactly flush with the inside surface of the window jamb.

3. First establish the angles for the mitered joints. Hold a piece of molding against the wall, the inside edge lined up with the window jamb.

4. *Holding it in place, draw two 4″ lines—with a sharp pencil—at about the places where the outside edges of the joints will occur on the wall.*

5. *Do the same with the next side of the window. Line the molding up with the inside jamb of the window and draw two 4″ lines where the outside corners of the joints will fall. The line will intersect with the other you just drew. Do the same on all eight sides of the window.*

8. *Now transfer the angle from the mark on the wall to a piece of molding. Hold the molding in position, against the wall, its inside edge lined up with the window jamb. With a sharp pencil, mark where the molding touches the joint on the window.*

9. *Still holding the trim firmly in place, now mark the other side, where it touches the two intersecting lines. Connect these two points on the molding by drawing a pencil line across its surface. Set the mitering knife or saw to this angle, or cut it by hand. Trim carefully along the pencil line on the molding.*

12. *If you're satisfied that the two angles match the pencil lines on the wall, tack the molding into position with two 4-penny finishing nails.*

13. *Continue around the window, matching each angle with each piece of molding. Tack the second piece into position alongside the first.*

6. *Line up a straightedge (we continued to use the molding) from the inside corner of the joint to the point where the pencil lines intersect opposite it. Trace this line with a pencil.*

7. *The line you've just drawn will bisect the angle of the two intersecting lines. This new line marks the angles to which the two pieces of molding must be cut in order to make the proper turn. Bisect all the angles in the same way.*

10. *Hold the molding up against the wall to see if the angle you've just cut matches the angle drawn on the wall.*

11. *Once you've matched the first angle on the molding, mark the wood for the second angle in the same way, and cut this down to size, matching it with the pencil line on the wall.*

14. *Continue with each piece in the same way. Do not assume that any two angles are alike. Each must be tailor-made for the specific angle.*

15. *If all eight pieces seem to fit comfortably together, drive in the nails and countersink them.*

16. We still had a gap to conceal between the molding and the window jamb, an exposed edge of gypsum wallboard. (If you've extended the jambs, you won't have this gap.) We cut eight pieces of beading to size—each end angled properly so that they made a tight joint.

17. We glued the beading and fastened it in place, bracing it with strips of wood until the glue dried.

18. The completed window. The hours spent trimming seemed worth it after we had finished the job!

grees. When we trimmed the door (see above), we had only two mitered joints to calculate. In an octagonal window you have to establish eight different angles in order to match up the eight pieces of molding. This is slow and painstaking work. (We figured, for example, that it took us about two hours to install the window and about five hours to trim it!) Nevertheless, the end result is very rewarding, well worth the time spent in making it right.

After installing our octagonal unit, we patched wallboard around it. With a utility knife, we scraped away the bumps and spackle from the gypsum so that the edge of the wall was perfectly flush with the inside surface of the octagonal window. If your window has been installed into a finished wall, chances are that the edges of the window jambs are exposed and are set back from the surface of the wall. This means you'll have to prepare the window before trimming by extending the jambs as we described in Chapter 19, "How to Trim Standard Doors and Windows." This is somewhat more complicated than a standard window. Here you'll have to extend eight jambs—not just three or four—matching each perfectly by angling the cuts so that no gaps appear between the joints. Once the jambs are flush with the surface of the wall, you're ready to begin.

First mark the wall on all eight sides so that you have a guide to follow for cutting the angles into the trim. Pick up a length of molding and hold it against the wall, lining up its edge with the inside surface of the window jamb. As you hold the inside edge along the window jamb, trace a line on the wall along the opposite edge of the molding. Use a sharp pencil for accuracy. Make two lines about 4″ long and place them on the wall just about where the angles between the joints will occur.

Now hold the molding along the next side of the octagonal window and mark the wall where the joints fall on this side as well, with two lines about 4″ long. Do the same on all eight sides of the window. When you've completed this, you'll find that each line intersects with its neighbors.

Now establish the angles. Line up a straightedge from the inside corner—where one window jamb is joined to the next—to precisely the point where your pencil lines intersect on the wall. Using the straightedge as a guide, draw a line from one point to the other, bisecting the angle on the wall. This line represents the angles needed for the two pieces of molding to join as they make the turn. Do this on all eight angles in the window, bisecting each in the same way. This is your road map.

Now that you can see what angles are needed

for which joints, it's simply a matter of transferring this information to the pieces of molding you are about to trim. Hold the first piece of molding up against the wall, lining its inside edge up with the edge of the window, and its outside edge with the two pencil lines. With a sharp pencil, mark the molding where the inside corner of the window touches the inside edge of the molding. Then mark the outside edge of the molding where it touches the two intersecting pencil lines on the wall. Remove the molding and connect these two points by drawing a pencil line on the molding.

Set the mitering box or knife to the angle marked on the molding. Lacking this, cut along the pencil line with a handsaw. Your cut must be accurate. The slightest deviation from the pencil line will throw off the joint. Check the accuracy of the cut by holding the molding against the wall and lining it up with the pencil line. When you are satisfied that you've matched the angle, mark the other end of the molding in the same way. Holding the wood in place, mark it on one side where it touches the joint at the window and on the other side where it touches the intersecting pencil lines. Connect these points and cut the angle accurately. Hold the wood against the pencil marks on the wall. If both sides seem accurate, tack it into place with 4-penny finishing nails. Proceed to the next piece of molding and follow the same method of establishing the angle. Con-

tinue on all eight sides. If the eight pieces seem to fit comfortably, anchor them into place by driving in the nails. Then countersink the nails.

If you've extended the jambs, your trimming job is complete when you've nailed in the eight pieces of trim. If your job is like ours in the demonstration, you will have a gap between the molding and the window jamb, an exposed edge of gypsum board on all eight sides. We concealed this gap with beading—the kind of molding you use when you conceal the edge of a screen on a door. We stained a long strip of this beading, cut it into eight pieces—each end angled for a proper fit—and then glued them into place. While the glue was drying, we braced the beading with strips of wood.

TRIMMING A BOW WINDOW

If trimming a small octagonal window can be an arduous task, trimming a large bow window is, by contrast, very simple. There seems to be no relationship between the size of a window and the difficulty of its installation, and its final trimming.

A bow window is different from a standard window only in the configuration of the stool. The jambs are extended as they would be in a traditional window; the casing is installed in the same way as well.

A stool for a traditional double-hung window

1. The bow window is ready for trimming.

2. *The edges of the jambs around the bow window are set back from the wall by about ½″.*

3. *The jambs have been extended—as they would be in any traditional window—so that their edges are flush with the surface of the finished wall.*

4. *Notch the extension jambs with a handsaw or utility knife for flush contact with the framing.*

5. *Since the stool sits deeply into the window, 1×6 pine was selected for trimming. Cut the board according to the same procedures as you would any traditional stool. Notch it to fit around the jamb and against the wall.*

6. *Since the stool is an important element in the design of this lovely window, the sharp edges at the corners are rounded off and shaped. The stool is butted against the unit for a deep window seat, anchored to the sill with 6-penny finishing nails.*

7. *After the stool is installed, casing is nailed around the perimeter of the window using the same method used for a traditional window. An apron is installed under the stool, angled slightly for a more distinctive appearance.*

is about 2½″ wide and is installed to block the seepage of air from beneath the window sash. A stool for a bow window is as wide as is desired —from 2″ to 12″—and is nailed flush with the window unit. Purchase a length of pine sufficient to span the window and wide enough to suit your taste. We used 1×6 pine. The length of the stool extends beyond the casing in the same proportion as for a double-hung window—about ¾″ beyond it on each side. Cut the pine to the correct length, and notch it to fit around the jamb and tightly against the wall.

Greater care should be exerted in shaping the edges of the stool. We rounded off the sharp corners in a shapely pattern on both sides of the window. Attach the stool to the framing with 6-penny finishing nails, and insert an apron below. (We angled the cut at both ends of the apron to give the window a more distinctive appearance.) Then install casing on the other three sides of the unit as with any traditional window. Countersink the nails, and paint or stain the window to finish it off.

8. The trimming on this large unit is complete, and the window is stained to match the other windows in the room.

Index

302